MUSCLE CARS

VIPER RT/10
VIPER

MUSCLE CARS

PETER HENSHAW

THUNDER BAY
P·R·E·S·S
San Diego, California

Thunder Bay Press
An imprint of the Advantage Publishers Group
5880 Oberlin Drive, San Diego, CA 92121-4794
www.thunderbaybooks.com

ISBN 1-59223-303-1

Library of Congress Cataloging-in-Publication Data available upon request.

Printed in China
1 2 3 4 5 08 07 06 05 04

Credits
Project Editor: Shaun Barrington
Designer: Cara Hamilton
Production: Don Campaniello
Reproduction by Classicscan Pte. Ltd, Singapore

All quotations in this book that are not accredited are from contemporary advertising copy. Running heads on the right-hand pages are guides to the motor divisions and models featured in the photographs.
All images by Garry Stuart except: Andrew Morland pp18-19, 44, 72-73, 77, 137, 277; Cadillac, General Motors 42; Ford Motor Co. 274-275; Mike Mueller 296; Ron Kimball Studios 419. With thanks to Mark Steigerwald, Curator of Watkin's Glen International Motor Racing Research Center, for providing the picture on page 297.

Contents

Introduction

"Just what is a Muscle Car? Exactly what the name implies. It is a product of the American car industry adhering to the hot rodder's philosophy of taking a small car and putting a BIG engine in it . . . The Muscle Car is Charles Atlas kicking sand in the face of the 98 hp weakling. It is the American man's answer to Susan B. Anthony. Wally Cox and Don Knotts reign supreme and Woody Allen can go home again."

*(*Road Test *magazine, June 1967)*

THAT QUOTE SAYS IT ALL. The concept of the muscle car really was, and always has been, as simple as that. Take the smallest, lightest bodyshell available, and squeeze in the biggest V8 that will fit. Stiffen up the suspension and beef up the brakes if you must, but they're just incidentals—muscle cars were about raw power and tire-smoking performance.

They didn't have the chassis sophistication of a Lotus or the lithe good looks of a Jaguar, still less the engineering integrity of a Porsche, or Ferrari's sheer exotic appeal. (The Europeans never made muscle cars.) But none of that mattered to the people who bought GTOs, Road Runners, Mustangs, and Chargers in the late sixties, the early seventies, and beyond. Raised on hot-rodding and drag racing, they wanted straight-line performance, the American way, and that's exactly what they got.

It's not hard to see why muscle cars were always a quintessentially American genre, though we have to go back a long way. In the very early days of motoring, American and European pioneers followed much the same path, and their rattling, flimsy contraptions looked pretty much what they were—horseless carriages. But their paths soon began to diverge. American cars grew bigger than their European counterparts. Bigger engines meant more cylinders, and American manufacturers pioneered the mass-produced six-cylinder engine, then the V8. Motorcycles followed a similar path—while most European manufacturers built small single-cylinder bikes, Harley-Davidson and Indian increasingly concentrated on big, fearsome V-twins.

The reason was simple. In the United States, a big and still-growing country, people just had to travel farther. A big engine in a large, roomy car wasn't just a luxury, it was a necessity, or seemed so at the time. So the American big three—Ford, General Motors, and Chrysler—became expert at offering big, powerful engines at low prices. Henry Ford built a cheap, mass-produced V8 from 1932, and though his archrivals didn't respond immediately, in the long term, they had no choice. The multicylinder route was true for upmarket automobiles too. In Europe, luxury cars were powered by straight 6s; in America, the rich drove V8s, V12s, and even 16s.

ABOVE: Plymouth Savoy, 1963. It may not look like a muscle car, but the 426 Max Wedge motor was an option.

So by the mid-1950s, America enjoyed an abundance of large, affordable engines, and the knowledge that surrounded them. That, in turn, affected motor sport. Heavy sixes and V8s didn't make for nimble track racing, but they were spectacular in straight-line acceleration. So drag racing and hot-rodding (which brought the big engine/small car formula down to a fine art) became central to the American motoring experience. Already, the foundations for the muscle car were being laid.

POWER RACE

BELOW: 1966 Shelby Mustang, one of the early GT350s. The Mustang was conceived as an affordable, good-looking coupe that could carry a family shopping or to the beach. Then Carroll Shelby recognized its potential, and a legendary line of Shelby Mustangs was born. They were only in production a few years, but their impact lived on: for 2005, Ford mimicked that '66 look in its latest Mustang.

The pace quickened in the 1950s. Those days are usually associated with the car as dinosaur. Great, heavy behemoths with sharklike fins and acres of chrome—not so much cars as an homage to excess, and certainly nothing to do with high performance. And yet, horsepower, and the image that went with it, was central even then. This was the jet age, and Detroit sought to emulate the jet planes that were just starting to take to the skies, not to mention the rockets that one day might put a man on the moon.

Just listen to the names of some of those V8s: Rocket, Powerpack, Firepower, Turbo-Fire. These were not intended for boulevard cruisers, though some of them may have ended up doing just that. Henry Ford's 1932 V8 had been revolutionary, but by modern standards the faithful flathead was somewhat underpowered. The 1950s saw an overhead valve coup, as every major American manufacturer launched an ohv V8 to keep up with a performance-hungry public.

Oldsmobile led the way in 1949 with the Rocket V8, the first genuinely new engine of the postwar era. The overhead valve Rocket could rev harder and faster than any sidevalve engine, V8 or not, and it made the Olds 88 one of the hottest cars

ABOVE: The beauty of muscle cars was that they took an unpromising base line, such as this Plymouth Belvedere, and produced something with supercar acceleration. Not many Belvedere GTXs were ordered with the expensive Hemi V8 option, but those that did could keep pace with a Ferrari or Porsche (though only in a straight line—early muscle cars often had soggy handling and poor brakes).

BELOW: The earliest muscle cars were three-box sedans, but Detroit soon realized that some buyers wanted svelte looks as well. Take this Dodge Charger fastback of 1966, which couldn't be mistaken for any sedan. Fake air scoops and "knock off" wheel trims underline the point: muscle cars were increasingly about looking the part.

available. Olds soon dropped their other engines, and would make nothing but V8s until 1964. Chevrolet didn't follow suit until 1955, but their 265 ci (4.3 liter) transformed Chevy's image. Their new small-block was nicknamed "the hot one," and could be enhanced by the addition of the "Power Pack" option—$59 brought a four-barrel carburetor, a special air cleaner, intake manifold, and dual exhausts, not to mention 180 horsepower. That same year, Chevrolet won the NASCAR series and dominated NHRA drag racing, while in the showrooms, had their best year ever.

The message was clear. Power and performance sold cars, and the great Detroit power race began in earnest. Chrysler was there too, having introduced their Firepower V8 back in 1951. This used hemispherical combustion chambers, which allowed bigger valves and deeper breathing, and hence more power. The Firepower wasn't the "Hemi" that would later become a muscle car legend, but it was its direct predecessor. Bigger cubes and more power followed, notably with the Red Ram (270

RIGHT: *The heart of any muscle car was, is, and always will be, the engine, as this '69 Pontiac GTO Judge demonstrates. The Judge was launched as a budget version of the mainstream GTO, so some equipment was missing, but it still came with a 366 hp 400 ci Ram Air III, not to mention bright colors and loud decals.*

ci, 193 hp) in 1955 and the D-500 later on. Ford wasn't quite so committed but had no intention of getting left behind, though they concentrated on the Thunderbird as their performance flagship.

In retrospect, the early T-bird is often seen as a bit of a cruiser, not a true sports car to rival the Corvette (though of course it outsold Chevy's two-seater by a huge margin). Even its standard 292 ci V8 offered over 200 hp, while the 312 ci Thunderbird Special upped that to 225 hp, and later to 245, 270, and 285 hp. The softly sprung Thunderbird couldn't match a Corvette around corners, but it was certainly fast in a straight line, and the ultimate T-bird would sport a supercharged V8 of 300 hp.

No doubt about it, the power race was in full swing, and some of these hotter engines were finding their way into American sedans as well. Take the

"Now, when you take three behemoth Supercars, all with curb weights around 3,600–3,700 pounds, and with a weight distribution of approximately 60-40, you can't expect Formula 1 handling."

(Motor Trend, *April 1970: Dodge Charger R/T, Mercury Cyclone GT, Olds Cutlass SX*)

Chrysler 300. Intended as a luxury two-door hardtop, Chrysler took it NASCAR racing, and in 1955 the 300 hp 300 (hence the name) was the most powerful production car on sale. The 300 didn't look like a sports car, still less like a muscle car, but it performed like one. Despite a curb weight of 4,000 lb. in 1955, ever increasing power gave it the muscle to cope. From that original 300 hp, power jumped to 340, then 355, and for 1962 the wedge-head 413 ci V8 was producing a claimed 405 hp.

With that sort of muscle, the Chrysler 300 could hardly be anything but fast, though this was despite its considerable bulk. Year after year through the 1950s, Americans had been happily consuming the mantra that bigger was better. Sure, there

RIGHT: Not all muscle cars improved with age. By 1969, the Shelby Mustangs had become largely cosmetic variations of the stock pony car. Early Shelby GT350s were fearsome things; fast, but noisy, hard riding, and difficult to drive on the limit. The '69 equivalent was softer, quieter . . . and sold in far greater numbers.

was more power than ever before, but more weight to haul around too. Fins sprouted higher, and wheelbases and overhangs got longer. Long, low, and wide was in.

But from 1958–59, there was a growing feeling that maybe it had all gone too far. In his book *The Insolent Chariots*, John Keats summed it up in graphic fashion. The driver, he wrote, "crouches to crawl into an illuminated rolling cave, and then reclines on a sort of couch, there to push buttons and idly wonder what might lie in front of the glittering hood while the sun burns into the eyes through the slanted windshield that is overhead." More to the point for Detroit, many Americans had turned away from the big three and were choosing small imported cars—Volkswagens

in particular. By 1960, one in ten new cars sold in the United States had been shipped there from overseas. It was an unheard-of figure.

So Detroit fought back with its own small cars. Not small in the European sense of course, but compact by American standards. Within a year or two, all of the big three had new compacts to sell. Chrysler's Valiant wasn't inspiring, more of a scaled-down big car, but the Chevrolet Corvair displayed genuine lateral thinking, with a rear-mounted flat-six motor that made it something of an upscaled, Americanized VW Beetle.

Right: A stock early '60s sedan? Not quite. Look more closely, and the roll cage and hood scoop show this Plymouth Savoy for what it is.

But the real success was the Ford Falcon. Simple, straightforward, and low cost, the Falcon aimed to provide the accommodation of a larger sedan, with fuel economy and running costs closer to that of a Beetle. It was the brainchild of Robert McNamara, president of Ford, but far from the stereotypical Detroit executive. McNamara was certainly no car nut—to him, cars were transportation, nothing more. This flew in the face of Detroit orthodoxy, and yet the Falcon was highly successful. Over 400,000 were sold in the first year, making it Ford's fastest-selling car of all time.

A Marriage Made in Heaven

That convinced the doubters. The American public was ready for a new generation of downsized cars, so the Valiant, Corvair, and Falcon were all followed by other Detroit downsizers. Over at Pontiac, all of the mainstream cars were made smaller and lighter, based on a new perimeter frame that cut wheelbases and lengths by a few inches. There was a new, smaller Pontiac to compete with the Falcon and Corvair as well—in those days, General Motors allowed their divisions to seriously compete with each other. It was the Tempest, compact and technically advanced, with an integral body/chassis and independent rear suspension, while the four-cylinder base engine was created by cutting Pontiac's 389ci V8 in half! A four-cylinder Pontiac? It was official—Detroit was finally making modern small cars.

So what has all this to do with muscle cars? Quite simply, the two vital elements that made up the muscle car revolution were now in place. On the one hand, big powerful V8 engines that offered 200–300 hp at reasonable cost. On the other, relatively compact, lightweight cars under whose hoods they would just about fit.

The new breed of compacts did something else as well, forming the base for the pony cars. When Ford introduced the Mustang in 1964, they might just as well have called it the Falcon Coupe, for all the Falcon parts they used. Sharing parts among

Left: Somewhere beneath that massive chrome air cleaner lies a muscle car legend. Chrysler's 426 ci Hemi V8 combined many cubic inches with the deep-breathing efficiency of hemispherical cylinder heads. The result was probably the most powerful street engine available.

ABOVE: Chrysler had the Hemi, Ford the Shelby Mustang, and Pontiac the Trans Am Firebird. Many muscle cars had an ultra-high performance variant, whose name became a force in itself. Such was the Z28 Chevrolet Camaro, which started out as a production racer, aimed at Trans Am.

models made a lot of sense, and many compact car components turned out to be ideal for the later ponies, which themselves became fully fledged muscle cars. So the advent of the early 1960s compacts is crucial to the muscle car story—if they hadn't existed, the muscle car in the form we know it would never have taken off.

Of course, the muscle car revolution didn't happen right away. Most people agree that the Pontiac GTO was the first true muscle car, but that didn't appear until 1964, a good few years after the compacts had first appeared. And, at first, it seemed as though compact buyers simply weren't interested in performance. There actually was a V8 option for the early Tempest (the Buick-built 215 ci unit of 155 hp) but only 1 percent of buyers chose it! But gradually, the initial excitement went out of the compact generation, and the buying public began to ask for more performance.

In 1963, Ford began offering a Falcon with the Fairlane 260 ci V8 slotted in.

According to a test by *Road & Track*, this mildly tuned 164 hp V8 in the lightweight Falcon added up to 0–60 mph in 8.5 seconds, and a top speed of 123 mph.

Meanwhile, Chevrolet introduced the Chevy II, a conventional compact to rival the Falcon, while the Corvair was transforming into a specialty sports coupe. At first, the Chevy II came with the same sort of power options as the plain-Jane Ford—a 90 hp 153 ci four and a 120 hp 194 ci six—but Chevrolet had something else up their sleeve. A factory-fitted V8 option didn't arrive until 1964, but well before then, it was possible to roll up outside your Chevy dealer in your II, and ask them to fit a 283 ci or 327 ci V8 off the shelf—the factory produced conversion kits to make this as easy as possible. The result was a true muscle car.

Or was it? Retrofitting the Chevy II with a V8 was an expensive business, and only the keenest types would go to the trouble of having their car out of action for a

LEFT: Few drivers left their muscle cars stock, though for many, the modifications amounted to bolting on a set of alloy wheels and applying some new pinstriping. Others took the modification game more seriously, as this Chevy Chevelle demonstrates. There are too many changes to list, and the supercharged V8, bursting alienlike through the hood, is just the most obvious.

"A young professional-type guy could easily turn on to any of these mature supercars. The Cyclone has the looks and performance, the Charger has the image and race-bred heritage, the Cutlass has the luxury. Too bad it isn't all together in one car."

(*Motor Trend*, April 1970: Dodge Charger R/T, Mercury Cyclone GT, Olds Cutlass SX)

week or two. Nor did the conversion include anything special in the way of trim, wide wheels, or interior. Some people liked it like that—most didn't.

No, it was the Pontiac GTO that finally brought all these things together in 1964: compact bodyshell, existing 389 ci V8, sporting trim, and a name to suit. And best of all, it was a factory job, so all you had to do to order one was check the appropriate box. The GTO was a massive success, and the muscle car was born.

So successful, that Pontiac's rivals soon came up with muscle cars of their own. Of course, some had been there all along, either with high-performance road cars—the Impala SS, the Corvette—or intended primarily for racing, such as special lightweight versions of the Galaxie or Pontiac's own "Super Duty" spec cars. But buyers soon became familiar with a whole host of names that would carve out their own legends: Chevelle SS, Gran Sport, Charger, 4-4-2, and Hemi. Parallel to these muscular sedans, the new breed of pony cars were also available with hot V8s: the Mustang, Camaro, Firebird, and Barracuda. They might not all fit the small car/big engine definition, but they were all muscle cars.

BELOW AND LEFT: ***Late-model Chevrolet Chevelle SS on the drag strip. Muscle cars were naturals for drag competition, being relatively affordable to buy and very quick over the quarter mile in stock showroom form, though for many, this was just the starting point.***

For the manufacturers, it was like Christmas. Not only did the buying public lap these cars up, but they were relatively cheap to build. Most of the parts came off the shelf, so it was just a case of picking the right engine, tranmission, and bodyshell and adding appropriate badgework, and you had a muscle car. That was reflected in those early interiors, which looked little different from those of the bread-and-butter cars on which they were based.

Unfortunately, much the same was true of the suspension, brakes, and steering. *Road Test* magazine tried the new generation of muscle cars in 1965 and found that they were fast all right, but lacking elsewhere. "Too little braking," was one comment; suspension "of the rubber band and marshmallow variety" was another;

RIGHT: Trans Am racing was another source of inspiration for muscle car owners, especially in its heyday of official manufacturer involvement in the late '60s and early '70s. The Pontiac Trans Am never actually raced, but made the most of its evocative name. This is a '73–'74 Super Duty 455, then the biggest-engined muscle car on sale.

steering had "the gearing ratio of the Queen Mary." Two years later, they tried again, and things were better. There were sway bars now, heavy-duty suspension setups, and even front disc brakes on most. Handling had improved, but sloppy suspension and featherweight steering still made some of the muscle cars a liability on high-speed corners. And disc brakes or not, stopping power still lagged far behind that of

European sports sedans. A Chevy SS was faster than a Jaguar but still couldn't stop or handle like one. It wasn't really until the end of the sixties that Detroit finally began to sort out the handling of its muscle cars. As we've said, that was all part of the appeal. Muscle cars could be rude, crude, and (with an inexperienced driver) unsafe, but many buyers, no sense in denying it, liked it that way.

"Even if we hadn't yet heard of quiche, it was clear that real men drove V8s."

(Motor Trend, 1988)

It couldn't last. The combination of young drivers with more enthusiasm than skill, plus powerful cars of less-than-perfect handling, led to many accidents. As a result, two things happened. Insurance rates skyrocketed for muscle cars, and some companies went so far as to refuse to cover young drivers altogether. And there were increasing calls for the muscle car craze to be curbed. In January 1970, the US Secretary of Transportation sought to have muscle car advertising curtailed.

By this time, muscle cars were out of tune with the times, with the advance of emissions and safety legislation, and the attiude to performance in general. But it would take an oil crisis to really kill the original muscle car. Detroit responded with a new generation of compacts—Ford's Falcon for the 1970s was the Pinto, while the Mustang II was smaller, lighter, and easier on gas than the original. It was no muscle car either, and the general view was that the age of the American performance car was over for good.

Except that it wasn't. Just as the early sixties compacts had gained ever bigger V8s as the buyers forgot about fuel economy, exactly the same thing happened a couple of decades later. The four-cylinder Mustangs and Camaros of the seventies and early eighties were gradually supplanted by V8s—everyone agreed that the Mustang GT V8 of the eighties was a little outdated and crude. But it was fast, fun, and affordable, so in a limited way, the muscle car was back.

As time went on, memories faded, and the Mustang, Camaro, and Firebird—arguably America's three remaining muscle cars in the late eighties and early nineties—carried on. Updated with new technology and more power, it really seemed as if the muscle car was back.

When Chrysler launched the Dodge Viper in 1992, that theory seemed vindicated. An 8.0 liter V10 power unit in an uncompromising sports car body and a soft-top to boot—who in 1974 or 1975 could have predicted that a muscle car like this would be on sale, and in demand, in North America again.

So is the muscle car back? Back in the seventies some thought it really had gone forever, and in a way they have been proved right. Performance cars are here in abundance, made in America and making the most of those hallowed old badges—even the GTO returned in 2004. (The Dodge Viper uses cubic inches rather than technological refinement to provide power in a very 1960s manner.) But these are not muscle cars in the spirit of the sixties, and they never could be. They are too high-tech, too expensive, and too competent. The original muscle cars were simple and crude by comparison . . . and cheap. The days when the man in the street could walk into a showroom, and for little more than the price of a family sedan, drive out in a rip-roaring 300 hp muscle car are gone forever.

Maybe, for the sake of safety and the environment, that's no bad thing, but we can still remember the golden age of the muscle car with affection.

***Right:** If anyone ever believed that the muscle car was dead after two oil crises, rocketing insurance rates, and a safety-conscious world, then the Dodge Viper proved them wrong. Not a muscle car in the old sense of a small sedan with a big V8, but the two-seat Viper still used sheer cubic inches to give stunning performance. An 8.0 liter V10 did the business.*

VIPER

"The interior and instrumentation is pure middle-class America . . . It is too bad Buick doesn't pay some close attention to the demands of this super-car market, because the Gran Sport has tremendous potential."
(Car and Driver, *April 1966, Skylark GS)*

General Motors

Were the Buick Gran Sports real muscle cars? They looked too understated for that. Hadn't they originated in William Mitchell's ambition to build a Buick to rival Jaguar? The head of General Motors was impressed by the British car's mix of elegance and power but was convinced that Buick could do the same job, cheaper. And no one calls the Jaguar a muscle car, do they? Buick, of course, had been in muscle car territory well before this. Way back in the 1930s, general manager Harlow Curtice ordered engineers to fit Buick's most powerful engine into the lightest body in the range. The result was the 100-mph Century, and Buick sales leapt to a healthy fourth, behind Chevrolet, Ford, and Plymouth.

Thirty years later, the Gran Sports most certainly were muscle cars, with authentically muscular big-cube V8s and 0–60 mph times as low as six seconds. They didn't shout their presence (late-model GSXs apart) and were understated in appearance, but then so were some other muscle cars. Muscle is as muscle does.

Firebird! Pontiac's pony car was a muscle car that both looked and acted the part, especially in later Trans Am guise.

PONTIAC
FIREBIRD

BELOW: The Riviera started out as an American Jaguar, or that was the intention. It succeeded as the first Gran Sport in 1965.

The first Gran Sport was launched in 1965, as an option on the standard Riviera, and unusually for a Buick, came with the choice of just one engine and transmission. Still, given what they were, Gran Sport customers didn't really need a choice. The engine was a 425 ci V8 with high 10.25:1 compression ratio, producing 360 hp at 4,400 rpm (a respectable 0.84 hp/ci) and a massive 465 lb ft at 2,800 rpm. This drove through General Motors's latest Hydra-Matic three-speed automatic transmission which, according *to Car and Driver*, was, "without question, the best automatic transmission in the world." A limited-slip differential and 3.42:1 rear axle ratio provided for a

RIGHT: "You can easily spend a party or two talking enthusiastically about the engine in Buick's new Riviera Gran Sport." (Pontiac advertisement, 1965)

16.2-second quarter-mile time, and 0–60 mph in 7.2 seconds. According to one magazine test, it could top 123 mph, so high-speed cruising should be a cinch for this American Jaguar.

None of this would have been much fun with the standard Riviera's roly-poly suspension, so part of the Gran Sport package was a heavier front antiroll bar, stiffer shock absorbers and springs, plus stiffer rear suspension bushings. With a higher-capacity dual exhaust to let the engine breathe and produce a pleasing V8 burble. Bill Mitchell had his Jaguar.

But the Riviera, although no monster on its 117-inch wheelbase, was no compact either, and the Pontiac GTO had made one thing abundantly clear—the most effective muscle cars were based on compacts.

So that's exactly what Buick did, transferring the successful Gran Sport concept on to the smaller Skylark for 1965. "There is mounting evidence that our engineers have turned into a bunch of performance enthusiasts," read one advertisement. "First they stuff the

"A 360 hp Wildcat V8 isn't all that's new with Riviera Gran Sport. But what a start . . . One of the new Gran Sports from Buick. You need not be a professional driver to qualify."

RIGHT: "A 360 hp Wildcat V8 isn't all that's new with Riviera Gran Sport," read a '65 advertisement for Pontiac's first car to bear that name, "But what a start." It went on to list all the extras that came as standard, concluding: "After all, wouldn't you rather have a Buick? One of the new Gran Sports from Buick." This later Riviera Gran Sport upheld the same concept of grace with pace.

Wildcat full of engine. Then the Riviera Gran Sport. And now this, the Skylark GS, which is almost like having your own personal-type nuclear deterrent." (They also described it as, "a howitzer with windshield wipers," so someone in the copywriting department evidently had a militaristic turn of mind.)

Being smaller and less heavy than the Riviera, the Skylark didn't get the same 425 ci engine, but its 401 ci V8 was only one step down. With the same high compression, it produced 325 hp, so it wasn't far behind the original Gran Sport on the test track either—*Motor Trend* recorded 0–60 in 7.8 seconds and 16.6 seconds over the standing quarter. As with the Riviera, the suspension was beefed up to suit, plus there were

"Buick GS-340. What the car enthusiasts are enthusiastic about."

RIGHT: For all its sporting aspirations (it wasn't really a muscle car for the hairy chested), the Gran Sport Riviera remained an elegant beast, setting the tone for all the '60s Buick GSs.

ABOVE: *A well-used GS readies itself on the strip, with what looks like wider than standard rear tires. This car lacks the stripes and spoilers that the later more flamboyant GSXs carried.*

LEFT: *The Gran Sport was never conceived as a drag racer, but like many muscle cars, that's what many of these models ended up doing. Their combination of abundant torque (465 lb ft in the original Riviera Gran Sport) and a slick automatic transmission did the business.*

dual exhausts. But there was evidence that the Skylark GS was aimed at more serious hot car enthusiasts, with wide tires, a beefed-up body shell (whether in coupe, hardtop, or convertible form), and a choice of six rear axle ratios. With a 4.3:1 rear end (not on Buick's standard list), racing slicks, headers, shimmed front springs, and a transmission kick-down switch, *Motor Trend* recorded a 13.42-second quarter, with a terminal speed of over 104 mph.

Nothing succeeds like success, and the Gran Sport idea was evidently successful, as Buick extended the option to the full-size Wildcat for 1966, with the now expected extras: a 340 hp V8, Positraction rear axle, and heavy-duty suspension. They paid it the ultimate compliment by promoting the Gran Sport from option status into a Skylark model in its own right. Pontiac did the same trick with the GTO when sheer demand overtook its option status.

Buick Skylark Gran sport 1966

Engine: *340-horsepower 401 cubic-inch V8*

Transmission: *two-speed automatic*

Steering: *recirculating ball*

Tires: *Firestone Super Sports 500 7.75 x 14*

Brakes: *four-wheel hydraulic 9.5-inch drums*

Suspension: *front independent, unequal-length wishbones, coil springs, antiroll bar; rear rigid axle and locating links, coil springs, antisway bar*

Wheelbase: *115 inches*

Track (F/R): *58/59in*

Weight: *3,550 lb.*

The new Skylark Gran Sport was no stripped-down muscle car. Like all the Gran Sports it was a little upmarket, so it shared trim with higher-level Skylarks—carpets, full wheel trims, full vinyl interior, and plenty of bright metal and subtle red stripes to underline the sports image. Power still came from Buick's 401 ci V8, though corporate politics demanded that the car be badged as a "400."

Why? GM head office had dictated that no midsize car be equipped with more than 400 cubic inches! If the 400's 325 hp wasn't enough, Buick offered a new 340 hp option, and the car still came in three body styles: hardtop (by far the most popular, with nearly 10,000 sold in 1966), coupe, and convertible.

"Get in with the In Crowd in a GS-400. The In Crowd knows what's happening, and what's happening is Buick '67."

So now there were three Gran Sports, but for '67 Buick expanded the range downward, with the 340. Still based on the Skylark, it was the company's first shot at a budget muscle car: "GS 400's running mate . . . for

Left: The biggest V8 ever to power a production Gran Sport: the 455. Unveiled for the 1970 model year, it made up one of the biggest-cube muscle cars ever. Claimed power was 350 hp, with torque peaking at over 500 lb-ft at 2,800 rpm That was without Stage 1 tuning, a factory-fit option.

ABOVE AND RIGHT: ***Look at me! Muscle cars got more garish in the early '70s, and even the gentlemanly Gran Sports had to follow suit, with the striped and spoilered GSX series. The hood-mounted tachometer is a real period touch.***

BELOW: It wasn't just stripes and spoilers; every GSX (it was a factory-fitted option on the standard Gran Sport) came with wide tires and a four-speed manual transmission.

people who look for a large measure of sporting flavor at a low price." In fact, the 340's status as a true muscle car is a little blurred, as the 340 ci V8 it offered was also available on any other midsize Buick at the time.

Sure, it came with a standard four-speed manual transmission, and there were plenty of red rallye stripes, red hood scoops, red rallye wheels, and (in case anyone hadn't got the message) those GS badges. But it was barely faster than any more sober Buick 340.

BELOW RIGHT: *The spoiler craze of the '70s was a direct spin-off from NASCAR racing, where ever higher speeds called for ever higher downforce.*

Not that this mattered too much. The whole point of the GS340 was an authentic sporty image (which it portrayed well), with lower insurance costs than the full GS400, a big bonus for younger drivers. Yet despite the milder motor and a more basic interior, it saved only $174 over the 400, and even heavy-duty suspension cost extra. Maybe it's not so surprising that the GS340 was totally outsold by the 400, by a factor of four to one.

Meanwhile, the GS400 had its own upgrade, with a new 400 ci engine. Pedants at Buick could relax—they were no longer breaking the "400" rule. On paper, power was still 340 hp, though performance nuts were opting for the four-speed manual transmission instead of paying $237 extra for the Super Turbine auto—it was a full second quicker to 60 mph. There were flashier wheels and more brightwork too, as Buick tried to make the GS look like more of a muscle car. There were even two simulated hood scoops, though overall the Buick retained its more subtle image, compared to, say, a Mopar muscle car or a Shelby Mustang.

The following year, the stripped-down 340 was upgraded with a 350 ci V8, now with 280 hp at 4,600 rpm and 375 lb ft at 3,200. Despite a price rise (now not far short of $1,000) and a downgraded three-speed manual transmission, it proved more popular than the 340, and Buick sold over 8,000 of them that year. The

Above: ***Whatever the external treatment, Gran Sports were quite cossetting inside—this was no stripped-out Road Runner or base-model Mustang. Plush vinyl seats, carpeting, and full trim tell the story. Note the U-handle transmission shifter.***

400 remained the performance flagship, and for 1969, enthusiasts could specify two extra levels of tune. Stage I was dealer fitted, and included a high-lift camshaft, tubular pushrods, heavy-duty valve springs, and a high-output oil pump, not to mention a big dual exhaust (the tailpipes were over two inches across) and a modified Quadrajet four-barrel carburetor. That added up to 345 hp at 4,800 rpm, giving a substantial performance boost over the standard GS400, and the motor was also fitted with an ignition governor to prevent over-revving, cutting in at 5,200 rpm. Rallye suspension and power front disc brakes could be added on top, and the rear axle choice was between 3.64:1 or 3.42:1. Stage II (the same as Stage I, but with a wilder cam) was only available over the counter—Buick dealers weren't allowed to fit it, as the hottest option wasn't recommended for road use, or indeed on any car fitted with a muffler.

By now, the muscle car power race was in full swing, though thanks to insurance and safety concerns, it wouldn't last much longer. There was still time for

Buick to announce the biggest-engined Gran Sport yet for 1970, and the GS 455 offered a 455 ci unit of 350 hp at 4,600 rpm. Torque was this big V8's strong point, at 510 lb ft, and it could push the biggest GS to 60 mph in about 6.5 seconds. But as ever, this wasn't enough for some (or for Buick, if it wanted to keep up with the muscle opposition), so the Stage I option was still there, though it was now a more thorough conversion, involving new big-port cylinder heads, blueprinted pistons, and nickel-chrome satellite steel valves. And all for just under $200. At 5.5 seconds 0–60 mph for the automatic transmission version, it was something of a performance bargain.

But Buick obviously still thought that the GS looked too boring and, in the same year as the 455, introduced the GSX option. This finally turned the Gran Sport into a look-at-me muscle car, available in bright yellow or white, with black hood, side stripes, and rear spoiler. There was a hood-mounted tachometer (a real muscle car badge of honor at the time) as well as a Rallye steering wheel, four-speed manual transmission, and wide tires. It certainly looked the part, but only 678 GS customers checked the GSX option box in 1970. It was still available in 1971 and 1972, but only to special order—a mere 124 GSXs were bought in 1971 and just 44 in 1972.

BELOW: A GSX certainly looked the part of a muscle car, but very few Gran Sport customers actually checked the box—little more than 100 in 1971 and a mere 44 in 1972. For real muscle car people, a loud and proud Mustang or Barracuda was more the thing.

But maybe with GSX, Buick misunderstood what the Gran Sport had been about. This was always the gentleman's muscle car. Seriously fast, but never flashy, reflecting its raison d'être in Bill Mitchell's Jaguar aspirations. Subtle or not, time was running out for the big GS in the early 1970s. Midsize by sixties standards, it was heavy and unwieldy for the more environment-conscious seventies, and for 1972 the V8s were downgraded to cope with US emissions laws, though they still came in 350, 455, and 455 Stage I forms. Net horsepower made the power cuts look bigger than they were, but the Stage I was now only 270 hp/390 lb ft. The end was near.

Move on ten years, and the climate had changed again. Despite two oil crises and stricter emissions/safety legislation that was here to stay, the early 1980s saw the first

BELOW: Gran Sports were naturals for the drag strip, long after production had ceased, as this recent shot of a GS shows.

glimmerings of a performance revival. Buick had already taken a tentative step in that direction with the Regal Grand National. It looked good, with its alloy wheels, T-top roof, and fancy paint job, but mechanically it was a standard Regal, and its 0–60 time of around 15 seconds could not have been less like a muscle car. Little more than 200 were sold, and Buick hastily dropped its "hot" Regal. The 1982 Regal Grand National was a special only available with a two-tone paint scheme with a silver mist upper body and charcoal gray lower body. The paint scheme was livened up with red pin stripping, and "Buick" decals on the rear quarters. Only 215 were built; which, as already pointed out, wasn't such a loss. The only engine option was a 4.1 liter V6 rated at a puny 125 bhp; though it did have the Gran Touring suspension system.

But in 1984 it tried again, and this time the Grand National (taking its name from Buick NASCAR racers) was back with a vengeance. The 3.8 liter V6 was turbocharged and fuel injected to produce 200 hp, enough to slash the 0–60 time to less than 9 seconds and boost top speed to around 120 mph. Still not in Shelby or Hemi territory perhaps, but a clear sign that performance was back.

The look had changed, too, and the Grand National now came with all-black paintwork, devoid of all decoration. The Grand National option cost $1,282, adding about 10% to the price of the standard Regal, though the price was cut for 1986.

In fact, the Grand National became something of a minilegend. By the time it was dropped in 1987, the Regal was Buick's last rear-wheel-drive car, and some mourned the passing of the all-black Grand.

As for the Gran Sport, that was later revived, and used on 1990s versions of both the Skylark and Regal, now in more compact front-wheel-drive form. These reverted to a more conservative image that was Buick's home territory—the GSX and Grand National had really been aberrations, for Buick's strength was not in producing muscle cars to rival Ford, Chevy, or Plymouth, but to build muscle cars that were acceptable for a different market that preferred quiet good looks to gaping hood scoops. The Gran Sports really were the gentleman's muscle cars.

CADILLAC: THE UNEXPECTED

Cadillac is not normally associated with muscle cars, for the very good reason that they never built any, at least not to the classic 1960s sense. Caddy finally did offer the Allante, though perhaps it would be more accurate to describe that model as a refined convertible that happened to have muscle car performance. But this didn't happen until the final year of Allante production, for just as the convertible came good, Cadillac dropped the whole project.

In a way, it's understandable. The Allante, begun with such high hopes, was showing every sign of turning into a full-scale, high-grade 100 percent lemon. The idea must have sounded good. Cadillac needed a classy convertible, a luxury two-seater, to compete with imports from Mercedes and Jaguar. To gain that Euro-credibility, the body would have to be designed in Europe, with power from an all-American V8. It was a well-worn formula that had been used many times before: European style coupled with American muscle.

But in the case of the Allante, the economics made little sense, even for a car that would sell for over $60,000 by 1993. Eldorado platforms were flown to Turin, Italy, by a special Boeing 747 freighter. Craftsmen at Pininfarina would shorten the platform and build the Allante's body onto it. Then the finished bodies were flown back across the Atlantic by 747 again, before being trucked to the GM Hamtramck assembly plant in Detroit.

The economics were crazy, but that might not have mattered had the original Allante been an object of desire. The trouble was, it was anything but. Most people liked the understated looks, but the plastic-dominated interior just didn't justify the $50,000 asking price. And Cadillac's 4.1 liter V8, mustering 170 hp, gave the Allante far from spirited performance. It would creep up to 120 mph, but 0–60 mph took 9.5 seconds, not enough to frighten any equivalent Jaguar or Mercedes.

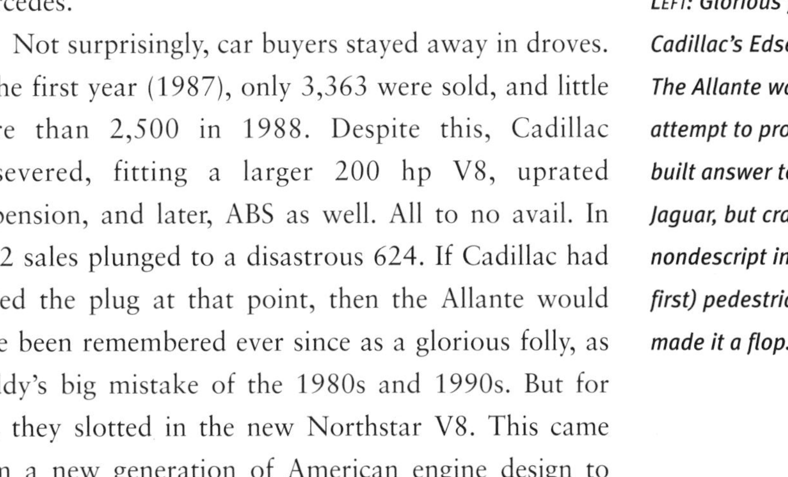

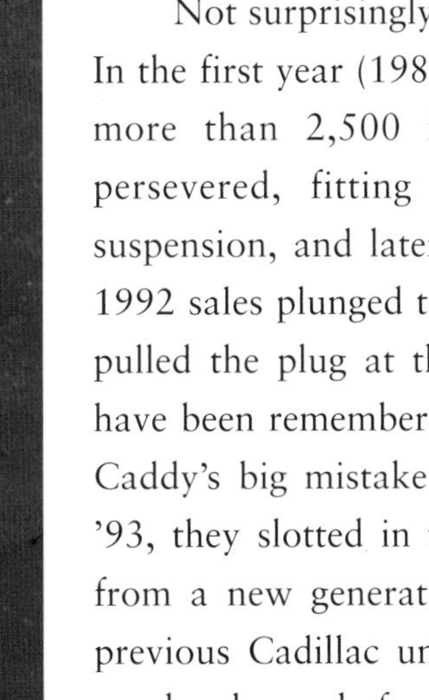

Left: Glorious folly? Or Cadillac's Edsel of the '80s? The Allante was a brave attempt to produce a Detroit-built answer to Mercedes and Jaguar, but crazy economics, a nondescript interior, and (at first) pedestrian performance made it a flop.

Not surprisingly, car buyers stayed away in droves. In the first year (1987), only 3,363 were sold, and little more than 2,500 in 1988. Despite this, Cadillac persevered, fitting a larger 200 hp V8, uprated suspension, and later, ABS as well. All to no avail. In 1992 sales plunged to a disastrous 624. If Cadillac had pulled the plug at that point, then the Allante would have been remembered ever since as a glorious folly, as Caddy's big mistake of the 1980s and 1990s. But for '93, they slotted in the new Northstar V8. This came from a new generation of American engine design to previous Cadillac units. A 4.6 liter V8, it had double overhead camshafts per cylinder bank, four valves per cylinder, and fuel injection.

The car was transformed, with a 0–60 mph time of just 6.7 seconds and a top speed of 145 mph. After recording those figures (which would equal many of the ultimate sixties muscle cars), *Road & Track* magazine declared that this was the fastest Cadillac they'd ever tested. As icing on the cake, it was chosen as Pace Car for the Indianapolis 500 that year, the honorary crown for any American performance car. Sadly, the American public seemed to have already made up its mind that the Allante was a nondescript luxury cruiser, and sales did not improve. So at the end of the '93 model year, when the Allante had finally achieved muscle car status, it also became history.

CHEVROLET: THE HOT ONE

BELOW: Corvettes dominated SCCA racing for a while, which helped to underline Chevrolet's strong performance image. This car is pictured at a 1990s meeting in England.

The Chevrolet muscle car story begins well before the sixties. They might have been General Motor's budget brand, the seller of cheap sedans and station wagons to rival those of Ford, but Chevrolet also had a strong performance image. It was natural that when the muscle car boom began, Chevy would be perfectly placed to take advantage of it. The combination of a reputation for perfomance and cheap base base models was a natural fit for muscle car creation.

RIGHT: *Many followed its exploits on the race track, but to many more the Corvette was always the ultimate American sports car. This convertible, under a bright blue sky, says it all.*

It was 1955 when Chevrolet spent $300 million on a dramatic renewal of its range, overseen by Harlow Curtice (now GM chief, and the same Curtice who had created the prototypical Buick muscle car in the 1930s). The new Chevys were carefully designed to look long, wide, and low, but this was only part of the change that transformed the company's image in a very short space of time. Chevrolet general manager managed to convince GM's overall Engineering Policy Committee that his division was "too six-cylinder minded." In short, that it needed a new V8. In February 1951, the committee approved, and Chevrolet's new V8 program was on. It was a turning point, for the small-block V8 that resulted would form the basis of Chevrolet

LEFT: *The first Corvette—let's be clear about this—was no muscle car, and any number of sedans were quicker over the quarter mile. But it was America's only real sports car for a couple of decades, and the muscle followed after just a few years.*

LEFT: *Small by American standards, the early Corvette was a size compromise between Detroit sedans and little European sports cars. With a lightweight fiberglass body, and styling influenced by the XK120 Jaguar, it looked like a winner.*

RIGHT: *Arguably, this was what held it back. The early Corvette was lumbered with the ancient "Stovebolt" straight-six, an ex-truck unit that could muster only 150 hp even in hot Corvette form. Later Corvette V8s made up for that.*

LEFT: *For 1964, all Corvettes were powered by the small-block 327ci V8, but in four states of tune. Base model came with a single four-barrel Carter carburetor and 250 hp, then the 300 hp L75. The L76 (11.0:1 compression, mechanical lifters) made that 365 hp, but the ultimate tune was the L84, with Ram Jet fuel injection and 375 hp.*

BELOW: *Sting Ray. This dramatic new styling for '63 was seen by many as the quintessential Corvette, and proved a fine performance flagship for Chevrolet—but Chevy wasn't the only "Hot One" by this time. Big-block V8s—the 396 and 427—soon followed.*

RIGHT: One-piece rear window marks this out as a '64-onward Sting Ray, as only the first '63 cars had that split window that looked great but was expensive to build, and made parking a nightmare. Either way, a Sting Ray's rear end shouted "Sports Car."

ABOVE: Until the arrival of the big-block in '65, Corvettes were more high-revving sports cars than true big-cube muscle machines. Offering a claimed 425 hp, the first 396 big-block made the highly tuned fuel-injected 327 superfluous. The 427 that soon followed claimed no more power, but had a torque advantage.

performance and muscle cars for the next ten years. The man they chose to design it was Ed Cole. It was a wise choice, as Cole was a GM man who had spent his entire working life with V8s, and already had a good idea of what Chevrolet needed. It would have to be overhead valve (the days of the flat-head V8 were rapidly disappearing), and he even had the capacity worked out. "[Harry] Barr and I were always fond of saying how we would do it if we could ever design a new engine," he later recalled in an interview for *Fortune* magazine. "We knew we'd like a displacement of 265 cubic inches and that automatically established the bore and stroke."

So confident were Cole and his colleague Harry Barr of their new Chevrolet V8, that the production plant and tooling were ordered before the prototype had even been started.

Their confidence was slightly flawed (the new engine used oil at a fair rate, and the rocker arms were noisy, though these faults were soon cured) but not misplaced, and the V8 had a huge impact. Journalist Tom McCahill described the Chevy V8 as "the hottest car of this brand ever to race down the turnpike."

ABOVE: Power bulge marks this out as a big-block Corvette—Camaro, Chevelle, and Impala also benefited from the 427.

Recognizing the engine's potential, Chevrolet rapidly offered a $59 "Power Pack" (four-barrel carburetor, special air cleaner, intake manifold, and dual exhaust). At Daytona Speed Week that year, the new car surprised everyone by topping out at 112 mph, and finishing second only to Cadillac. McCahill was impressed all over

Above: ***This "bubble top" Bel Air coupe might not look like a muscle car, but with a 409 under the hood, it most certainly was.***

again, ranking Chevy alongside the Ford Thunderbird, Chrysler 300, and Jaguar D-Type as one of "the four biggest sensations of the week." Bob Lund later confirmed that the new power unit had transformed Chevrolet's image "from being a relatively unexciting car . . . to a very exciting car in the mid-fifties and late-fifties . . . It was all brought about by the introduction of that V8."

"You're protected by all kinds of new safety features; your ride's smoother and your steering's easier; your music's in true stereo on tape or radio; you've never looked better, going the Chevrolet Way."

In 1955, "that V8" had earned Chevrolet the nickname, the "Hot One." For 1956, its own slogan declared, "The Hot One's Even Hotter." The 265 ci V8 was given a further boost up to 205 hp, as the Super Turbo-Fire V8, thanks to a four-barrel carburetor, high-lift camshaft, and 9.25:1 compression ratio. That was just the beginning. The following year, a 283 ci V8 was launched, with a larger bore and stroke than the 265, and replacing the smaller unit in all but its lowest-powered 162 hp form. The new motor came in five different power levels: 185 hp, 220, 245, and 250 . . . and 283 hp. That top figure was the really big news, as Chevrolet had set a new record, building the first production engine to offer one hp per cubic inch. Rochester Ram-Jet fuel injection helped Chevrolet's latest V8 reach that magic figure. It's also worth noting that the original 265 V8 had been the "Hot One." Now, barely two years later, its replacement offered over 70 percent more power! Years before the classic muscle car era began, a power race was already underway.

ABOVE RIGHT: Given a long enough straight, the aerodynamic bubble top could nudge 150 mph, when 409 powered.

FAR RIGHT: Squared-off for '62, the Impala was Chevrolet's flagship car, and still offered the Super Sport option, though this was a purely cosmetic collection of stripes, badges, and wheeltrims.

That fuel-injected 283 also found its way into the Corvette, which had suffered from a distinct lack of performance, being saddled with Chevrolet's economy engine, the ageing Blue Streak six. This was doubly embarrassing, as the Corvette was touted as a true two-seat sports car, and looked the part too, yet Ford's softer Thunderbird V8 was decisively faster. Not any more. *Road & Track* found that the new engine in the Corvette, as well as being "quiet and remarkably docile," could rocket the lightweight sports car to 60 mph in just 5.7 seconds.

"From the distinctive front end styling to the smart new wraparound taillights, the Impala SS demands attention."

But just to show that not everything went Chevrolet's way, 1958 saw the introduction of an even larger V8, the 348. Built to beat Ford's Interceptor Special 352 V8, it claimed 280 hp in Super Turbo-Thrust form, with triple two-barrel

RIGHT: The SS option was available on both coupes and convertibles, but real muscle car character came with the legendary 409, which came in 380 hp or 409 hp guise, the latter named "Turbo-Fire," with lightweight valve train. Either way, buyers had one of the fastest cars on the street.

LEFT: Conceived as a compact, the Chevy II soon grew in size and was available with a range of muscular V8s. From 1968, with a Camaro-sized engine bay (the whole car was upsized that year), this included big blocks as well as the 327 and 350s. A 396 Turbo-Jet with 350 hp or 375 hp was available from the factory, though tuners soon discovered that a full-power 427 would slip into the space just as easily.

BELOW: Chevrolet's answer to the Ford Falcon, the Chevy II, offered a wider range of V8s than the plain-Jane Ford, including a 350 hp 327. Milder versions were available.

carburetors and a 9.5:1 compression. But the real-world performance didn't live up to that promise, and to make things worse, the new engine weighed 110 lb. more than the 283, and was actually slower in practice. At Daytona that year, the 283 was nearly 5 mph faster.

Matters were rectified midyear, with 348s in a higher state of tune. The "Law Enforcement Engine" came as a 300 hp unit with single four-barrel carburetor, or as

RIGHT: *"SS" still stood for "Super Sport" in Chevrolet badge-speak, and meant more complete instrumentation, bucket seats, plus those all-important badges.*

315 hp and triple two-barrels. Both had a high-lift Duntov cam, solid lifters, and ultra-high 11.0:1 compression. It did the trick, and Chevrolets with this engine could reach 60 mph in 7 seconds, and top 135 mph. By the time the 1960 model year rolled around, the 348 was producing 350 hp in top Super Turbo-Thrust form, now with dual valve springs and very careful assembly.

So the 348 had finally passed the 1 hp/ci milestone as well, but the really big news of the year was Chevrolet's new 409 V8. An early production example was taken to the Winternationals drag racing championship at Pomona in California. Don Nicholson blew the opposition away with a quarter mile of 13.59 seconds. A legend

RIGHT: *If you wanted performance to go with the SS finery, the only answer was a hot 327 V8, now with 11.0:1 compression ratio and 350 hp, and 360 lb ft. In short, it was the Corvette small-block that was shoehorned into this compact sedan, and the result was 0–60 mph in 7.2 seconds and a 15-second quarter mile.*

Above: Despite the badges, trim, and that hot V8 under the hood, there was no disguising the origins of the Nova II, a simple and economical sedan.

had been born. The 409 would become such an iconic engine that the Beach Boys would write a song about it.

The early 360 hp 409 was derived from the 348, with a larger bore and stroke, but it was quickly withdrawn after only a handful had been made. In 409 form, the old 348 block gave only marginal thickness and was difficult to produce. But in 1962 it was back, this time with its own all-new block, cast alloy cylinder heads, and larger intake valves. The result was a power boost to 380 hp with a single four-barrel

LEFT: In 1966, a newly sports-conscious market made that "Super Sport" script and the red "SS" badge highly desirable, though the 350 hp V8 wasn't a compulsory part of the package.

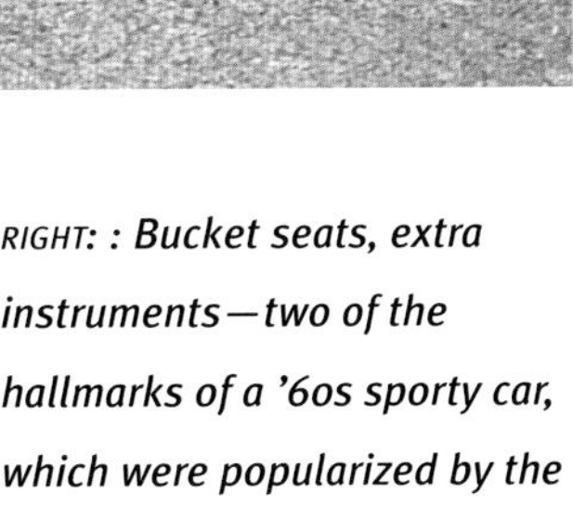

RIGHT: : Bucket seats, extra instruments—two of the hallmarks of a '60s sporty car, which were popularized by the Mustang.

carburetor, and 409 hp at 6,000 rpm if you specified twin four-barrels. Once again, a Chevrolet V8 had hit that magic 1 hp/ci figure, and more drag race records began to be broken.

With ultralow rear-axle ratios, astonishing acceleration was possible. When *Car Life* tested a drag-prepared 409-powered Bel Air Sport Coupe, it recorded 0–60 mph in 4.0 seconds. The car then stormed on to 100 mph in just 9.4 seconds!

RIGHT: Hood bulge denotes a big-block Corvette from '65 onward. The side-mounted exhaust was a new option that year, at $134.50—perfect for throttle blipping at red lights!

A 409 could be ordered in just about any Chevy listed in 1961, including station wagons, though the Bel Air was a good choice for street racers, thanks to its relatively low weight and good aerodynamics—150 mph was possible, given a long enough straight. The midsize Impala could be had with a 409 as well, though Chevrolet decided to make the most of its sporting credentials with a new Super Sport option for the Impala. This was a complete package that included power brakes with sintered

BERRY MOTOR CARS, LLC

LEFT: The second-generation Corvette caused a sensation when it was launched, bringing together influences from stylist Bill Mitchell's Mako Shark show car and the E-Type Jaguar (Mitchell himself drove a Jag). It was one of the first cars to be designed with the aid of a wind tunnel.

BELOW: That sleek fastback looked superb, both in pictures and in the metal, though hauling heavy cases into the trunk via the passenger compartment took some of the glamour out it. Neither the roadster nor the coupe had a trunk lid.

LEFT: Rare beast. The split rear window marks this car out as one of the original '63 Corvettes. This styling feature, based on a seam that ran down the center of the car, from the hood bulge rearward, was highly controversial at the time—it was intended to resemble the tail of a real stingray. It disappeared for '64.

metal brake linings, power steering, heavy duty springs and shocks, 7,000 rpm tachometer and Super Sport trim. It added up to a good value at $54. Of course, you didn't have to have a 409 as well (and only 142 '61 SS Impalas were so equipped), and extra-power options kicked off with the 340 hp four-barrel 348. A triple two-barrel 348 offered 350 hp while the 360 hp or 380 hp 409s were available too. Pay around $500 extra, and you got the full-house 409, with twin four-barrel carburetors and that

***Below:* Restyled for 1968, the Chevy Nova still came with the option of large, muscular V8s.**

genuine 409 hp. Even in SS trim, the Impala sport coupe didn't look like a muscle car, but it certainly performed like one.

Much the same could be said of the Corvette. Today, muscle cars of the sixties are seen as sedans and coupes, but the Corvette was clearly a two-seater sports car. On the other hand, it certainly performed like a muscle car, at least once Chevrolet had equipped it with the small-block V8. In fact, it was the fastest U.S.-built road car on sale, thanks to its lightweight fiberglass body. It had benefited from that first fuel-injected motor, the one that extracted 283 hp from 283 ci. Less powerful engines were available too, but by 1962 the ultimate Corvette was powered by a 327 ci small-block V8 (a development of the 283), still with Rochester fuel injection and enough power to take it to 60 mph in around six seconds.

Many Corvettes were raced, and in an attempt to get around the AMA racing ban of 1957, racing parts began to find their way onto the Corvette factory options list. If parts, however special, were factory-

BELOW: Longer and wider than before, the freshened-up Nova also sported new fastback styling influenced by that of the Chevelle. If you insisted, the base engine was still a straight six (and in fact most customers checked that box), but a whole range of V8s were there too, a 325 hp version of the 327 and later, 350 or 375 hp 396s.

Below: Chevy IIs with the hottest V8s lent themselves well to drag racing. They were lighter in weight than the full-size sedans and relatively affordable, with factory-fitted V8s that offered stunning off-the-line performance.

fitted, they were not subject to the ban. So the 327 V8 came in three versions, the most powerful of which was a virtual racing engine, with an unheard-of 360 hp—this broke the 1 hp per cubic inch, and then some! Other exotic parts could be ordered to make the factory Corvette race-ready, such as wild "Duntov" camshafts (named after Corvette racing guru Zora Arkus-Duntov), aluminum-cased transmissions, and super-large fuel tanks. The Corvette still eschewed those new-fangled disc brakes, but everything else was on offer to make the drums as effective as possible: power assistance, dual circuits, sintered metallic linings, and Ram Air cooling. Of course, very few Corvettes were actually ordered with all this equipment, but enough for the car to dominate B-production SCCA racing, at least until the AC Cobra came along.

For '63, the Corvette was transformed into the Stingray. With its sharp edges, hidden headlights and striking looks, the new car had a huge impact. It was built to

ABOVE: This shot of a Chevy II Nova shows how radical changes often are to drag racers. By 1970, the ultimate Nova SS option was code-named RPO L78, which brought the 396 V8 in 375 hp form—over 5,000 Nova buyers opted for that in 1970, with less than 2,000 going for the slightly milder 350 hp version.

RIGHT: This earlier Nova has been heavily modified for the drag strip, with a roll cage, big fat rear slicks, and a massive hood scoop to keep two hungry four barrels supplied with untold cubic feet of fresh air.

ABOVE: *Despite the radical modifications, the original Chevy II Nova body is almost as it left the factory. Not that street-bound Novas would be under-equipped—tick the right boxes on the order form, and your compact Chevy could come with four-speed manual transmission, limited-slip differential, and heavy-duty suspension.*

LEFT: *Hard to believe that the Chevy II started out as an economy car to meet and beat the Ford Falcon, not to mention the VW Beetle. The first engine options were a 90 hp four or 120 hp six, though you could go to the trouble and expense of having your Chevrolet dealer retrofit a V8.*

Chevrolet
JEGS

LEFT: Drag racing has always been central to muscle car culture, as this Chevrolet Biscayne demonstrates—just look at the distortion on that rear tire! Trans Am and NASCAR had their followers, but competing at the strip was something anyone could do, almost anywhere. Some of the cars were almost stock, but extra horsepower and fatter rear tires were essential for really quick times.

BELOW: As its popularity grew through the fifties, Detroit's big three began to offer cars (or parts) to make their products quicker on the strip. Some of these were thinly disguised racers, barely road legal, and are now pulse-quickening collectors' items. The result was a generation for whom the standing quarter-mile time was the most important figure on any car's checklist.

LEFT: Biscayne 427. Drag racing's FX class (which later led to the funny cars) opened up new opportunities for radical changes. Moving the rear axle forward was one (expensive) option, shifting weight distribution rearward and thus improving traction.

perform under the skin too, with independent rear suspension and the 327 V8 offered in four levels of tune: 250 hp, 300 hp, 340 hp, or (with fuel injection and 11.25:1 compression) 360 hp. Not only that, but Corvette owners could buy a closed coupe for the first time. Sales doubled from around 10,000 a year to over 21,000 in 1963. Despite Chevrolet taking on a second shift at the St Louis assembly plant, some eager buyers had to wait two months for delivery of their new Stingrays.

BELOW: A 1968 Corvette. Even without that badge, what else could this be? This was the convertible's heyday too, before safety fears put a temporary stop to ragtops.

RIGHT: Look closely—"Chevrolet Motor Division: Disc Brakes"—still something to boast about on the wheel hubs in the mid '60s.

But the Corvette couldn't afford to stand still, and right through the sixties, it kept up with the muscle cars sprouting around it. For 1964, the top-injected 327 now produced 375 hp at 6,200 rpm and 350 lb ft at 4,400 rpm, that high-rpm torque peak indicating the V8's high state of tune. The following year, when Corvette sales hit another new record, there were all-round disc brakes at last. This was just as well, as 1965 also saw the first big-block Corvette, with the 396 ci V8 also offered in the full-size Chevy and the Chevelle that year. It claimed 425 hp but only lasted a year, as in '66 Chevrolet upped the stakes yet again, with a 427 V8 of 390 or 425 hp. Both came with four-speed manual transmissions as standard, with standard or close ratios respectively. Despite more equipment (power steering, power brakes, electric windows), the latest Corvette, at

CHEVROLET CORVETTE *1968*

Engine: *Base 300-horsepower 327 cubic-inch V8; through four further options to L88, increases to 430-horsepower (probably 560) and 427 cubic-inch V8*

Transmission: *three-speed automatic, three-speed manual, or four-speed manual*

Steering: *recirculating ball*

Wheels & tires: *15 x 7-inch stamped steel rims with Firestone 9.20 x 15*

Brakes: *11.7-inch discs*

Suspension: *front short arms with coil springs; rear independent triple-link arms with transverse leaf springs and lateral struts*

Wheelbase: *98 inches*

Height: *47.9 inches*

Weight: *3,419 pounds (L88)*

3,270 lb., was only slightly heavier than the fifties lightweight. *Car Life* tested a 425 hp 427, and measured a 14-second standing quarter, plus a 5.7-second 0–60 time. Make that 5.5 seconds in '67, when the top Tri-Power 427 was up to 435 hp. Restyled in 1968, the Corvette retained the same 427 options, including the racing-only aluminum-headed L88 427—430 hp officially, but unofficial estimates ranged from

560 hp to nearly 600! But this was the high point for hot Corvettes. New legislation was starting to bite, and power figures leveled off. That didn't stop Chevrolet from introducing a big-block 454 V8 in 1970, in mild 390 hp form or as the hotter LT-1. Another option was a tuned-up small-block, the 350 V8 with 370 hp and 380 lb ft, while for '71 the 454 options were 365 hp or 425 hp. For the rest of the 1970s, the Corvette had to comply with tighter legislation and a harsher economic climate.

Let's go back to 1960, when America seemed to be growing tired of big cars, overladen with chromework and burdened with massive fins. Ford's Falcon had shown the way to the new type of American compact car, with much of the space and comfort that U.S. customers expected, but with running costs closer to those of a VW Beetle. Chevy had no choice but to respond, and that same year Ed Cole gave the go-ahead for a Falcon rival. It would combine, "maximum functionalism with thrift," providing "good basic transportation for the American family."

When it appeared the following year, the new Chevy II compact appeared to be exactly that. Plain, conventional, and straightforward, its standard power unit was a 153 ci four of 90 hp, while a 120 hp six-

LEFT: The drag racer, poised at the start of the strip, started life as a Chevelle, Chevy's intermediate sedan placed just one step up from the Chevy II. It was seen by many as a natural successor to the famed '55–'57 Chevys.

BELOW: Chevrolet's first attempt to make a muscle car out of the Chevelle, by fitting the 327 V8, was turned down by GM's head office. But they relented, and the 327 in both 250 hp and 300 hp forms soon joined the options list. The Chevelle would go on to become one of Chevy's leading muscle cars.

"Everyone has a bit of swashbuckler in him. And one sure way to bring it out is to get behind the wheel of an all-new Malibu Super Sport."

cylinder unit was optional for a few more dollars. So far, so functional, but did Chevrolet have an alternative agenda for its little compact? Maybe: despite the Chevy II's avowed sensible nature, the company made it very easy to transform it into a mini muscle car.

A V8 factory option didn't come on stream for three years, but well before then, Chevrolet was selling special conversion kits that allowed any dealer to fit a Chevy II with any 283 or 327 V8. From the start, the Chevy II/Nova had been designed to accept these hotter engines. The 170 hp 283 was a modest enough power boost, but in theory the 360 hp 327 would fit just as snugly under the Nova's hood, and some did. It wasn't a cheap conversion—one Los Angeles dealer quoted a price of $1,555 for the complete 327 job, including a four-speed manual transmission and Positraction rear axle.

ABOVE: *The Chevelle also came as a neat convertible, here in SS trim, which, as ever, added some trim, badges, and other sporty accouterments for extra image. But that was all cosmetic, and the ultimate performance option in 1966 was the "Z16," a highly modified car with the 396 V8—production was limited.*

LEFT: *Chevelle buyers could choose a two-door or four-door sedan, plus this fastback coupe, as well as the open top. More to the point for muscle car freaks, the meaty 396 cubic-inch V8 was now a series production option, and the SS396 Chevelle would later become a model in its own right.*

BELOW: Look closely—this is no muscle car. That little "307" badge on the fender denotes fitment of Chevy's 307 ci V8, a nice enough unit, but it was the entry-level V8, just one step up from the base-model straight sixes. Collectors prefer the big-cube Chevelles, but SS trim, a four-speed manual transmission, and the convertible body can also boost the value.

LEFT: If the 396 ci Chevelle seemed like a true muscle car, there could be no doubting the 454 unit launched in 1970. The figures that mattered (in hot LS6 guise) were 450 hp and 500 lb ft.

The Chevy II/Nova was also beefed up with stiffer front springs (to support the heavier engine), a front antiroll bar, rear traction arms, and sintered brake linings. Still, a top-power 327 Nova would be quite a handful—in other words, a true muscle car. And, of course, some buyers liked the fact that the car still looked almost completely standard. Unless bystanders spotted the 200-mph speedometer and dual exhausts, a 327-equipped Nova looked for all the world like the standard, friendly, four-cylinder car, until the driver fired up and put his foot down.

There was clearly money to be made here, so, from 1964, Chevrolet offered the V8 as a factory option, along with sporty SS trim to make it less of a quiet man's

Below: Hood stripes, wide styled wheels, and quick-release hood catches—for the Chevelle SS454 handsome is as handsome does. Make that 0–60 mph in 5.4 seconds, and 13.8 seconds over the quarter.

muscle car. The six-cylinder Nova was still by far the most popular choice, but the V8 was here to stay.

One early main option was a relatively mild 275 hp version of the 327, but in 1968, the Chevy II Nova was restyled. Now slightly wider and longer, it shared its platform and many underpinnings with the Camaro. That meant a Camaro-sized engine bay, so any Camaro engine would fit. So new options that year were a 295 hp 350 ci V8, and the big 396 ci unit, this offering 350 hp and 415 lb ft that, incidentally,

SS
Radial T/A
BFGoodrich

LEFT: Many consider this to have been the best of the Chevelle muscle cars. In 1970, Car and Driver *readers voted it the best muscle car of all, and Chevy's SS454 brochure for '71 predicted that the car was, "sure to stay around." Well, it did for a few years, but not in that original 450 hp form. Rocketing insurance rates, plus new emissions and safety legislation, forced Chevrolet to rein in its big-block Chevelle.*

Below: Hood bulges became a virtual art form on late '60s muscle cars. A plain bulge wasn't enough any more, and manufacturers vied with each other to offer the coolest, most threatening, or simply biggest bulge in the market. The Chevelle's "Cowl Induction" system was relatively restrained, with its rearward-facing intake.

meant it was packing nearly four times the power of the original four-cylinder Chevy II. Maybe with an eye on adverse publicity, Chevrolet didn't actually advertise this engine, but it was available all the same.

Not that there were many takers. Of the many thousands of Nova buyers in 1968, fewer than 5,600 paid extra for the SS package and only 667 opted for the full-house 396. Drag racers were a different story, and it didn't take them long to figure out that the Nova's engine bay would also accept a 427.

The Chevy II Nova wasn't the only compact Chevrolet muscle car. The Chevelle wasn't actually a true compact, more of a midsize car, but it was smaller and lighter than the full-size models. So with the right sort of V8, it had the makings of a muscle car. The Chevelle was one of GM's new A-body cars launched for 1964, alongside the

ABOVE: The cliché, "This is the view that other drivers saw" (i.e. a fast-retreating rear end) was true most of the time for the SS454 Chevelle. This was (almost) the biggest-engined muscle car on sale, and was the high point of power and performance, before the insurers and the government called a halt.

Right: A 1970 Chevelle SS454 tire spins its way off the line. In its aspect, character, and performance, the biggest-engined Chevelle was pure muscle car, but it was joined in 1970 by the more elegant Monte Carlo, based on the same components as the Chevelle, including an SS454 option. Very few (less than 3% percent) Monte Carlo buyers opted for it, most preferring to treat this as the luxury coupe it was intended to be.

SS
N98·TYH

ABOVE: The Chevelle changed for 1971, with a new single-headlight, twin-level grille. But although the muscle car was under fire and the fully equipped SS could be had with 350 and 400ci V8s, the 454 survived. "Don't panic," went the brochure, "there's still an SS454." As for the SS pack, that brought special suspension, power front disc brakes, wide wheels and tires, stripes, badges, and bulges.

Pontiac Tempest (from which the GTO would spring), the Oldsmobile F-85, and the Buick Special. All four were based on the same components, part of a new strategy at GM to save money by sharing parts between its divisions.

It was a clever piece of packaging: the Chevelle was four inches shorter and narrower than a full-size Chevy, yet it lacked only one inch of interior space by comparison. Engine choices began with the 120 hp six, and although V8s were optional from the start, these were restricted to a 195 hp or 220 hp version of the 283, the latter with a four-barrel carburetor. However, it wasn't long before Chevrolet began applying its Chevy II experience to the new car.

Not that the Chevelle was without any performance pretensions. "Everyone has a bit of swashbuckler in him," went the advertisement for the Chevelle SS. The SS (it stood for "Super Sport") package brought an electric tachometer, Positraction rear axle, sintered metallic brake linings, four-speed manual transmission, and front bucket seats. And, of course, lots of SS badging.

Later in the year, Chevrolet backed up the SS image by adding 250 hp and 300 hp 327s to the options list, though this was just the start of big-engined Chevelles. For

BELOW: The times might have been a little straitened, but nearly one in four SS-equipped Chevelles were ordered with the 454 option in 1971—that's over 19,000 cars. The two alternative 454s were slightly derated to 365 hp and 425 hp (or 285 hp and 325 hp under the new net measurement system), so they were still true muscle cars.

SS
19 TEXAS 70
HPP·862

LEFT: A 1970 Chevelle SS454 blasts off the line, but it would soon be joined by more economic (though less muscular) alternatives. The "Heavy Chevy" Chevelle was one of the first "appearance" muscle cars, which looked the part but came with a smaller V8 to cut insurance costs. Base engine in the Heavy Chevy was the 200 hp 307—options went up to the 300 hp 402, but the full-house 454 was banned.

"The SS 396 is not the fastest car or the best handling, but it is possibly the best compromise of them all, especially when its relatively low price is considered."

(CAR AND DRIVER, *APRIL 1966*)

1965, the company offered limited numbers of 396-engined Chevelles, but you had to search to find one. The Chevelle SS396 wasn't advertised at first, and production quantities were strictly limited, partly because Chevrolet had made many changes under the skin, and producing the big-block Chevelle (its option code was Z16) in big numbers would have been an expensive business—only 201 were built in that first year.

For 1966, the SS396 became a regular option, available in three states of tune: 325 hp, 360 hp (capable of 0–60 mph in 7.9 seconds), and the special L78 option with 375 hp. Despite a 0–60 time of 6.5 seconds, fewer than 100 of the L78 Chevelles were ordered, a recurrent market reaction in muscle car history. The hottest V8s of all—the L78s, the Boss 429s, and Hemis—attract most attention now

LEFT: Happier times: Back in 1967, a Chevelle SS396 was one of the fastest cars American customers could buy, and at $2,825 for the basic coupe, was something of a bargain as well. For that, you had a 325 hp version of the famous big-block, plus a three-speed manual transmission, though there were endless options, including nine different rear axle ratios.

LEFT: Chevrolet sold over 63,000 SS Chevelles in 1967. That was actually down slightly from the previous year, but it still made this one of the best-selling muscle cars. And no wonder, with a sub-15-second standing quarter, and 0–60 mph in 6.5 seconds. That was with the ultimate 375 hp 396, though the tuning parts had to be fitted at the dealer, not on the production line.

LEFT: *Nineteen sixty-nine, a year after the fundamental Corvette restyle, though underneath it's much the same ladder frame and all-independent suspension. The Sting Ray fastback has gone, replaced by this tunnel-roof coupe with a removable rear window. Smoother, more aerodynamic than the original, but better looking? You decide. Color choices included tuxedo black, silverstone silver, and safari yellow.*

ABOVE: *Naturally, the Corvette offered more power than any sedan-based muscle car at the time. The big-block 427 V8 alone came in four versions: the base L36 (10.25:1 compression, single four-barrel carburetor) offered 390 hp and 460 lb ft. Add three Holley two-barrels, and the L68 had 400 hp, though peak torque was quoted as the same. L71 used solid lifters and a higher compression for 435 hp, while the ultimate L88, with sky-high 12.5:1 compression, gave an estimated 560 hp.*

CORVETTE
TEXAS
B23·BJC
THE LONE STAR STATE

LEFT: The Corvette's simple rear end treatment, used from 1968 on, is obvious in this shot of a drag racing convertible. For over half a century, the drag strip has allowed owners of fast road cars to compete over the quarter mile, and a whole drag racing culture surrounds muscle cars that can be driven to the strip, raced, and driven home. This road-registered Corvette is typical, and an L88-engined version could trip the lights in well under fourteen seconds.

455
350

LEFT: It looks impressive now, but in the early '70s, when this Corvette was built, America's only sports car was under pressure to clean up its act. Chevrolet persevered with the 464 ci V8 option though.

ABOVE: Looks just like a Ferrari Dino with the tunneled roof and those four round lights, though maybe that was the whole point. Not only that, but the hottest Corvettes offered Ferrari-style performance at a fraction of the price.

BELOW: Road tires, road registration, and even the external luggage rack is still in place, but this '73 Corvette is ready to blast down the drag strip. Coupe Corvettes like this were now outselling the convertible.

> “Those tweedy-capped purists who have been accusing Detroit’s performance cars of being ill-handling hogs capable of little more than straight-line travel have had their legs kicked out from under them by the Chevelle.”
>
> (CAR AND DRIVER, FEBRUARY 1970)

because they offered so much power. But at the time, they only sold in comparatively small numbers. Still, milder versions of the SS396 Chevelle became one of the standard muscle cars through the 1960s, and in 1969 over 86,000 of them were sold.

Even the 375 hp version wasn’t the fastest Chevelle any more, however, for that year saw an SS427 available to special order through GM’s Central Office Production Order (COPO) system. This was intended to cater to special fleet orders—100 Novas with a nonstandard transmission, for example—but could also be used to fit the largest possible V8.

BELOW LEFT: The insurance-sensitive Heavy Chevy was not a great success in 1971, and more customers opted for the full-strength SS Chevelle.

BELOW: Single headlights and a simpler exterior treatment identify this as a '71 Chevelle SS; you could still have the 454 in its final full-power form.

Most, if not all, of those 427 Chevelles went to dealer Don Yenko in Canonsburg, Pennsylvania. Yenko was also the man behind a run of 427-engined Novas. Meanwhile, the 396 Chevelle had been overtaken by younger muscle cars, and for 1970 Chevrolet announced an official SS454, which would be the ultimate big-block Chevelle muscle car.

Right: *Chevelle Malibu coupe, with the "wrap-over" front end used by the intermediate Chevrolet from 1968. Malibu was always the top-of-the-range Chevelle coupe, and as such was the most desirable recipient of the Super Sport option pack and the biggest, most powerful V8s. SS 396 versions had a matte-black finish along the rocker panel—this is a lesser-engined Malibu.*

BELOW: The pre-wrap-over Chevelle sported this body from '66, with no-nonsense squared-off lines and very subtle tunneled roofline. It kept the same 115-inch wheelbase as the '64 original, but looked larger and more imposing. The Chevelle, of course, was just one of four A-body cars from General Motors, though in the Chevrolet tradition, it was cheaper than its cousins from Pontiac and Oldsmobile.

RIGHT: One of those four A-body cars was the Pontiac Tempest, which formed the basis for the GTO. It was the success of that milestone muscle car that spurred Oldsmobile to offer the 4-4-2 and Chevy the SS 396, though neither achieved the same iconic status—being first always counts for a lot. But in the meantime, thousands of Chevy enthusiasts were happy enough with their interpretation of an early muscle car.

564
HARRY'S
FORD

RIGHT: Chevelle Malibu convertible, a comfortable and stylish open-top four-seater. Add the SS 396 option though, and it was transformed into a real muscle car, one of the fastest available in the mid-'60s. The 396 V8 was actually derived from the legendary 409, but with a shorter stroke of 3.76 inches to lose those 13 cubic inches. Why bother? Well, GM had a policy of not allowing V8s of more than 400 ci into any intermediate body, so a sub-400 big-block was worth developing.

LEFT: Initially, the 396 was offered in three different versions, starting out with the L35, which used a 10.25:1 compression ratio to produce 325 hp and 410 lb ft. Pay a little extra, and the L34 added dual exhausts, higher-lift cam and forged alloy crankshaft, for 360 hp and 420 lb ft. But for muscle car fans, the L78 was better still, with an 11.0:1 compression, even hotter cam, bigger tailpipes, and other add-ons, to produce 375 hp at 5,600 rpm, though peak torque was slightly less, at 415 lb ft. That was enough for 0–60 mph in 6.5 seconds.

RIGHT: A somewhat subdued SS396 Chevelle coupe, without the racing stripes and vinyl roof that characterized the 1970 version, though the Chevelle was always relatively restrained by muscle car standards. Its hood scoop was understated and rear facing, and it never succumbed to the early '70s craze for spoilers. Understated maybe, but an SS was the only means of specifying the big-cube 454 V8. Parking lights mounted on the front edge of the fenders identify this as an early '70s example.

SS

LEFT: Simple, clean profile of the SS Chevelle, without spoilers at either end and looking all the better for it.

SS
TEXAS
B01 TSX

LEFT: Take away the SS badge, and this could be a base-model Nova—the hood bulge was subtle, the general look unadorned. Bigger and heavier than before, but the Nova SS still made a fine muscle car, especially with the 350 or 375 hp 396 V8 under the hood.

Again, not many people paid extra to own the ultimate—fewer than 4,000 in 1970, and only "a handful" (according to author John Gunnell) ordered the top-spec 450 hp version. But for those who did, a 0–60 time of 5.4 seconds, and a 13.8-second quarter made this the fastest road-going Chevelle of them all.

Chevelle was never going to be the answer to the daunting sales figures set down by Ford with the all-conquering Mustang. Something less derivative would be needed, and after some delays, Chevrolet did not shirk the challenge.

RIGHT: The base Nova V8 cost just $2,503 in 1970 coupe form, but that brought the relatively mild-mannered 307 cubic-inch motor. For a little under $300, buyers could upgrade to the Nova SS package, which brought a 300 hp 350 ci V8, as well as dual exhausts, power front disc brakes, and wide wheels and tires, plus dress-up parts. Not enough? The 350 hp L34 396 cost another $184 on top, or the special 375 hp L78 an extra $316. In 1970, one in three Nova SS buyers paid extra for the biggest-block motors.

BFGOODRICH

ABOVE: Like every other compact, the Chevy II/Nova had grown out of its economy car roots, a sign of the hedonistic '60s.

Camaro: The General's Pony Car

There was one thing that Chevrolet management disliked more than anything else—coming second to Ford. When the Mustang was introduced in April 1964, when crowds gathered outside Ford showrooms and the whole of America seemed to be talking about the new pony car, it looked as if Chevy had been wrong-footed in a big way. That was confirmed when Mustang sales figures began to come through. With over 400,000 cars sold in its first (albeit extended) model year, the Mustang proved a phenomenal success, something that Chevrolet simply could not ignore.

BELOW: Camaro, General Motor's Chevrolet answer to the Mustang, though it debuted a full eighteen months later than the Ford pony car. Chevy management decreed that the Camaro be better looking than a Mustang, with more room for four people, faster, better to drive, and less expensive to buy. It had a good shot at all of those things, though never conclusively knocked Mustang off its pony car pedestal.

Not that GM's top-selling division had been ignoring sporty cars. As early as 1962, the division's chief designer, Irv Rybicki, had been working on a smaller sporty car based on Chevy II components, to meet and beat the foreign imports. A prototype was built, and the project had high-level support from none other than GM's overall styling vice-president, Bill Mitchell. But it was vetoed by Bunkie Knudsen, the division general manager. "What we don't need right now," he said, "is another car." However, a couple of years later Knudsen himself commissioned a similar project, this time to test public reaction. But this time his boss, Jack Gordon, was the man who said no.

BELOW: Being pace car for the Indianapolis 500 was an honor for any muscle car, and the Camaro got its first chance in 1967. Unlike Ford, Chevrolet didn't build thousands of replicas for sale, just 104 Camaro RS/SS convertibles for VIPs to use in race month.

Conceivably, if the 1962 project had gotten the go-ahead, Chevy could have beat Ford to market with a Mustang beater.

But they didn't, and now Chevrolet's top brass were looking at early Mustang sales figures and wondering what the hell they were going to do about them. They didn't wonder for long, and less than six months after the Mustang's debut, a full-scale project was underway. But they couldn't rush a Mustang copy straight out. Sure, the "Chevrolet Mustang" (already code-named **XP-836**, and later the "F-car" in honor of the car in its sights) would have to be a sporty four-seater, but cloning the Mustang wouldn't convince anyone to buy it.

BELOW: SS, for Super Sport, had long meant performance for Chevrolet owners, ever since the first Impala SS back in 1961. So, of course, there was a Camaro SS, available as an SS 350 package for $211. That brought the new small-block V8 offering 295 hp, beefier suspension, wide red-stripe tires, stripes, and louvers.

Instead, they could target the pony car's weak points and aim to better them. The Mustang was undeniably cramped for four, so the F-car would be longer, wider, and lower, with more space inside. It would be faster and better to drive, and every version would be cheaper than the equivalent Mustang. As if that weren't enough, it had to be better looking as well. Not everyone liked the Ford's sharp edges, so the new Chevy would be softer, with more flowing lines—more "fluidity" in GM parlance. A full-size clay model was finished and photographed next to a Mustang in December 1964, four months into the project. By mid 1965, running prototypes were being driven on the road, and an intensive program of testing continued through the winter of 1965/66. Much of this nuts-and-bolts work was complete by the spring, with the new car on target for its autumn launch as a 1967 model.

One thing that helped speed up the design process was that, just like Mustang, the new Chevy made full use of existing components to cut both costs and development time. Chevrolet straight sixes and V8s would provide the power (all existing engines apart from a new 350 V8), while transmissions came off the shelf as well. One thing that was new (and set the car apart from the Mustang) was a front subframe in addition to unitary construction. This allowed more effective isolation of engine roar, vibration, and tire noise. There were some teething problems, notably with scuttle shake and door sagging on the convertible, but most of these were overcome.

“*The Camaro was built to be all things to all people, as a result, it was a disappointment*”

(Car and Driver, *March 1968*)

But the F-car didn’t have a name yet. For something so dependent on the image

*Below: The 350 was all very well, but it wasn't enough to keep up with a Mustang 390 or Barracuda 383. So Chevrolet made the big-block 396 an option (it fit right in, and there was no need to bulk the car up to fit a big-block, as Ford had to do with the '67 Mustang). This cut the 0–60 mph time to less than 7 seconds (*Motor Trend* magazine recorded 6 seconds), though in '67, the SS 396 was outsold by the cheaper 350 by five to one.*

it portrayed, this was a crucial factor. The code name "Panther" had supplanted the less-than-inspiring XP-836, and everyone assumed that this would make it into production. After all, what better rival could there be for a Mustang than another wild animal with teeth?

It was not to be. At the time, General Motors was conducting its low-level warfare with Ralph Nader, and naming a new car "Panther" was thought to be too provocative.

Instead, GM researchers (which, according to one source, consisted of Chevy managers Bob Lund and Ed Rollert leafing through French and Spanish dictionaries) began searching for an alternative. They wanted something vaguely exotic and European, and found it in "Camaro," which translated as "comrade." As it happened, a journalist later discovered that there were other, less fortunate, translations, but the Camaro was so well received that no one seemed to care.

At its late 1966 launch, the Camaro was welcomed as the first of a new generation of Mustang rivals (Pontiac, Chrysler, and American Motors would all produce their own within a very short time). Many thought that it was better looking

RIGHT: Just like Ford, Chevrolet offered a six-cylinder pony car as a price leader, but those V8s stole the headlines, especially the 302 ci Z28.

BELOW: Like a Panther, ready to strike? The Camaro certainly suggested power and grace, but the code name "Panther" didn't make it into production.

than a Mustang, and Chevy made the most of its less aggressive, more flowing lines by often showing women at the wheel in advertisements—they wanted both sexes to buy Camaros. Inside, the design team had tried to give the impression of a fighter plane, something that flattered the driver into pilot status. In any event, only the higher spec Camaros got this sporty interior, but it certainly impressed in the showroom. The car handled better and had more space for people and their luggage.

LEFT: Completely restyled for 1970 (though introduced midseason) and with a Ferrari-like front end, the Camaro faced an uncertain future. The convertible was dead (some thought these would soon be outlawed anyway), though engine options remained much the same, notably with the 300 hp 350 and 350 hp 396, both with Supersport SS or Rallye Sport RS trim.

And this wouldn't have been a true Mustang rival without a wide choice of options: different engines, transmission, colors, detail parts, and special packages were always part of the Camaro buying experience.

At first, there were five engine choices, all of them Chevrolet-sourced: two sixes, the familiar 327 V8 in both 210 hp and 275 hp form, and a new four-barrel 350 that claimed 295 hp. "Over 3,200 pounds of driving machine," boasted the advertisement, "nestled between four fat red-stripe tires, an SS350 carries the 295-horsepower 350-cubic-inch V8 . . . Try one on at your Chevrolet dealer's. It's a ball and a half."

Ball and a half it might be, but 295 hp wasn't a high enough figure to out-muscle the Camaro's big rivals. At 7.8 seconds 0–60, and with a 15.4-second quarter, the SS350 was fast, but not superfast. A couple of years before, that would have been more than enough, but the power race was moving fast, and even fresh new cars like the Camaro couldn't afford to get left behind. So just two months after the launch, Chevrolet added a new 396 ci alternative to the Camaro's long list of options. Actually, there were two of them, the 325 hp L34 and 375 hp L35. According to *Motor Trend*, the latter cut the Camaro's 0–60 time to 6 seconds, with a 14.5-second quarter. The SS396 was certainly fast, though in 1967 the 350 still outsold it by more than five to one.

So the road-going Camaro was taken care of, but racing sells cars too, and never more so than in the late 1960s, when the Trans Am series was rapidly becoming a proving ground for the new breed of pony cars. Whatever won at Trans Am usually benefited in showroom sales. GM was still abiding by the SCCA ruling, which banned factory-sponsored teams (though, along with Ford, it was helping out leading privateers by the back door). But there was nothing to keep it from building an extraspecial ready-to-race Camaro, which could be sold to private teams.

CHEVROLET CAMARO *RS350 1969*

Engine: *300-horsepower 350 cubic-inch V8*

Transmission: *four-speed manual*

Steering: *recirculating ball*

Tires: *F70 x 14*

Brakes: *hydraulic front discs, rear drums*

Suspension: *front independent, coil springs; rear live rear axle, single-leaf semi-elliptic springs*

Wheelbase: *108 inches*

Track: *(F/R): 59.6/59.5 inches*

Weight: *3,435 pounds*

> "Some of the [Z28] Camaro's appeal is right down at the basic bad-boy level, too. Around town, the exhaust sound is a perfect replay of our high-school ideal."
>
> (Car and Driver, FEBRUARY 1993)

So the Z28 was born. At first, Chevrolet intended to use its existing 283 ci V8, which was well within the 305 ci class limit imposed by the SCCA. But it soon became clear that a 283 Camaro would stand no chance against the 302 ci Mustangs, which had been built with just this ruling in mind. So Chevrolet took a look at its parts bin and combined the 327 block with the 283 crankshaft. This resulted in a short-stroke, high-revving V8 with a capacity of 302 ci—just perfect, as far as Chevrolet was concerned. Corvette L79 cylinder heads were added, with big valves and dual exhaust ports. There was a high-rise aluminum intake manifold, uprated ignition, and a Holley four-barrel carburetor. The result was 350 hp at 6,200 rpm and 320 lb ft, enough to win Trans Am races, which, of course, was the whole point.

In theory, any Camaro customer could check the Z28 box on their order form and use their racer on the road. It was fully road-legal after all, and the interior was fully trimmed, though you couldn't have air conditioning, even as an

RIGHT: The hardtop was always the best selling Camaro of the '60s, as most buyers preferred its practicality to the soft-top convertible. Chevrolet did consider a fastback Camaro too (to rival the equivalent Mustang), before dropping the idea. An intriguing fastback/estate got to the mock-up stage as well, but both ideas were unlikely to generate big sales, and GM chose to keep things simple.

option—deadly serious racers could also delete the heater. Performance? Magazine tests found the Z28 capable of sprinting to 60 mph in less than 6 seconds, and the standing quarter in less than 14 seconds. So despite its smaller V8, this was the fastest Camaro you could buy—more to the point, it was quicker (just) than the equivalent Mustang. The Z28 motor was also listed at an attractive $358, which wasn't much to pay for a specially built engine. In reality, other compulsory options came with it, things like heavy-duty suspension, a close-ratio four-speed transmission, 3.73:1 rear axle, and power front disc brakes. That pushed the price up to $4,100, or nearly double that of the basic Camaro coupe. Not surprisingly, few people apart from race teams bought the early Z28—it would make up just 3 percent of Camaro sales.

But bottom line for the Camaro—maybe even more important than winning races—was showroom traffic. When the figures came in at the end of its first year, the sales total stood at around 200,000. It hadn't toppled the Mustang off its pedestal, but it was enough. Meanwhile, Chevrolet's designers began working on alternative Camaros. A proposal for a fastback was rejected, probably because Chevrolet

BELOW: Z28, the most revered Camaro of them all. It started out as a means for Chevrolet to smoke the Mustang in Trans Am racing. To qualify, Trans Am cars had to be in series production, so the hot Z28 package was made an option on the stock Camaro. Ready to go, it was nearly double the price of a basic coupe, but included a special 302 ci V8, heavy-duty suspension, close-ratio four-speed transmission, 3.73:1 rear axle, and power front disc brakes.

management had had bad experiences of investing good money in fastbacks that then sold in small numbers. In any case, the Mustang fastback was outsold by the hardtop by a factor of four or five to one. More innovative was the idea for a high-performance estate, with a Kamm rear end. It looked attractive, but again, the top brass could see only a limited market for a muscle wagon with less space than a traditional station wagon. They were probably right.

Still, sticking with just two body styles—the hardtop and convertible—didn't seem to hurt Camaro sales, and in 1969 over 235,000 of them left Chevrolet showrooms. The car was also voted top sporty car of the year by readers of *Car and Driver* magazine.

Meanwhile, some Camaro customers, especially the drag racing crowd, were pleading for more power. Chevrolet's big-block 427, with 400+ hp, would easily fit under the Camaro's hood, but the factory was too busy building standard cars. Chevrolet dealers like Don Yenko in Pennsylvania had been fitting 427s to Camaros since 1967, with a choice of 435 or 450 hp. But Yenko and the other specialty dealers couldn't keep up with demand, so he persuaded Chevrolet to supply them from the

factory, albeit through the COPO (Central Office Production Order) system. Just over 1,000 of these COPO 427 Camaros were built and sold through specialty dealers like Yenko, Fred Gibb, and Nickey Chevrolet. The price wasn't out of court—between $3,500 and $4,500 depending on specification—though now these rare, big-cube Camaros are worth six-figure sums.

BELOW RIGHT: ***A special short-stroke high-revving V8 was part of the Z28 package. Chevy engineers knew that their stock 283 V8, while within Trans Am's 305 ci class limit, simply wouldn't have been competitive. Combining the 327 block with the 283 crankshaft produced the short-stroke 302, with 350 hp at a frenetic 6,200 rpm.***

Not that the factory was against big-cube Camaros on principle. That same year, it built a very small number of cars with a special all-aluminum version of the 427 V8. Dealer Fred Gibb was heavily involved in drag racing and wanted to build an aluminum-engined Camaro for the Super Stock class. NHRA rules stipulated that at least fifty had to be made, but Gibb managed to persuade Chevrolet general manager Pete Estes to supply them, promising to buy them all. With half an eye on the Mustang Boss 429 (also built with drag racing in mind), Estes agreed.

The ZL1s, as they were termed, were all delivered by the COPO system (of course), and all came with the Rallye Sport package, power brakes, power steering, tachometer, and many other special parts, as well as the aluminum 427. The price had shot up from the agreed $4,900 to over $7,000, but Fred Gibb still bought those fifty cars. An additional nineteen ZL1s were delivered to other dealers. Was it worth it? Well, according to *Super Stock* magazine, a ZL1 could cover the standing quarter in just 10.41 seconds, with a terminal speed of 128.1 mph. So as far as drag racers were concerned, the answer was probably yes.

Nineteen seventy was the high point for affordable Chevrolet muscle. In their respective classes, the Camaro, Corvette, Nova, and Chevelle all arguably led the field, but for 1971, Ed Cole announced that all GM cars would soon have to run on unleaded fuel, in preparation for catalytic converters. That meant lower compression ratios, retarded timing, and less power. At the same time, insurance rates (especially

for younger drivers) were starting to make muscle cars untenable—this wasn't cussedness on the part of insurance companies, just an economic reaction to the accident rates of young, inexperienced drivers in high-powered (sometimes over-powered) cars. Safety legislation was tightening up too. In short, the glory days of unrestricted muscle cars were on their way out.

Into all of this, Chevrolet launched the Mk2 Camaro. It looked lower, wider, and more European than the original, and, for the time being, hung on to its high-power options. As well as a token six, there were 307, 350, and 396 V8s of 200, 250/300, and 350 hp respectively. As for the Z28, this was no longer a homologation special for Trans Am racing, but the badge was so well respected that it was kept on as a

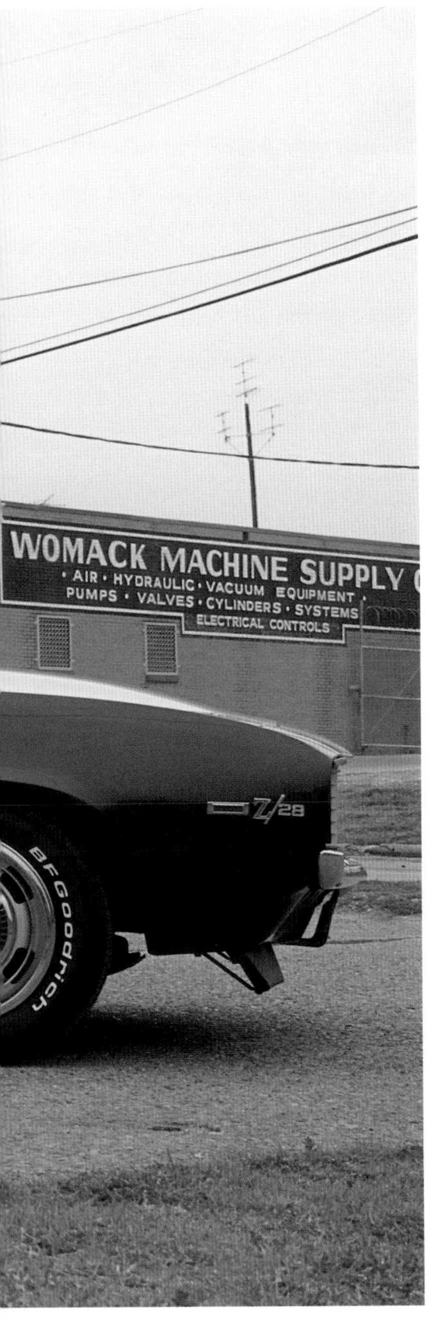

genuine road car. So its special qualifying 302 ci power unit was dropped in favor of a hotter version of the 350, with 406 hp. It wasn't as fast as the original Z28, and *Sports Car Graphic* recorded a 0–60 time of 8.7 seconds (though *Motor Trend* managed 7 seconds), but it still fit the bill. Camaro sales fell that year, at just under 150,000, though that was a decent second-place behind the Mustang.

In 1972, the Camaro was almost dropped altogether. New federal bumper regulations meant very expensive changes, and given the car's low sales (by GM's mass-production standards), these just weren't worthwhile. The early 1970s were a good time for Chevrolet in general, as they broke all sales records, with John DeLorean at the helm. In that context, the Camaro was clearly slipping. But they survived. At the eleventh hour, Chevy engineers found a cheaper way to get their Mustang rival to meet the new regulations, and it was reprieved. Sales slumped that year and only recovered slightly in 1973. Then the 1974 oil crisis arrived—surely this was finally the end for the Camaro?

Oddly, they gained a new lease on life. By Detroit standards, the Camaro was a relatively compact, fuel-efficient car, and U.S. drivers running from their gas guzzlers flocked to buy it—over 135,000 were sold that year. The advertising reflected this new world of gas saving and the 55-mph limit. Gone were all references to excitement, adrenaline, and horsepower. "As long as you've got to go slower," went one slogan, "you may as well do it in style." In 1975, the Z28 was dropped altogether. The crisis soon faded in public memory. Chevrolet began sponsoring IROC (International Race of Champions), a celebrity race in which all the well-known faces drove Camaros. And the Z28 returned for 1976, its advertising losing all trace of those touchy-feely oil crisis days: "Intended for the macho enthusiast . . . aggressive, quick, agile, and dependable." For muscle car nuts, it must have seemed like the good old days were back. Power began to creep up again, and Camaro sales carried on climbing, to 200,000 in 1977 (finally overtaking the Mustang), then to almost a quarter of a million.

LEFT: The original Z28 was a low production special, aimed specifically at racers, and just 3 percent of Camaro customers ordered one. It was one of the fastest road cars on sale, with a 0–60mph time of less than six seconds and a standing-quarter in the thirteens. In fact, the Z28 became something of a legend, and in milder form was a standard model in the Camaro range for many years, alongside its long-term sparring partner, the Mustang Boss (which it outlived, by the way). Oh, and it won the Trans Am Championship in 1968.

"If you like playing with blocks, try this. With Chevrolet's Turbo-Fire 409 V8 block you can build to great heights. Say, 340 hp, 400 hp. Or, with the ingredients shown here, 425 hp. Isn't playing with blocks fun?"

> ***"The Lime Rock pit straight is a wavy, gray blur. Up front [on the Camaro Z28] two roaring Holleys are trying to suck a hole in the atmosphere. 'A 7000 rpm red line? Christ Almighty, it's gonna burst.' But it doesn't, and Sam Posey snaps the shift lever into fourth at seven grand as the speedometer climbs past 110 in one of the absolute wildest street machines ever to come out of Detroit."***
>
> (Car and Driver, *July 1968)*

Then just as it seemed like the American performance car was back, the second oil crisis hit, and it was 1974 all over again. This time the Camaro didn't fare so well, and sales slumped again.

Chevrolet's answer to this new uncertain world was a new Camaro in 1982. It still had rear-wheel drive with a V8 option, and its sharper lines bore a strong family resemblance to the 1970s car. But underneath, there was radical change. Ten inches shorter than the old car, the 1982 Camaro was a full 500 lb. lighter as well. And while there was a V8, the base engine was a 155 ci four, something of a culture shock for muscle car fans, but necessary for Chevrolet to keep up with the Corporate Average Fuel Consumption regulations. There was also a 173 ci V6 of 102 hp, and a 305 ci V8 in 145 hp and fuel-injected 165 hp form.

The latter came as part of the Z28 package, which *Motor Trend* voted Car of the Year. Once again, power outputs began to creep up. An L69 High Output V8 was optional, which produced 190 hp at 5,800 rpm, enough for 0–60 mph in 7.2 seconds. With brakes to match the power, the Z28 for the eighties could accelerate up to 100 mph, then come to a stop again, all in 23.8 seconds. After a short break, the IROC series was back on stream, and for 1985 Chevrolet launched a special edition IROC-Z28, with the V8 hopped up to 215 hp, lowered suspension, gas-filled shocks, and ventilated disc brakes.

Just to underline the fact that performance was back in fashion, the Z28 accounted for nearly half of all Camaro sales in 1986, and the following year, Chevy uprated the IROC with a 220 hp 348 ci injected V8, borrowed from the Corvette. Performance really was now back up to 1960s levels, with 0–60 mph in 6.3 seconds, and a standing-quarter of 14.5 seconds. As ever with the hottest engine options, it wasn't possible just to have the V8. The latest IROC-Z28 came with a whole list of options that were in fact compulsory. A limited-slip differential, four-wheel disc brakes, upgraded four-speed transmission (still automatic though), and an engine oil cooler all had to be paid for as well, and together they doubled the cost of the option. Still, *Hot Rod* magazine thought the result was worth it: "the closest facsimile to a full-bore road-racing car you'll ever drive." In short, the muscle car was back with a vengeance.

Meanwhile, what of the Corvette itself? Like every other muscle car, this had been forced to draw in its horns a little during the seventies, but like the Camaro, it survived. Unlike the Camaro, there was no talk of a radically downsized and depowered Corvette, no ultra-economical four-cylinder version. Instead, the Corvette treaded water for a few years, its V8s pegged back to suit legislation and the general climate. Then, in the early 1980s, as things began to relax, Corvette horsepower began

BELOW: Beneath the escaping motor, model alloys, and paint lives a mid-'70s Camaro. It nearly went in 1972, when new bumper regulations loomed but was given a new lease on life by the energy crisis—hard to believe, looking at this car, but in the mid-'70s, the Camaro was sold on its fuel economy.

Below: Sign of the times (1). In 1975, the Corvette convertible was dropped (though it would later return), and for a while, this was as close to fresh-air motoring as a Corvette driver could get, though the T-roof was a good compromise between wind in the hair and hardtop protection. With the roof panels in place and the windows wound up, this was effectively a hardtop.

to climb once again, and by 1987, Chevrolet was offering a twin-turbo V8 Corvette with 345 hp.

But the turbo car wasn't built by Chevrolet (the conversion was done by Callaway Engineering). To celebrate a return to hedonism, it needed an in-house flagship, something to inspire the public. And it had to be the world's fastest production car. That was quite an ambition, but Chevy was better placed than ever before to do it. Lotus Engineering, with its many years of experience building highly tuned engines, was now a General Motors subsidiary, so when the head office told the English engineers to design an all-new performance V8 for the Corvette, that's exactly what they did.

The result was the all-aluminum LT5, and the Corvette it was fitted to was named ZL-1, "King of the Hill," with good reason. Typically Lotus, the new V8 combined high tech with high-revving power. There was sequential fuel injection, an

RIGHT: Sign of the times (2): A time-traveling driver from the '60s would ask where this '73 Corvette had lost its bumpers. From 1973, U.S. legislation decreed that all new cars be fitted with standard-height bumpers that could withstand a 5 mph impact without damage. The Corvette solution was elegant, with body-color deformable sections that blended into the car's lines.

11.0:1 compression ratio, and four valves per cylinder, with twin overhead cams per bank. The induction system showed some clever new thinking, with three valves in the throttle body: one small one that gave good response at low revs, and two gaping big ones for when full power was needed. Each was controlled electronically, so it was possible to "lock out" the full-power valves. Why? Well, in the unlikely event of using the ZL-1 to teach a learner driver, it might be useful.

Keep those power valves plugged in, and the ZL-1 produced 375 hp at 6,000 rpm, plus 370 lb ft at 4,800 rpm. *Motor Trend* tested the car and found it to be the fastest production Corvette yet, with a 12.8-second quarter-mile time and 4.4 seconds to 60 mph, both from a standing start. Keep on accelerating and the ZL-1 would wind up to a top speed of 180 mph. Backing all of this up was a six-speed manual transmission, adjustable dampers, ultra-low-profile Goodyear Eagles, and a luxurious interior. No wonder the ZL-1 cost twice as much as a standard Corvette, though it was still much cheaper than the equivalent Ferrari or Porsche. Was it the fastest production car available at the time? Well, no one seemed to be sure, but it was a close-run thing.

But the ZL-1's moment of glory was relatively brief. There was huge interest from the magazines at first, and orders flowed in during 1990–91. Thereafter they tailed off and only trickled in for the next three years. By then, Chevrolet's in-house efforts were nearly as fast and certainly cheaper to build—the specialty LT5 was built by marine engine specialists Mercury, who had lots of experience with aluminum motors.

The ZL-1 had done its job, putting the Corvette firmly back in the top league of performance cars, but for 1996, Chevrolet had a new flagship. The Grand Sport Corvette had no multivalve cylinder heads or clever throttle bodies. It was not designed in England or made by Mercury, and even used good old-fashioned pushrods instead of overhead cams. Despite this, it was remarkably effective. High compression aluminum heads, a new camshaft, and other changes produced 330 hp, which on paper looked a little pale next to the outgoing ZL-1. In practice though, the Grand Sport was nearly as fast. Chevrolet claimed a 13.8-second standing quarter, and

OPPOSITE AND BELOW: In the wake of the first energy crisis, Chevrolet's marketing made an abrupt U-turn, and the Corvette was apparently transformed from a rubber-burning sports car into a luxury grand tourer. Leather upholstery, air conditioning, and electric windows joined the options list, while the big-block 427 and 454 were dropped. There were plans for a mid-engined replacement, but these were dropped, and in 1975 chief engineer David McLellan vowed to keep the Corvette forever front engine/rear drive.

4.7 seconds to 60 mph. In blue with white racing stripes, it looked the part of a special (Corvettes had raced in these colors in 1963), and more to the point, was little more than half the price of its exotic forbear.

In fact, muscular performance was spreading throughout the Chevrolet range, even pickups. The SS454 pick up of 1990 was a high-performance take on the regular C1500 truck, and kicked off a whole new generation of muscle trucks in the 1990s. Chevrolet fitted a 454 ci V8 of 230 hp, enough to propel this 4,700 lb. commercial vehicle to 60 mph in 7.8 seconds. The SS454 was a great success, selling 14,000 in its first year.

Remember the Impala SS? It was back (in name at least) in 1994, on a hopped-up version of the Caprice Classic sedan. At the heart of the conversion was the 350 ci 260 hp LT1 V8 plucked straight from the Corvette and Camaro. Fuel injection, 10.5:1 compression ratio and an electronically controlled four-speed automatic gave the Impala a 15.4-second quarter mile and a 0–60 time of 7.1 seconds. Not Porsche territory, but respectable enough for a 4,200 lb. full-size sedan, and it actually made the 1990s Impala SS quicker than the original SS396. The whole package was based on that of the police-specification Impala, which included beefed-up suspension with deCarbon gas shock absorbers, four-wheel ventilated disc brakes, and wide alloy wheels with P255/50 BFGoodrich Comp tires. Of course, the police don't get a

RED HOT
JGN 863T
AND HI-PO

luxurious or sporting interior, so the SS was decidedly ordinary, with no tachometer, a column shift, and bench front seat, though bucket seats and floor shifter were added in 1996. It looked more special on the outside though, thanks to those wide alloys and the use of body color instead of bright work on all the details, plus a rear spoiler. In all, nearly 70,000 Impala SS cars were sold in three years, before America's last rear-wheel-drive muscle sedan was dropped in 1997. Who knows, maybe some of those 70,000 buyers had been boys in the early sixties, old enough to remember the original Impala SS that they had dreamed of owning.

The Impala was rear-wheel drive, but this was rapidly becoming restricted to

BELOW: For 1991, General Motors declared a loss of over seven billion dollars, but the Corvette had survived against some pretty long odds. All Corvettes got wider wheels and tires for 1993.

specialty cars, to big sedans . . . and Corvettes. For 1997, the fifth generation Corvette stuck to this traditional layout. Engineers Dave Hill and John Cafaro had been considering a mid-engined layout, but research found that Corvette customers believed there was only one way for a Corvette to be: front-mounted V8 engine, with rear-wheel drive. But they did mount the transmission in the rear to achieve a perfect 50/50 weight distribution.

The 1997 Corvette still used a fiberglass body (another Corvette tradition) based on a full-length perimeter frame. Using fewer parts than the old Corvette, this was far more rigid, allowing better ride quality without upsetting the handling. A longer wheelbase and wider track allowed more room for people and luggage. The latest Corvette managed that neat 1990s trick of looking both modern and retro at the same time.

Did the Corvette C5 still qualify as a muscle car? The answer had to be yes. Its standard 350 ci V8 offered 345 hp and 350 lb ft, which was plenty. Enough, according to *Motor Trend*, for 13.3 seconds over the quarter mile and 0–60 in 4.7 seconds. Although it was of a familiar capacity, this was actually a new engine; still a pushrod V8, but stronger and more rigid, with lower emissions and fuel consumption.

However, muscle car fans of the 1990s would surely have been more interested in the Z06 Corvette. Named after Zora Arkus-Duntov's marvelous Z06

BELOW: Unlike the pony cars, there was no suggestion of an economy four-cylinder option. It might be more efficient, but this was still a Corvette, so the stock engine was the 350ci small-block V8 with Cross Fire Injection. Electronically controlled, this produced 205 bhp at 4,300 rpm, and was able to evade the "Gas Guzzler" tax, thanks to overdrive on second, third, and fourth in the four-speed manual transmission—you could still have a lower 3.33:1 rear axle though.

BELOW: Still front engine/rear drive, still a 350 cubic-inch V8 under the hood, and still one of the fastest cars made in the United States. The seventh-generation Corvette—Z06—was launched in 1997 with a all-new body, chassis, and drivetrain. A strong and rigid chassis based on a pair of hydroformed rails carried the sleek new body, which was still of fiberglass, so some things hadn't changed.

Corvettes of 1963, the 2001 version was, just like them, road-legal but ready to race. It was designed to appeal to amateur racers who liked to take to the track at weekends. It was 117 lb. lighter than the standard Corvette, thanks in part to a titanium exhaust system (the first mass-production car to be so fitted). The Active Handling system brought electronic traction control responding to side slip as well as wheelspin.

In fact, the Z06 Corvette was light years away from the classic muscle cars in conception. In the sixties, muscle cars used off-the-shelf parts as a quick route to affordable performance. The Z06 was too high-tech and expensive to be part of that tradition. But no one could doubt that it was fast.

Power came from an LS6 (another name from muscle car history) 350 ci V8, this one based on the aluminum LS1, and now blasting out 385 hp at 6,000 rpm. It was mated to a new six-speed manual transmission, which permitted a top speed of 171 mph, the standing quarter mile in 12.6 seconds and 0–60 mph in just four seconds. Whether or not it qualified as a muscle car, the twenty-first century Corvette was one of the fastest cars you could buy.

ABOVE: ***An extra eight inches in the wheelbase improved ride quality, while the transmission was mounted in the rear to improve weight distribution—a six-speed manual joined the options list. The 350 V8 (cast in aluminum) was 44 lb. lighter than the previous LT1, but delivered an extra 45 hp. Launched as a hard top only, the Z06 Corvette was joined by a sleek convertible in 1998.***

In the meantime, the Camaro, which had survived two oil crises and the death and rebirth of the modern muscle car, had been rebodied and relaunched in the mid-1990s. A smooth, rounded body consisting of composite panels sat on a steel substructure. There was a new front suspension and rack-and-pinion steering, while the base engine was now a 208 ci 160 hp V6—that fuel crisis four had long since faded away. And, of course, there was a Z28, now with the LT1 348 ci V8 with aluminum cylinder heads and 275 hp.

Like Corvette, the Camaro had gone high tech, and as the Z28 headed for the twenty-first century, it came with a six-speed manual transmission and ABS brakes. There was also a speed limiter, which ensured that the car wouldn't exceed 108 mph in fourth, fifth, or sixth gears. Opt for the Z-rated tires however, and you got the full 150 mph of which the car was capable. Either way, it was still the fastest factory-built Camaro ever, with a 14-second quarter and 0–60 in 5.3 seconds, according to *Car and Driver.* By 2000, the engine options included a 200 hp V6 and the 348 ci V8 in 305 hp or 320 hp form.

So all those barroom rumors that modern high-tech muscle cars would never match the good ol' boy variety were baloney.

Oldsmobile: 4+4+2 = Muscle

BELOW: The 4-4-2 was Oldsmobile's answer to the phenomenally successful Pontiac GTO. Just as the GTO was based on the A-body Tempest, so 4-4-2 grew out of Olds's own A-body car, the Cutlass.

Chevy, Ford, Pontiac—mainstream Detroit motor manufacturers with a strong tradition of building affordable performance cars. And Oldsmobile? A car for the middle-aged and middle class. Yet Oldsmobile was first with a modern overhead valve V8 after World War II, and the others followed in its wake. A significant point in the muscle car story, because V8s like that laid the basis for the sixties muscle cars that became legends.

It was 1949 when Oldsmobile announced its new V8 named Rocket, a time when most US manufacturers were still using updated prewar designs. The jet age was dawning, and with a name like that, it was clear what Olds was selling its new engine on—performance. It revved higher and made more power than the old-school V8s, and endowed the Model 88 with impressive performance. It was so successful that Oldsmobile stopped building sixes altogether, and sold nothing but V8s until 1964.

Let's move on to 1964. Pontiac has just launched the GTO option package on the midsize Tempest. It's an immediate success, and GM stablemates Chevrolet immediately look around for a means of responding. The Tempest is an A-body car, and so is the Chevrolet Chevelle, and the Oldsmobile F-85 Cutlass (and, for that matter, so is the Buick Special). So Oldsmobile take the quickest route to offering their first muscle cars, and heat up the A-body. Where Pontiac created the GTO and Chevy the Chevelle SS, Oldsmobile announce the 4-4-2.

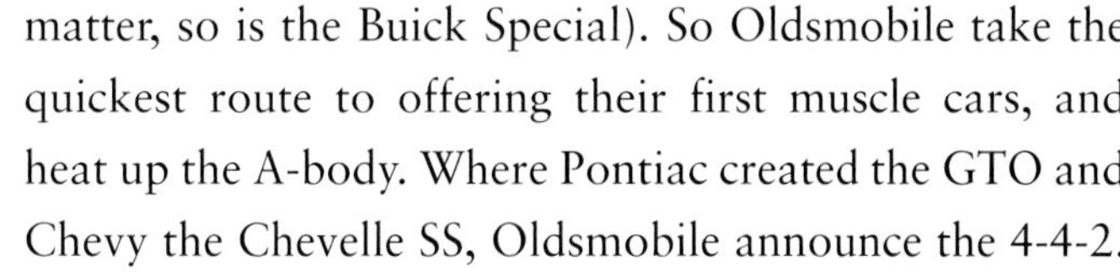

At first, the 4-4-2 was only a modest step up from the standard Cutlass, with an extra 20 hp. Its full official title was "Optional number B-09 Police Apprehender Pursuit." Fortunately, Oldsmobile came up with a snappier name, and explained it in advice to salesmen as follows:

> 4-BARREL CARBURETION—plus high-lift cams boost the power of the "4-4-2" Ultra High-Compression V8 to 310 hp—up 20 hp over the Cutlass V8.
> 4-ON-THE-FLOOR—the stick-shift syncromesh transmission captures every power advantage both up and down the entire gear range.
> 2 DUAL EXHAUSTS—complete dual exhaust system features less back pressure for better performance . . . aluminized for longer life.

*BELOW: That hood badge simply wasn't associated with hot cars in the early 1960s (despite the pioneering Rocket V8 of a decade earlier), but the 4-4-2 changed all that. Not quite as powerful as a GTO, with 310 hp on early cars, but it was at least as fast—*Motor Trend *reckoned it was slightly quicker to 60 mph, at 7.5 seconds, with a 15.5-second standing quarter.*

BELOW: *The 4-4-2 was an option package on both hardtop and convertible Cutlasses, with the same extras applied. This soft top has period-styled wheels.*

Four on the floor, four-barrel carburetor, and dual exhaust—the 4-4-2 pressed all the right buttons for hot car nuts of the time. Included in the package, which cost a reasonable $285, were heavy-duty springs and shocks, a rear stabilizer bar, and higher quality rod and main bearings.

Motor Trend tested one of the early 4-4-2s and found that it was slightly quicker than a GTO, despite giving away 15 horsepower to the Pontiac. A sprint to 60 mph took 7.5 seconds (GTO, 7.7), and the quarter mile 15.5 seconds (GTO, 15.8). *Car Life*

BELOW RIGHT: *It might have started out as a hopped-up Cutlass, as this badge shows, but the 4-4-2 was so popular that Olds made it a model in its own right.*

did the same job, and concluded that, "No better Oldsmobile has rolled off the Lansing assembly line in many a year and though it isn't quite the sports car that corporate brass likes to think it is, it doesn't miss by much."

"Police needed it—Olds built it—pursuits proved it."

Pontiac and Chevy, of course, had fitted bigger engines, and that's what Olds did to the 4-4-2 the following year. It actually created a new size of V8, reducing the bore size of the new 425 ci unit to four inches, which produced a nice round 400 ci, not to mention 345 hp at 4,800 rpm, and no less than 440 lb ft at 3,200 rpm. Carburetion was still by a single four-barrel Rochester, and acceleration times had been cut to 6.5 seconds to 60 mph, and exactly 15 seconds over the quarter, according to a test by *Car and Driver*. The 4-4-2 option was available on the basic F-85 coupe as well as the Cutlass coupe, hardtop, and convertible. Over 25,000 customers checked the 4-4-2 option box in 1965—it was a hit.

Even staid Olds knew that the secret of competing with the GTO was to offer a little more power each year. So for 1966, a slight increase in compression ratio boosted the peak to 350 hp. Later that same year, a triple two-barrel carburetor setup was offered as well,

ABOVE: Later (1970–71) 4-4-2 convertible. Being Cutlass-based, Oldsmobile's muscle car mirrored the updates on that familiar intermediate. What didn't change was its reputation as the best-handling muscle car of the '60s, which was praise indeed when many of these hot V8s still suffered from soft, wobbly suspension and inadequate brakes.

for which they claimed 360 hp. That cut the quarter-mile time to 14.8 seconds, and *Car Life*, which recorded that time, described the 4-4-2 as, "the civilized supercar." They had good reason, as the package now included seat belts, a padded instrument panel, windshield washer with two-speed wipers, carpeting front and rear, bucket seats, a courtesy lamp . . . and so it went on.

In fact, for those who didn't want their 4-4-2 too sporty, a Turbo Hydra-Matic three-speed automatic was optional in 1967, at an extra $236. If one insisted, even the bucket seats could be deleted in favor of a conventional bench. But for most 4-4-2 buyers, those essential muscle car cues were what made the car so desirable: the special wheels, Red Line tires, and 4-4-2 badging. The whole package (including the engine and heavy-duty suspension) cost $184, though it didn't include a four-on-the-floor transmission any more—that cost another $184 extra. For the really committed, a limited-slip differential came in at $42.

Meanwhile, General Motors had decreed that none of its cars (Corvette excepted) could be sold with Tri-Power, the triple two-barrel carburetor setup offered on the 4-4-2 for '66. This left Oldsmobile without an extra-performance option, so it added the W30. This would become famous in muscle car circles as the hottest 4-4-2 from the factory, though the first 1967 W30 only added ducting to the hood louvers, the idea being to add a ram effect to the air intake. Olds actually claimed 360 hp for this setup, the same as the old Tri-Power, though acceleration tests showed that the

ABOVE: Palms, a clear sky, and a 4-4-2 convertible—but why isn't the top down? Sadly, the 4-4-2's career as a separate model was drawing to a close.

LEFT: Checking out the opposition? By the late 1960s, there were a couple of extrahot options on top of the stock 4-4-2. One was the Hurst/Olds, a collaboration between tuner George Hurst and an Olds dealer, which involved squeezing the division's biggest 455 ci V8 into a 4-4-2. In Force Air form, and with lots of special parts such as a high-lift cam and Ram Air cylinder heads, this delivered 390 hp at 5,000 rpm and 500 lb ft at 3,600. Only 515 Hurst/Olds were built in 1968, but Super Stock *magazine reported a 109 mph quarter mile, covered in just 12.9 seconds.*

Oldsmobile 4-4-2 1966
Engine: *350-horsepower 400 cubic-inch V8*
Transmission: *four-speed manual*
Steering: *recirculating ball*
Tires: *7.35 x 14*
Brakes: *four-wheel hydraulic with front discs, rear drums*
Suspension: *front independent, unequal-length wishbones, coil springs, antiroll bar; rear rigid axle and locating links, coil springs*
Wheelbase: *115 inches*
Height: *53.8 inches*
Weight: *3,960 pounds*

W30 was about a second slower to 60 mph and over the standing quarter.

For 1968, Olds paid the 4-4-2 the ultimate compliment and made it a model in its own right, just as Pontiac had done with the GTO. Coming as a Holiday hardtop, sports coupe, and convertible, it was easily recognizable from the dual exhaust exiting through the rear bumper. At a scant $63 more than the stock hard top, the Holiday hardtop was by far the most popular 4-4-2 in 1968, with nearly 20,000 sold.

The suspension wasn't changed, but it didn't need to be, as the 4-4-2 had long been acknowledged as one of the best-handling muscle cars available. *Car and Driver* put one up against a Chevelle SS, GTO, Fairlane GT/A, Skylark GS, and Comet Cyclone, and declared it to be, "far and away the best-handling car of the six," managing second place on the handling course despite being down on power. A new 400 ci V8 now came in four states of tune: 290 hp or 325 hp with automatic, or the full 350 or 360 hp manual, though a three-speed

ABOVE AND LEFT: This Holiday hardtop was a later option for the 4-4-2, with the existing coupe and convertible.

RIGHT: Aside from the low-production Hurst/Olds and W30, most 4-4-2s left the factory with the stock 400 ci V8 in 325 hp four-barrel or 290 hp two-barrel form—the two barrel was later dropped, for fear it would dilute the 4-4-2's muscular image. The top power option was Tri-Power, three two-barrel carburetors offering 360 hp.

BELOW: *The W30 (this is a stock 4-4-2) officially gave just five extra horsepower than standard in 1970, with 370 hp at 5,400 rpm, though you could hardly mistake one for the other—two large rectangular air scoops gaped out of the fiberglass hood, delivering ram air to a low-restriction intake. Transmission was a close-ratio four-speed manual with Hurst shifter, though the Turbo Hydra-Matic was optional, suitably tweaked to give higher-speed upshifts.*

transmission (not the original four) was still the standard fitment.

Meanwhile, General Motors was keeping a tight rein on the performance aspirations within its ranks, and wouldn't allow Olds to fit its largest V8, now a 455 ci, to the 4-4-2. But George Hurst, of Hurst Performance Products, suffered no such restrictions, and did just that. It worked so well that he persuaded an Olds dealer (with the help of Olds officials, it has to be said) to produce clones.

"Snarls softly and carries a big stick. Awesome is the word for it."

The first Hurst/Olds offered 390 hp at 5,000 rpm and 500 lb ft at 3,600 rpm, though it wasn't as simple a conversion as just slotting in the 455. It had a special crankshaft, modified distributor, a high-lift camshaft, and hand-assembled Ram-Air cylinder-heads. A modified Turbo Hydra-matic was part of the package (it could be shifted like a manual), as was a special silver-and-black paint job. *Super Stock* magazine found the Hurst/Olds could return a sub-13-second standing quarter, and over 500 were sold.

So successful was the marriage, that there would be Hurst/Olds for several years yet. There were 10 years that Hurst/Olds were built, spanning 21 years, from 1968 to

ABOVE: The 4-4-2 in its most popular Holiday hardtop form. For 1970, the hard top was also available as the Rallye 350, an attempt to offer a milder alternative to the 4-4-2 and W30, cheaper to buy and easier to insure. Based on the Cutlass S (in coupe as well as hardtop form), it majored on looks instead of performance. Bright yellow paintwork, big spoiler, and sporty striping made it stand out, and a 310 hp 350 V8 was stock, though you could have the W31 Force Air package as well.

"The 4-4-2 is a beautifully balanced automobile . . . strong and exceedingly comfortable, and it exhibited some of the most civilized handling we've found in a domestically built car."

(Car and Driver, April 1966)

1988. During those production runs, less than 16,000 total cars were built, so a Hurst/Olds is a pretty rare beast.

There were few changes to the standard 4-4-2 for 1969, apart from some mild image enhancing. The economy two-barrel option was dropped (it was diluting the car's image) and the W30's torque, for an unexplained reason, fell by nearly 10 percent, to 400 lb ft. Maybe that was why W30s made up only 5 percent of production that year. There was a new W31 too—a milder, slightly cheaper version of the original aimed at younger drivers—but it was not a success, and only 1 percent of 4-4-2 buyers chose it. The Hurst/Olds went from strength to strength though, and over 900 were sold in the 1969 colors of white and gold. *Motor Trend* considered the '69 "The hairiest Oldsmobile."

The 4-4-2 and W30 were joined in 1970 by the bright yellow Rallye 350. Milder than the 4-4-2, this was a bright and breezy all-yellow option on the Cutlass, with a 310 hp 350 ci V8. Like Pontiac's GTO Judge, it sought to combine flashy muscle car looks with a cheaper mechanical package, both to buy and insure. It certainly looked the part, but wasn't a great success, with only around 3,500 sold. The 4-4-2 wasn't faring so well either, and less than 8,000 were sold in 1972, its last year as a separate model. Like the Buick Gran Sports, the 4-4-2 had always been the gentleman's muscle car, not quite as fast as some, but with better manners.

As for the Hurst/Olds, these became increasingly dress-up kits in the early 1970s (the Shelby Mustang was suffering a similar fate at the same time), and they ceased altogether in 1975. But the partnership was revived in '79, with a special version of the downsized Cutlass Calais. No supertuning, but the latest Hurst did have a 170 net hp 350 ci V8 (powerful by GM late seventies standards), with a whole host of image enhancers: gold paint, gold aluminum wheels, a Hurst Dual-Gate shifter, and appropriate badging. In the mid-eighties, you could still buy a Hurst/Olds, and the coupe

Right: The 4-4-2 wouldn't have been much of a muscle car if it had never been picked as pace car for the Indianapolis 500. Its moment of glory came late, in May 1972, in the form of white convertibles with suitable graphics, not to mention the 455 ci V8. The cars were actually supplied by Hurst, as mainstream manufacturers were drawing back from racing involvement at the time.

of 1984 featured no fewer than three automatic transmission selectors: one for automatic changes and the other two for manual selection of first and second gears. Hurst, one of the key names in the muscle car movement, had always been about shifters.

Pontiac: Where It All Began?

The consensus is that Pontiac started the whole muscle car boom, with the 1964 GTO. As we've shown, a V8-fueled power race was up and running long before then, though the GTO remains a milestone car, one that combined a big V8 in a smaller bodyshell, with many of the sporty accouterments that gave muscle cars such tremendous showroom appeal.

But the Pontiac muscle story really starts back in 1954, when its big, bulbous sedans and station wagons—the Chieftains and Star Chiefs—were powered by a straight-six or lumbering flat-head straight eight. However, Pontiac engineers were readying an all-new overhead-valve V8 (which was just as well, since Oldsmobile already had one and Chevrolet was about to launch its own ohv V8).

It arrived in '55, a 288 ci power unit that came with a mild 7.4:1 compression ratio and 173 hp. That was with manual transmission—auto transmission buyers had an 8.0:1 compression and 180 hp to make up for the inefficiency of the slush-box. The V8 itself was state-of-the-art for the time, designed by Clayton B. Leach and Ed Windeler, with iron, easy-to-cast block, five main bearings, and hydraulic valve lifters. This wasn't Pontiac's first V8 (it had offered a flat-head back in 1932) but was the first with overhead valves. It may not have had quite the impact of Chevrolet's "Hot One," which debuted the same year, but the new V8, along with all-new bodies for that year, did help to transform Pontiac with a more sporting, youthful image. So much so, that within a few months of the V8's introduction, the company had launched an optional "Power Pack," consisting of four-barrel carburetor and dual exhausts. "Powered to match its future-fashioned style!" went the advertisement: " . . . 200 HP performance—the most power per dollar of any big luxury car."

Above: Pontiac's GTO (this is the Tempest coupe on which it was based) is generally accepted to be the first muscle car. There had been hot V8 sedans before, of course, and lots of them, but the GTO laid down a formula copied by countless others. The combination of an intermediate or compact sedan with a big-cube V8 proved to be a potent one.

Pontiac got another shake up the following year when Simon E. "Bunkie" Knudsen arrived to head up the division. At forty-three, he was the youngest divisional manager in General Motors and would be the proverbial new broom, sweeping Pontiac clean of its old traditions. He famously stated that although one couldn't sell an old man's car to a young man, the other way around was a different story. If no one believed it then, surely they must have been convinced when the Mustang sold to people of all ages. So Pontiacs would be increasingly youth-oriented, and Bunkie was the perfect boss for the exciting new V8 era.

In keeping with this, the V8s were growing in size and power. The Chieftain V8 was of 317 ci and came in 192 or 205 hp, dependent on transmission type. For the Star Chief, a four-barrel carburetor was added, boosting power to 216 or 227 hp. But that was just the start. An "extra hp" version was announced in March 1956, of the same displacement but with two four-barrel carburetors, and many other changes such as 10.0:1 compression, new valve timing, a bigger fuel pump, high-tension valve springs, and so on. This 285 hp "NASCAR" engine was actually aimed at stock car and drag racing, and only 200 cars were sold with it. The veteran speed record holder, Ab Jenkins, recognized its potential, and took a NASCAR-powered Chieftain coupe

to Bonneville Salt Flats, where he set a new twenty-four-hour record, covering 2,481 miles at an average of 118.37 mph.

Meanwhile, the road-going Pontiacs weren't being neglected, and in 1958, fuel injection was made an option on the top-line Bonneville. It cost a steep $500 extra, but was an exotic thing to have at the time, and 310 hp was claimed, a figure confirmed by *Motor Trend* magazine. The Bonneville also had a capacity boost, so even the standard four-barrel carb motor produced 285 hp, or 300 hp with the Tri-Power option. But Pontiac hadn't forgotten the impact of its NASCAR engines. Racing may or may not improve the breed, but it can create some great publicity, especially if you win. The sport of drag racing (then still an almost solely American series) was growing year by year. Born out of the unofficial street races, it was increasingly well organized by the newly formed National Hot Rod Association (NHRA), and watched by bigger crowds. NASCAR was still a huge draw.

Despite the AMA's (Automobile Manufacturers Association) voluntary ban on factory involvement (with the laudable aim of keeping racing affordable), most manufacturers couldn't resist giving it a try. And none more than Pontiac, where three car enthusiasts held top positions. As divisional bosses go, Bunkie Knudsen was still a relatively young man; Chief Engineer "Pete" Estes shared his vision of a vigorous, youth-oriented Pontiac, as did the young John Zachary DeLorean. There was no question of building expensive one-off race cars, especially to compete in the production classes, but what Bunkie, Pete, and Zachary could do was offer special options, ostensibly road-legal but really intended for racing.

These were the "Super Duty" parts, all based around Pontiac's overhead valve engine, often with the Tri-power triple carburetor setup. Super Duty parts weren't available in production cars, but were sold over the counter, and if customers wanted to use them to build up a superhot road car, well, that was up to them. These parts were first offered in 1959, aimed at improving the longevity of the 389 ci V8 under race conditions, as well as its power. So there was a four-bolt block as well as all the usual horsepower parts, plus an aluminum intake manifold and header-type exhaust manifolds. For 1960 there were new cylinder heads with big valves, and forged high-compression pistons. By 1961, with further parts on stream, the 389 made 368 hp.

BELOW: By the standards of later muscle cars (especially those of 1969–70) the original GTO was restrained indeed. No spoilers, no stripes, and even the GTO badges were subtle in the extreme. Few visuals were added to this Tempest Le Mans coupe to turn it into a GTO, but they were enough to transform its image.

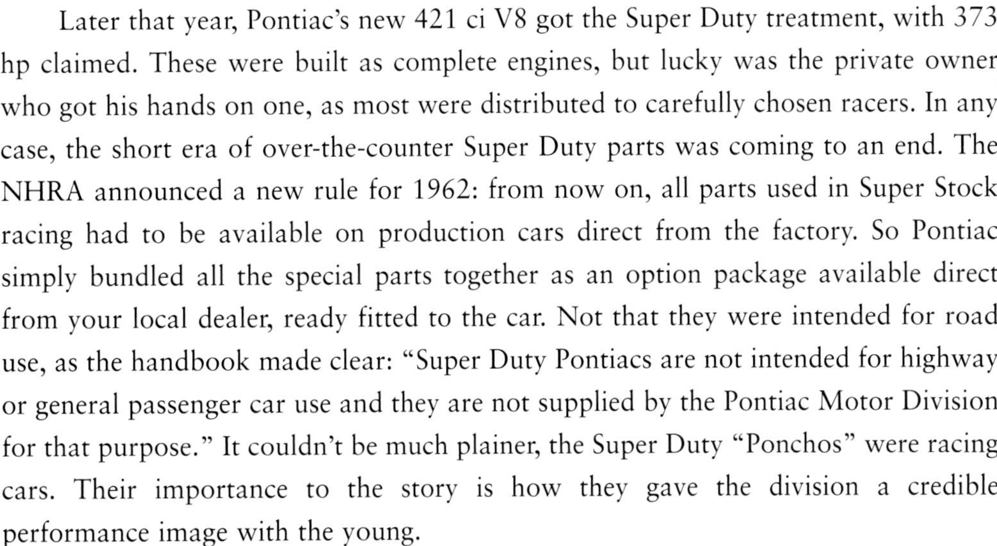

Later that year, Pontiac's new 421 ci V8 got the Super Duty treatment, with 373 hp claimed. These were built as complete engines, but lucky was the private owner who got his hands on one, as most were distributed to carefully chosen racers. In any case, the short era of over-the-counter Super Duty parts was coming to an end. The NHRA announced a new rule for 1962: from now on, all parts used in Super Stock racing had to be available on production cars direct from the factory. So Pontiac simply bundled all the special parts together as an option package available direct from your local dealer, ready fitted to the car. Not that they were intended for road use, as the handbook made clear: "Super Duty Pontiacs are not intended for highway or general passenger car use and they are not supplied by the Pontiac Motor Division for that purpose." It couldn't be much plainer, the Super Duty "Ponchos" were racing cars. Their importance to the story is how they gave the division a credible performance image with the young.

As a package, the 1962 Catalina Super Duty used the 421 ci V8 with a 405 hp rating (Pontiac's most powerful factory engine yet). An 11.0:1 compression ratio did the trick, along with dual four-barrel carburetors, big valves working polished ports with dual springs, forged aluminum pistons, an aluminum intake manifold with low-restriction air cleaners, solid lifters, and a McKellar cam. It was certainly a strong engine, with a forged crankshaft and big six-quart oil capacity.

So that was the engine, but Pontiac also sought to pare weight to a minimum by offering aluminum fenders, hood, and bumper as optional parts—even the bumper brackets could be pared down to save precious ounces. Thus equipped, Pontiac's adman (and part-time racer) Jim Wangers took journalist Roger Huntington along for a quarter-mile ride in a 421 Super Duty. They managed a 13.9-second run, and a breathless Huntington calculated that the car's true power, given its weight and acceleration, was more like 465 hp than 405.

BELOW RIGHT: There were sports variations on stock sedans before the GTO, and this Le Mans was the sportiest version of the Pontiac Tempest. What the GTO brought was a new level of performance to intermediate sedans—not for nothing did Pontiac steal a Ferrari name when it came to badging.

But the end was near, and in 1963 GM implemented its own no-racing ban. Unlike the 1957 nod-and-a-wink ban, this one was serious, and Pontiac was given just six weeks to get rid of its remaining Super Duty parts. So that was the end of their brief but glorious career. But before that came into effect, the 1963 Super Duty Catalinas, Grand Prixs, and Tempests (eighty-eight cars in all) were the most radical yet. The 421 came in for yet more tuning, with higher intake ports, oval-shaped exhaust ports, larger valves, and 12.5:1 compression cylinder-heads—a few cars had 13.0:1 compressions. The cam was still a McKellar with solid lifters, and transistorized ignition was added. Officially, this all added up to 410 hp, but one estimate puts the actual output as 540–550 hp.

Weight saving was taken a step further too now, with aluminum trunk lids and Pexiglass windows. With detail aluminum parts like the splash pans, radiator core supports, and bumper mounts, another 100 lb could be trimmed off the bulk of a Catalina. This went to an extreme with the "Swiss cheese" cars, whose chassis were drilled with holes to save yet more weight—fifteen Swiss cheese Catalinas were completed before the head office racing ban came into effect, though no one tried to pretend they were production cars. In F/SX (factory experimental) class drag racing, one of these recorded an 11.91-second quarter mile, driven by Arnie "Farmer" Beswick.

Today, the Super Duty Pontiacs are collectors' items and a car with racing history (or any of the very rare Swiss cheese Catalinas) can command a six-figure sum. But the real significance of the Super Duty Pontiacs was that they gave the badge a new credibility with young buyers—Pontiacs were simultaneously cool . . . and hot, which was a neat trick if you could work it. In short, the time was ripe for the GTO.

GTO: Origin of the Species

The Pontiac GTO really was the car that kicked off the muscle car boom. Of course, there had been performance cars before. The V8 power race had been running for a decade or more, and from the late 1950s, Pontiac and others began building lightweight, super-tuned cars. These were all very well, but until the GTO came along, those top-power V8s had only been fitted to heavy, full-size cars. Lots of them were sold on their performance, but they were just too large and unwieldy to be true performance cars. The road-legal racers like the Super Duty Pontiacs went too far the other way. Blisteringly fast, they were also blisteringly expensive and really needed a dedicated mechanic to keep them up to snuff.

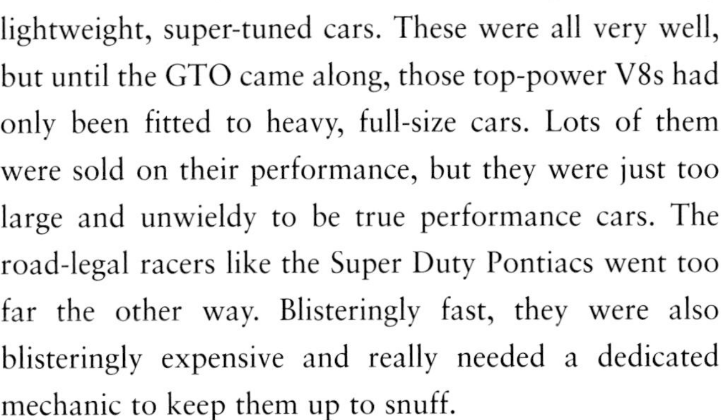

BELOW: In the '60s, most American-made cars were face-lifted every couple of years, or even every year, and the GTO's first freshen-up happened in 1965, with vertically stacked twin headlights. The nose was cleaned up again the following year, and given an all-new look for '68. This '66 example could be had with the 360 hp Tri-Power V8.

That was where the GTO came in. Squeezing a full-size V8 into an intermediate car gave impressive performance, and yet the GTO was friendly and tractable, as happy to trundle into town to collect the groceries as to burn down the drag strip. It was as comfortable as any other production car and could be serviced by any Pontiac dealer. And using off-the-shelf parts, it was affordable too, at $2,700. So all the elements of the quintessential muscle car were there in the GTO—fuss-free high performance in a sporty-looking package, with a reasonably low price.

The GTO wasn't part of a long-term strategic plan—there were no focus groups or painstaking market research. Instead, it came about via a number of factors, among which gut feeling played a significant part.

Let's take the people first. Remember how the enthusiastic trio of Knudsen, Estes, and DeLorean had come up with the Super Duty Pontiacs? Bunkie

Above: Early muscle car interiors made little concession to making the occupants feel special. The Mustang might have made a point of offering bucket seats, a floor shift, and sporty three-spoke steering wheel as standard, but this Tempest coupe didn't. It would be years before full instrumentation came as standard.

Knudsen had moved on, but Pete Estes had taken his place, with John DeLorean as Chief Engineer. They were joined by engineers Russ Gee and Bill Collins, plus adman/racer Jim Wangers. All were hot car enthusiasts, and all were keen to use performance to boost Pontiac's image. With GM's racing ban in place, they were looking around for something else that would do the same job.

With hindsight, all the hardware was already in place. In 1961, the Tempest was Pontiac's version of the new GM A-body intermediate, along with the Chevrolet Chevelle, Oldsmobile F-85, and Buick Special. It was designed to take advantage of the growing small car market, and its base engine was a 195 ci four-cylinder unit of 110 hp. This was actually half of the existing 389 ci V8, and was available in 120, 140, and (with four-barrel carburetor) 155 hp versions. And there was a lone V8 option, the Buick 215 ci, also of 155 hp. Otherwise, the Tempest was quite innovative, with independent rear suspension, rear-mounted transaxle, and a unitary body/chassis. More to the point for our story, it was a good 400 lb. lighter than a full-size Pontiac.

The Tempest was reasonably successful, but Americans' enthusiasm for small domestic cars began to wane after a couple of years, so for 1964 the latest Tempest had grown, with a 115-in. wheelbase and a conventional perimeter chassis. There was something else too. The '64 Tempest was designed to share more parts with the rest of the Pontiac range, which made it easier to swap components around . . . including engines. Not only that, but all the Pontiac V8s, from the 326 to the 421, were the same size externally, which made them even easier to fit. And finally, 1963 had seen all the Pontiac V8 engines lose a little weight, so fitting a larger one into a smaller car would be less likely to upset the handling. It was almost as though fitting out the Tempest with a big V8 was meant to be. History does not record who actually had the idea, but it was surely one of the "Young Turks" who decided that a 389 ci V8-powered Tempest would be an ideal image booster for Pontiac.

There was just one problem. GM's head office put a general ceiling on power-to-weight ratios, decreeing that no car leave the factory with less than 10 lb. per cubic inch. For the Tempest Le Mans, that meant the 326 ci V8 was the largest permissible, and the beefier 389 was outlawed.

However, John DeLorean and his fellow engineers found a way around this. They discovered that GM's Engineering Policy Committee only had to approve new models. If the 389 V8 was made an option on the Tempest two-door LeMans, it would bypass the committee altogether. So that's what they did, and the plan worked. Though when it was announced, the GTO option came as a complete package, not just the engine. To distinguish it from any other Tempest, there were GTO badges on the grille, fenders, deck lid, and glove compartment, plus dummy air vents in the hood and simulated engine-turned aluminum dashboard inserts. Special six-inch-wide wheels were fitted with low-profile red-stripe tires, and the standard three-speed manual transmission could be upgraded to a Muncie close-ratio four-speed. Suspension-wise, there were beefier springs, specially valved shock absorbers, and longer rear stabilizers.

BELOW: The muscle car would never have existed had it not been for Detroit's expertise in building relatively light and compact cast-iron V8s at low cost. It was a Detroit tradition, stemming from Henry Ford's pioneering of a mass production V8 in the 1930s, and the result was a horsepower per dollar rating that was unbeatable.

Right: 1965 GTO on the drag strip—the hood scoop is a later addition, though the car did get a scoop that year. The standard V8 remained Pontiac's 389 ci unit, offering 335 hp on a 10.75:1 compression ratio. That was enough for a 0–60 mph time of 7.2 seconds, but even quicker acceleration was available with the 360 hp Tri-Power, with three two-barrel carburetors and longer-duration camshaft.

But the engine was central to the GTO concept, and it did not disappoint. Rather than just slip in the standard 389 V8, DeLorean and crew boosted it with 10.75:1 cylinder heads from the 421HO (High Output) V8, plus bigger valves, a wilder cam, and freer-flowing exhaust system. A heavy-duty cooling system, starter, and battery were standard. The result was 325 hp at 4,800 rpm with the standard four-barrel carburetor. That was, just to put it in perspective, almost three times the power of the original base-model Tempest! And if that wasn't enough, the triple carburetor Tri-Power system offered 360 hp.

To say that the GTO had impact would be a gross understatement. It caused a sensation, making the cover of countless magazines and Pontiac the marque of the moment. And no wonder. Even the standard 325 hp convertible would sprint to 60 mph in 7.7 seconds, while a Tri-Power hardtop made that 6.6 seconds, with a 14.8-second standing quarter. Of course, the wily Jim Wangers made sure that press cars were good examples of the breed, and some were tuned Royal Bobcat GTOs. Whatever, the press loved it, and one magazine famously put a Pontiac GTO up against its Ferrari namesake. To the horror of Ferrari purists across the States, the Pontiac won! Bet that generated a few column inches in the editorial pages.

At the end of its first year, the GTO option had sold to well over 30,000 buyers, with over half of those going for the hardtop. The following year, Pontiac moved over 55,000 hardtops alone, with a total of 75,352 GTOs finding buyers. Pontiac had a serious hit on its hands.

But the management knew they couldn't stand still, and that the GTO's rapturous reception would invite a whole string of GTO-clones from its competitors. Vertically stacked headlights in taller front fenders gave the '65 GTO a different look, and Rallye wheels were a new option. Perhaps more relevant to most buyers was a small but

Pontiac GTO 1966

Engine: *360 hp 389 cubic-inch V8 (335 hp standard)*

Transmission: *four-speed manual*

Steering: *recirculating ball*

Tires: *Firestone Super Sports 500 7.75 x 14*

Brakes: *hydraulic drums, 9.5-inch-diameter front and rear*

Suspension: *front independent, unequal-length wishbones, coil springs, antiroll bar; rear rigid axle and locating links, coil springs*

Wheelbase: *115 inches*

Height: *53.8 inches*

Weight: *3,620 pounds*

significant power boost, thanks to a new camshaft, improved cylinder heads, and a revised intake manifold. The standard four-barrel 389 now delivered 335 hp at 5,000 rpm, though claimed output for the Tri-Power stayed at 360 hp. Later in the year came a Tri-Power with Ram Air, which still claimed 360 horses but did have better performance at speed.

So successful was the GTO that for 1966 it became a model in its own right, though of course it was still basically a Tempest with a hot engine. It was actually a few dollars cheaper this year, and the coupe started at $2,783, rising to $3,082 for a convertible, though the interior now included fake walnut inserts on the dashboard. Those prices were without extras, and there were certainly plenty of those on the GTO order form. The standard dashboard, for example, was bare, offering just a speedometer and fuel gauge, so many drivers paid extra for the Rallye gauge option, consisting of a 7,000 rpm tachometer and water temperature and oil pressure gauges. You couldn't have disc brakes (yet), but Pontiac would happily sell you aluminum-finned drums to give the hard-worked standard brakes a helping hand.

There were no mechanical changes, but Pontiac still sold more GTOs than ever in 1966: over 10,000 coupes, nearly 13,000 convertibles, and not far short of 74,000 hardtops. Mustang apart, that made it the best-selling muscle car of them all. Quite an achievement, when you consider that this was an increasingly crowded market.

RIGHT: Not rocket science. Squeezing the big 389ci V8 into the intermediate Tempest made the GTO what it was, though maybe "squeeze" is the wrong word, as there seems to be plenty of room in the engine bay. The Tempest's base engine, remember, was a 195 ci four, though that was based on half the 389 V8—so fitting the full-size motor was a kind of poetic justice.

LEFT: From the start, the GTO was available as a full convertible, as well as a hardtop or coupe, still with four seats and the same performance add-ons as its fixed-roof cousins. But like all convertibles, it was always the priciest body style, and sales were lower as a result. In 1965, when Pontiac sold just over 11,300 GTO convertibles, over 55,000 plain hardtops found homes.

Ford was now offering 390 and even 427 V8s in the Fairlane and Mercury Cyclone, while the new Chrysler Hemi was just coming on stream. Despite this, GM began to enforce its capacity ceiling with more vigor, though they did raise the intermediate limit (as applied to the Tempest/GTO) to 400 ci.

In fact, there were signs that Pontiac needed to look over its shoulder. In April 1966 *Car and Driver* held a giant six-car contest for the major muscle cars. The GTO had the most power, despite having the smallest engine, but that was thanks to its Royal Bobcat tuning package. This dealer-fitted setup included richer jets, thinner head gaskets (to increase compression), and a retuned distributor. That was all very well, but it turned the well-mannered 389 into a recalcitrant beast, reluctant to start and a real gas guzzler. Standard GTOs weren't like that, of course, but they shared the test car's suspension. Severe axle tramp was, "bordering on the uncontrollable," and in circuit testing, "the suspension is certainly too soft . . . it tends to float and bounce in corners."

In 1967, the GTO façade began to crack slightly, with sales falling for the first time. Not that you would have known it from the options list. The 400 ci V8 (bored out from the 389) was now standard across the

BELOW: This '66–'67 GTO is substantially standard, despite its reincarnation on a modern drag strip. Even the hood scoop is just as it left the factory, and only those modern wheels denote the passage of time. This car also appears to have lost the grille-mounted parking lights that were fitted in those years.

range, but came in an astonishing twelve versions, if you counted manual/automatic transmissions. There was actually a new economy option, with a two-barrel carburetor and a modest 255 hp, though not surprisingly only 4 percent of GTO buyers chose this option, which came with an automatic transmission only. The standard unit with four-barrel carb still claimed the same 335 hp as the 389, while a new 360 hp 400HO took the place of the old Tri-Power. Another directive from head office had banned the use of triple carburetors, so the HO came with a 288/302

Right: Even without the optional Tri-Power V8, the stock GTO could be expected to turn in a standing-quarter time of around 15.4 seconds. Even by twenty-first century standards, that's fast.

> **"The Judge can be bought. For a lot less bread than a lot of those so-called performance cars, we hasten to add. Surprised? The Judge is full of them. Like a standard 366-horse 400-cube Ram Air V8 with Quadra-jet carb. Coupled to a standard 3-speed, fully synched, manual gearbox. Stirred by a standard Hurst T-handle shifter . . . The Judge. It's a steal."**

camshaft, and free-flowing exhaust. Finally, there were variations on the Ram Air theme, which used a functional hood scoop to direct cold, dense air straight into the carburetor. As ever, these did not claim any extra power, but added speed at speed, if that makes sense.

As if that wasn't enough, the GTO buyer had the choice of ten different rear axle ratios and countless detail touches. Dealers could fit everything from a luggage carrier to a trash basket (the latter in red, blue, black, or beige), and there were over eighty items fittable at the factory, from air conditioning to cruise control and something called a "Safeguard speedometer." The options game became a part of the muscle car buying experience, and every manufacturer played it. Fun for some buyers, but a nightmare for production planners, parts men, and dealers. Perhaps more relevant to most buyers was the availability of front disc brakes, which had vented discs and came with dual circuits.

With a new prosafety climate (even John DeLorean was toning down his public pronouncements) and a horde of new competitors, one might have expected the GTO to sink further in 1968, but, in fact, sales bounced back slightly, to 87,000. It was even voted Car of the Year by *Motor Trend*, but then the GTO did have a fresh new image for '68, sharing the Tempest's new bodyshell, with a 112-inch wheelbase and classic long hood/short deck looks. The headlights were hidden as well, Camaro-style, behind vacuum-operated doors in the grille—all very well until an air leak developed in one side, allowing the Pontiac to "wink" its way down the street. Endura bumpers also made the front end look cleaner. Made of high-density urethane-elastomer, they could be molded to body shape and painted. When hit at low speed, they would spring back into shape without damage. In a TV advertisement, John DeLorean graphically demonstrated this by repeatedly hitting the front end with a sledgehammer!

Inside, the interior was all-new, with a three-pod instrument panel (though you still had to pay extra for a tachometer) and wood grain trim. There were tweaks to the V8s to cut emissions, but power outputs were up, to 265 hp for the two-barrel token economy option and 350 hp for the more popular four-barrel. Ram Air became

BELOW: GTO sales suffered from the all-conquering Plymouth Road Runner, which offered a true muscle car experience at a low price. The Judge was Pontiac's response, which majored on looks instead of creature comforts—the stripes, decals, and rear spoiler were all standard, and in '69 you could have any color you liked as long as it was bright orange!

Ram Air II, with bigger intake ports and freer-flowing exhaust ports in new cylinder heads, a hotter cam, and bigger valves. These only brought an extra six horsepower.

Nineteen sixty-nine was the year of the Judge, which was Pontiac's response to Plymouth's stripped-down, good-value Road Runner. Initial thoughts had been to build a really low-price GTO, by taking the Tempest 350HO (already available) and naming it the E/T (as in a quarter-mile elapsed time). It would bypass the soaring insurance rates for true muscle cars and attract younger drivers to the Pontiac fold. It was a good idea that came from the Ad Hoc Committee, which consisted of half a dozen of Pontiac's "Young Turk" engineers, plus the ever-present Jim Wangers. But John DeLorean vetoed it. To be credible, he said, any Pontiac muscle car had to have a 400 ci V8.

So the Judge wasn't quite as bargain-basement as the stillborn Tempest E/T, instead concentrating on a loud appearance and go-faster parts at the expense of

Below: It might look orange, but the official term was "Carousel Red. " Even when Pontiac offered other colors, this was still the most popular.

luxury. Eighty percent of Judges came in the flamboyant Carousel Red, with matching stripes and those pop art decals. A 60-inch rear spoiler completed the Judge.

Jim Wangers and his ad team had a field day with that name. They were barred from using "Here comes da Judge," a catchphrase from the TV show *Laugh-In,* but Wangers and company came up with some pretty good alternatives. "The Judge can be bought," read one (which the American Bar Association didn't like at all), "for a lot less bread than a lot of those so-called performance cars, we hasten to add."

Under the skin though, the Judge was the real deal. It came with the 400 ci V8 to Ram Air III spec (which brought 366 hp), heavy-duty suspension, Rallye II wheels, and G70 x 14 tires, so it had the performance to live up to its looks. Incidentally, the Ram Air system now had an added convenience factor. If it rained, the gaping hood scoops could be closed by switches inside the car. Before, the driver had to stop, dive into the trunk, and find those clip-on covers he hadn't used since the last storm.

Car and Driver tested six of what it termed the "Econo-Racers" in January 1969: the Judge, Chevelle SS396, Hemi Road Runner, Cyclone CJ, a Fairlane Cobra, and Dodge Super Bee. So how did the Judge do against the opposition? It's tough to say, as the test car turned out to be a hybrid, a sort of prototype with a 1968-spec engine that wouldn't have passed 1969 emissions standards. It also had seven-inch-wide wheels in place of the usual six-inch. *Car and Driver* wisely decided to exclude it from performance testing, for the good reason that it wasn't like any Judge that a

PONTIAC GTO THE JUDGE 1969

Engine: *366 hp 400 ci V8, Ram Air III*

Transmission: *four-speed manual*

Steering: *re-circulating ball, power assisted*

Tires: *Goodyear Polyglas G70 x 14*

Brakes: *Front 11.1 in vented discs, power assisted; rear 9.5 in drums, power assisted*

Suspension: *Front independent, unequal-length wishbones, coil springs, antiroll bar; rear rigid axle, trailing arms, coil springs*

Wheelbase: *112 inches*

Height: *52.3 inches*

Weight: *3,898 pounds*

***BELOW:* Body-color soft front end with twin headlights marks this out as a 1970 GTO, here in Judge form, an option that continued for that year. It was an option pack rather than a model in its own right, and checking the box brought a 366 hp Ram Air V8, Rally II wheels, G70-14 fiberglass-belted tires, T-handle transmission shifter, rear spoiler, black grille, and those all-important stripes and decals.**

1969 customer could walk into a showroom and buy. So it wasn't much of a consolation when the dressed-up GTO scored equal first in those things that could be rated, the driver's controls and instrumentation. For the record, the all-conquering Road Runner scored an easy win on acceleration, braking, and handling, with 17 points. The Super Bee and Fairlane managed 11 points apiece, and the Chevelle and Cyclone, 10 points.

Judge apart, there were few major changes to the GTO that year, though Ram Air IV was now the ultimate power option, with a claimed 370 hp thanks to improved intake ports, a higher-lift cam, and limited-travel hydraulic lifters. But the glory days were over for the GTO, and the Judge was something of a loud swan song. Even with 7,000 Judges sold in '69, overall sales slumped by 20 percent. Evidence of ever-tightening emissions and safety legislation, those spiraling insurance rates, and a public that was ending its brief but intensive love affair with high performance. All these things virtually destroyed the mass market for muscle cars. GTO sales slumped by half, to 40,000, in 1970, and a mere 10,000 would be sold in 1971, by which time the car was being outsold by the plain Tempest by ten to one.

Despite the unhelpful climate, the GTO had a macho facelift for 1970 (which

***Below left:* By the time the Judge came along, the GTO was already past its peak, overtaken by younger, more compact muscle cars—the GTO had grown in girth and weight in just a few years. But the Judge brightened up the range, and was a dream for copywriters: "The Judge can be bought."**

RIGHT: *Ram Air was all the rage in the late '60s, and that foam wall around the air cleaner made an airtight seal between intake and hood, channeling dense cold air into the engine.*

BELOW: *That rear spoiler measured sixty inches across, and reflected a growing interest in aerodynamic aids stemming from their use in NASCAR. Whether it actually did any good is anyone's guess.*

RIGHT: Heavily modified Firebird sits hunched on the line, awaiting the green light. Pontiac was a late entrant to the pony car market, and was forced to take a variation of Chevrolet's Camaro to compete, though it used Pontiac's own engines.

evidently didn't work), with fatter wheel arches and a more aggressive front end. And, in what seemed even more out of tune with its times, Pontiac fitted the biggest-possible 455 ci V8—GM had finally lifted its 400 ci limit on intermediate cars. However, the 455 was far from frenetic, being a relaxed and torquey V8, in a lower state of tune than 400, offering 360 hp and over 500 lb ft. For horsepower fanatics, the 400 Ram Air IV was still available. There was a belated attempt to improve the handling as well, with a rear antiroll bar and larger front bar, while the suspension mountings were beefed up and the power steering had a new variable-ratio setup. Despite unchanged spring rates, it added up to a great improvement, though you still had to pay extra for disc brakes. In Europe, front discs were now fitted to the humblest family sedans, but the big GTO stuck with drums.

"If you can stop drooling for a moment, we'd like to tell you what's propelling that Firebird 400 in the picture. What it is, is 400 cubes of chromed V8. And what it puts out is 325 hp. The point being, that Pontiac Firebird 400 was designed for heroic driving . . . Of course, if the 400 is too much car for you, there are four other Firebirds to choose from. Lucky you."

For 1971, the GTO began showing signs of winding down. Pontiac's muscle car flagship was the Trans Am, and it wasn't inclined to throw money at the GTO—it wasn't even advertised in the mainstream magazines that year. Compression ratios were dropped all around, to accept regular fuel, and Ram Air III and IV went the way of the dodo. The easy-going 455 V8 was now the hottest GTO option, at 335 hp, while the standard 400 offered 300 hp.

ABOVE: *Pencil-thin rear lights and the twin-headlight front end identify this as a Firebird instead of a Camaro. The Firebird was popular, but never really caught the public's imagination in the way the Mustang did. The later Trans Am built up quite a following though.*

So it was hardly surprising that only 10,532 GTOs found buyers that year, nor that Pontiac relegated it to option status for '72. In a way, the GTO was back to where it came from, as a performance option on the Tempest, though sales were a fraction of the early figures. In any case, it was a purely cosmetic package now, as a Tempest could be ordered with the same V8s. The GTO option swapped to the Le Mans coupe for 1973, and early suggestions that a 310 hp Super Duty 455 would be an option came to nothing—those engines were reserved for the Firebird and Trans Am.

No one would have been surprised if the GTO had died then and there, but Pontiac decided to give it one more chance, as the hot option on its X-body economy car, the Ventura. The Ventura GTO looked promising: 800 lb lighter than a Le Mans, so 200 hp from a 350 ci V8 should make for sprightly performance and better mileage. It even had a vibrating scoop atop the hood and certainly looked the hot rod part. Alas, the Ventura wasn't especially fast (16 seconds over the quarter) and still guzzled gas at the rate of 12 mpg. Sales were up on '73, but not by enough, and the Ventura GTO didn't reappear in 1974. But it inspired '70s hot rodders to discover that a 400 or 455 V8 would slot straight in. Big engine/small car is where the GTO started out. Years later, in 2004, Pontiac launched its all-new GTO. This V8 coupe, with a $32,000 price tag, all-aluminum LS1 V8, and high-tech traction control, wasn't the same sort of affordable performance as the original. But the GTO was back.

The Firebird & Trans Am

Pontiac, Plymouth, Chevy, Dodge, Olds, AMC, Buick. They all had cause to be upset by the huge success of the new Mustang in 1964. It set a new record for first-year sales, and there really were crowds gathered outside Ford showrooms. But maybe Pontiac had cause to be more disgruntled than most. After all, it had virtually invented the muscle car, with the '64 GTO, and successful though that was, its sales were a fraction of those of Ford's new pony car.

The trouble was, for all its popularity, the GTO still looked what it was, a hotted-up Tempest. The Mustang offered something else. It had four seats but looked like a proper sports car, and Ford's rivals had no choice but to come up with a Mustang beater, and quickly. Over at Chevrolet, they lost no time, and just four months after

BELOW: In pony car tradition, the Firebird offered a wide range of engines, starting with a low-priced budget straight six to attract buyers into the showroom, plus plenty of options to bump up the price when they got there. This Firebird, you won't be surprised to hear, is not powered by any sort of straight six. Most drivers went for one of the V8s.

the pony car's launch, they were hard at work on the car that would become the Camaro, a four-seat pony car out of the Mustang mold.

At Pontiac, John DeLorean had different ideas. He wanted a two-seat sports car, and a design project began under the codename XP-833. It would have a plastic body, and be smaller and more economical than a Corvette. A prototype was built, the Banshee Fastback, a sleek little sports car with pop-up headlamps, looking more like something out of the seventies than 1964.

But a prototype was as far as it got. GM top brass vetoed the idea, saying they didn't want any in-house competition. They were probably right. The market for two-seat sports cars, despite the high profile of cars like the Corvette, the MGs, and Jaguar

BELOW: Ignore the rear lights, and it's clear that the Firebird shared its body with the Camaro, being wider and more generous in size than the Mustang it was aimed at. Neither Firebird nor Camaro though, succeeded in toppling the original pony car from its throne.

XKs, was actually quite small, certainly in comparison with the huge economies of scale Detroit was used to. Remember the Mustang had started out as a little two-seater, until Lee Iacocca realized that it wouldn't sell in the required numbers and ordered that it be stretched into the four-seat pony car.

So no sports car for Pontiac, but GM's top management weren't about to deny the division its own pony car. There was just one thing; they'd have to tag on to Chevrolet's pony car project. By now, of course, the Chevy project was far advanced, so Pontiac engineers would have little influence on the design. The body was already finalized. "Ultimately, it just made good economic sense to handle the project this way," wrote Bill Holder and Phillip Kunz in *Firebird and Trans Am*. "Pontiac didn't like the decision, but that was the way the game would be played."

The Chevrolet also had a name already—Camaro—but here, at least, Pontiac did have an ace up its sleeve. Back in 1954, it had built a one-off turbine concept car, the sort of show vehicle that US manufacturers were in love with in the fifties. This used an early version of the Firebird logo, and the name sprang from there. Also, PMD (Pontiac Motor Division) engineers weren't limited to simply sticking their own badges onto a Chevrolet. They had to keep the fenders unchanged but could reshape the nose and tail a little. So they added a split front grille, after the style of the GTO (and now a recognizable Pontiac trademark) with twin headlights—the Camaro used single lights, or hid them under the grille. At the rear, the Camaro's conventional rear lights were ditched in favor of two narrow horizontal strips. A Pontiac archive picture shows a prototype with the remodeled nose and tail, though badged as a "GM-X."

All this work succeeded in giving the Firebird its own identity (or as much as possible, given the design constraints), but it delayed its launch by several months. So while the Camaro was unveiled to the public on schedule, in September 1966, it was February 1967 before the Firebird was finally ready. Pontiac's new pony car had been born under the shadow of its Chevy cousin—could it survive?

"After this," said the full-page advertisement for the new Firebird, "you'll never go back to driving whatever you're driving." It went on in a tone familiar to a generation of copywriters. "400 cubes of chromed V8 . . . designed for heroic driving . . . heavy-duty three-speed floor shift, extra sticky suspension and a set of duals that announce your coming like the brass section of the New York Philharmonic." Above the purple prose was a full-color picture of a bright blue Firebird 400 blasting down a deserted mountain road. The driver was depicted as happy, but alone, implying that this was a car for serious drivers. When advertisers wanted to depict a slightly softer image, they put a passenger in as well, sometimes with the woman in the driving seat. (Same-sex pony car couples were a bit too radical, even for the late sixties.)

To compete with the Mustang and Camaro, there had to be a full range of Firebirds, and there was. All five of them used Pontiac's own engines, which may seem odd given the lengths to which GM wanted to go to promote parts-sharing and economies of scale. Why have different engines when they were hidden away under the hood? GM divisions, of course, had long had a strong tradition of independent

BELOW: Mildly modified Firebird hard top, though of course there was a convertible on offer in the late '60s as well. A less common option was the six-cylinder Firebird Sprint—the torquey 326 ci V8 was a more popular choice.

engineering and tough in-house competition. Also, there was even more of a case for bespoke power units in enthusiast cars like the Firebird and Camaro. The buyers of these cars were engine-conscious; for many of them, the nuts and bolts under the hood, and where they came from, really mattered. So similar though they were, the GM pony car cousins did generate loyal followings of their own, and having an authentic Pontiac, or Chevrolet, motor was part of the appeal.

Back to those five Firebirds. The base car (at just $2,600) was powered by Pontiac's 230 ci straight six and an overhead cam unit delivering 165 hp. Next up was

the Sprint, and this was unique among muscle cars in using a more highly tuned six instead of a V8. Most manufacturers offered the six as a base power unit, but really just as a means of tempting buyers into the showroom with a low sticker price. Once there, a salesman would do his best to sell the customer a V8 with all the options.

The Firebird Sprint aimed to provide a high revving, sporting six in the European tradition. That 230 ci power unit was tuned up with a Rochester four-barrel carburetor, high-lift cam, 10.5:1 compression ratio, freer flowing exhaust, and air cleaner. It all added up to 215 hp, with a floor-mounted three-speed stick shift as standard (less sporting Firebirds had a column-shift), plus firmed-up suspension.

More popular than the Sprint was the more traditional 326 ci V8, slightly more powerful at 250 hp but with a lot more torque (330 lb ft, peaking at a nice low 2,500 rpm). It also cost less than the Sprint, but it too could be given more sporting credibility via the options list: floor-mounted shift, a center console, and front bucket seats were just the obvious items. As was true of the Mustang and Camaro, a basic Firebird without any options at all was little more than a rebodied sedan, complete with bench front seat, sparse instrumentation, and that column-shift. Human nature being what it is, not many buyers left them that way.

The softly tuned 326 was probably the most relaxed Firebird, but to climb into true muscle car territory, you had to opt for the 326HO or 400. The HO added a Carter four-barrel carburetor to the 326 V8, plus a dual exhaust and 10.5:1 compression ratio, which

BELOW LEFT: That well-known Firebird logo, here in back-lit form. Some said the Firebird was always partially hidden beneath the Camaro's shadow, but the car did build up its own following, and that emblem was a natural as a supersize hood decal, which would come later.

Above: *V8 options for the early Firebird included the stock 326 ci V8 of 250 hp and 330 lb ft, but a hotter, higher compression version with four-barrel carburetor made that closer to 300 hp. The ultimate in '67 was the Firebird 400, with 325 hp: there are no hood scoops on this car, so it wasn't one of those.*

Left: *Unlike its in-house cousin, the Camaro, Pontiac's Firebird never took to the fashion for hidden headlights, sticking with the conventional twin-light setup for its first few years. The body-color front end identifies this as a post-'69 car.*

"Announcing Pontiac's new pony express. Firebird Trans Am."

took power to 285 hp—that was a fairly modest 14% boost—but many believed that the 326HO was underrated, with a true figure of around 300 hp. To mark it out as an HO, this Firebird had appropriate badging and long body stripes. Finally, the ultimate Firebird at launch was the full 400, with 325 hp. Gaping hood scoops came as standard, but they were just for show unless you specified the optional Ram Air. And if that wasn't enough, Pontiac also offered a unique hood-mounted tachometer on all the Firebirds, something else that differentiated it from the Camaro. With the tacho needle quivering and those two scoops gulping in air to feed a hungry, roaring V8, the Firebird drivers could be in no doubt that they were piloting a true muscle car.

So the early Firebird pressed all the right buttons, and over 82,000 were sold in its first year, which sounds quite respectable. Except that Chevrolet sold more than twice as many Camaros (with five extra months on sale), and Ford was still the pony car leader with over 475,000 finding homes in 1967. Pontiac had some way to go.

BELOW: Fat racing stripes, vinyl roof, hood scoops, and spoilers—this Firebird Trans Am has just about every appearance extra that an early '70s hot car nut could wish for. Restyled for 1970, the range was simplified, with the six-cylinder Sprint dropped and a new luxury Esprit introduced. Even with the muscle car under pressure, the Firebird's real strength was in the big V8s, the 400s and 455s.

It sought to redress the balance in '68 by boosting the six to 250 ci (which meant more power for the base unit, and more torque for the Sprint), and the 326 V8 up to a full 350. The latter now offered 265 hp in mild-mannered two-barrel form, and 320 hp as the high-compression four-barrel HO. The 400 got a power boost too, but only a slight one, to 335 hp, so maybe paying $435 extra was a bit over the top. Some people did though, and for the good reason that at the time this was the biggest-engined pony car on sale. A dealer-tuned Camaro 396, or a factory-fresh Z28, offered plenty more power, but for some buyers, sheer cubic inches counted more than anything else.

Pontiac Firebird 350 1969

Engine: *265 hp 350 ci V8*

Transmission: *three-speed automatic*

Steering: *recirculating ball, variable power assisted*

Tires: *F70 x 14*

Brakes: *front discs, power assisted; rear drums, power assisted*

Suspension: *front independent, coil springs; rear rigid axle, multileaf semielliptic springs*

Wheelbase: *108 inches*

Height: *49.6 inches*

Weight: *3,642 pounds*

With the Firebird and Camaro sharing so much, one might expect their magazine road tests to have read very similarly as well. Like identical twins getting the same school report. They didn't. In October 1967, *Road Test* magazine pitted a Camaro and Firebird against a Mustang, Dodge Dart, Cougar, and Barracuda. While admitting that the two GM cars "come out of virtually the same mold," they stated that "most drivers like the F-Bird better than the Camaro SS 396 for handling. There are several subtleties that induce this preference." Specifically, the Firebird had a rear spring stabilizing system, which the Camaro didn't, so it kept better control of the rear axle—axle tramp, or hop, was always a Camaro weakness. It also had multileaf rear springs and staggered shocks, which helped. In March '69, *Motor Trend's* five-way test put the Firebird third, ahead of its cousin.

The real standoff came in *Car and Driver*, March 1968. "The Camaro," they concluded, "was built to be all things to all people, as a result, it was a disappointment . . . For sheer enjoyment and confidence behind the wheel, the Firebird was almost in a class by itself." That must have been an especially sweet victory for Pontiac engineers—despite tagging on to a Chevrolet project late in the day, they seemed to have done a better development job. The sales figures must have been cheering too, with over 100,000 Firebirds sold in 1968.

For 1969, there were more power boosts, to 230 hp for the Sprint and 325 hp for the 350 HO (the latter with larger valves and a higher lift cam). That left the base 400 looking only slightly more powerful than the top 350, though it was a lot more torquey, at 430 lb ft. The 400's optional Ram Air was given a boost too, with a new

Ram Air IV, including a hotter cam, aluminum cylinder heads, and special valve train. It cost a substantial $832 extra for a quoted 345 hp, which made for a decidedly expensive 10 hp advantage over Ram Air III.

But the really big news that year was a new variation on the Firebird theme. A mere 700-odd were sold in 1969, and its launch hadn't gone according to plan, but its name would eventually overshadow that of the Firebird itself—Trans Am. The car that would become a legend among muscle cars was originally intended as a bona fide racer in the popular Trans Am series. The idea was to enter a Firebird-based car, win the championship, then sell a road car spinoff named after the series.

The only problem was that Pontiac didn't have a competitive V8 to suit the series' 303 ci capacity limit. The engineering design department got down to work, and in the meantime, Firebirds raced using Chevrolet Z28 engines. But Pontiac's own motor took too long to develop, and by the time it was ready, the rules had changed, and it wasn't legal to race. PMD decided to go ahead and launch its Firebird "Trans Am" at the 1969 Chicago Auto Show anyway, though instead of a special racing-derived V8, it used the stock 400. And the car named after the race series had never actually raced.

So the early Trans Am was little more than a Firebird 400 with a spoiler and a different paint job. Admittedly that paint job was something special—white with blue racing stripes running the length of the hood,

BELOW: Muscle car, mid '70s style. The Pontiac Can Am was a limited-production machine, based on the idea of a 1975 concept car, the All-American Grand Am. In production, it was based on a Le Mans coupe, but the conversion was carried out by the Motortown concern, not by Pontiac itself. The 200 hp (net) 400 ci V8 was borrowed from the Trans Am.

Right: Like many '70s muscle cars, the Can Am was as much about appearance as performance, hence the all-white body with orange graphics, the shaker hood scoop, and Rallye II wheels. Automatic transmission, air conditioning, tinted glass, and AM/FM stereo were all part of the package as well.

roof, and trunk lid. There were two big hood scoops and two more extractor scoops behind each front wheel, while the large rear spoiler was calculated to produce 100 lb. of downforce at 100 mph. There were suspension changes too: heavy-duty springs, a stabilizer bar, and seven-inch-wide wheels, so it wasn't just a cosmetic job after all.

There must have been some at Pontiac who doubted the wisdom of the Trans Am. Not only was it the race car that never raced, but the company had to pay SCCA (Sports Car Club of America) a five dollar royalty on each one in return for using the Trans Am name. As it turned out, of course, the name became more associated with the car than with the race.

Both Firebird and Trans Am (they developed side by side) were restyled with a single-headlight front end for 1970. The range was rejigged and simplified, with the

BELOW: Keeping the faith. While other muscle cars downsized and turned all meek and mild in the '70s, the Firebird and Trans Am stood their ground. Sales actually increased from '74 to '79.

Sprint being dropped altogether and the basic Firebird receiving a Chevy six in place of the Pontiac one. The Esprit was a new luxury model, with the 350 V8 as its base power plant, albeit in soft low-compression two-barrel guise, with 255 hp. The three 400s were rationalized down to a single Formula 400 Firebird, with 330 hp or 335 hp (the latter with Ram Air III) options. They also had Trans Am style suspension that year. As for the Trans Am itself, this had Ram Air III as standard, but its exterior appearance was muted a little, with smaller, smoother spoilers. A Shaker hood scoop and Rallye II wheels ensured that the Trans Am didn't get too discreet.

RIGHT: Introducing a big-cube Super Duty 455 in the wake of the oil crisis was either brave or foolish, depending on your point of view. Few members of the buying public were impressed enough to buy.

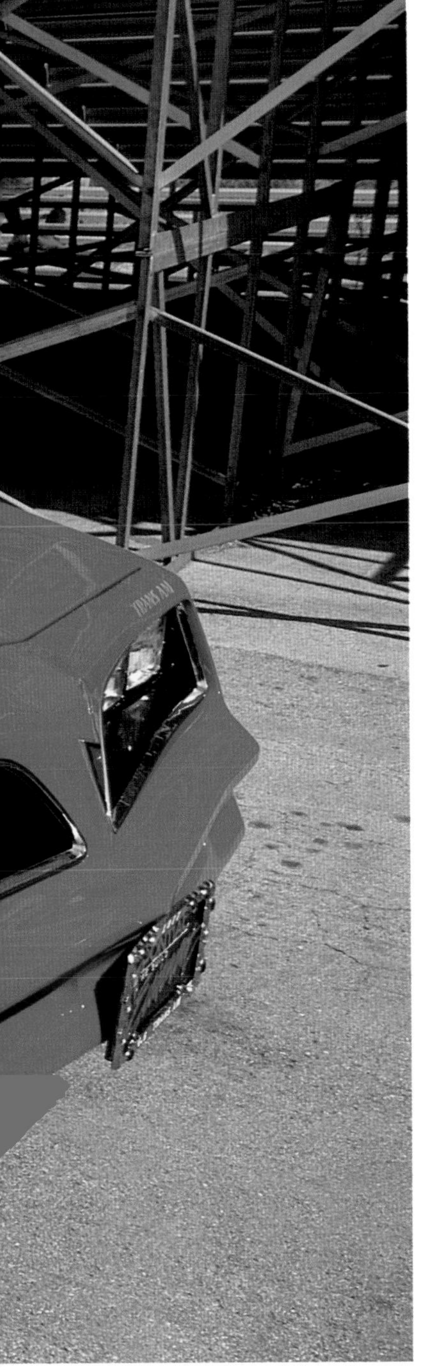

The early 1970s were not happy times for any muscle cars, with stricter legislation, soaring insurance rates, and public opinion swinging back in favor of smaller, more sensible cars. (These things come in cycles—exactly the same thing had happened at the beginning of the sixties.) But while other muscle car makers were trimming back on power and toning down their advertising, Pontiac introduced the mighty 455 ci V8. In terms of horsepower, it wasn't actually as mighty as it seemed, with 325 hp in two-barrel form, or 335 hp as a four barrel. But they did enable the Firebird to claim back the biggest-engine crown, and those 455s were very beefy, supplying 455 lb ft of torque.

It was a brave move and was applauded by enthusiasts, but in terms of actually selling cars, the 455s were a flop, contributing little to overall sales. Even adding a Super Duty 455 (recalling those no-holds barred tuning parts of the early sixties) did not bring customers flocking to Pontiac showrooms. The Super Duty was no cosmetic muscle car, with many internal engine changes and 310 hp net, which made it 360-370 hp on the old measurement system. In fact, it was overtuned, and the original was too dirty to pass emissions legislation. Pontiac hurriedly substituted a milder cam, and once derated to 290 hp, the SD was legal to sell.

But, despite the 455s, the Super Duty, and yet more rejigging of the range (with detuned V8s and a cheaper Formula 350, giving muscle car looks with lower insurance), the Firebird/Trans Am was going through its worst patch ever. In 1972, fewer than 30,000 cars found homes (a tiny number in Detroit terms), and there was talk of dropping the range altogether. The Super Duty did go, then the base 455 as well. There were similar fears over the Camaro. It was just as well they didn't drop it, as in 1974, Firebird sales began to claw their way back up again. Ironically, given the anti–gas guzzler climate, the Trans Am became the best-selling model. Over 10,000 were sold that year, 27,000 in '75, nearly 47,000 in '76, and 69,000 in '77. In 1979, the Trans Am's best year ever, 117,108 left Pontiac showrooms. That year, over 200,000 Firebird/Trans Ams of all types were sold.

There was one very good reason why the Firebird and Trans Am continued to sell well in the late '70s. Other muscle cars had toned down, downsized, or disappeared altogether, but the Pontiac, with its four rectangular headlights, fat tires, and loud colors, still looked the part. The V8s might be detuned (though power was starting to creep up again), but by specifying the W50 body kit, buyers could make their Firebird look just as macho as any late sixties muscle car.

BELOW: Starting out as a limited-edition addendum to the Firebird range, the Trans Am later became a model in its own right. Early cars were repainted Firebird 400s with stiffer suspension, but the marque created its own following and became one of the longest-lived muscle cars of all.

It didn't last though, and in the wake of the second oil crisis, sales slumped again by more than half in 1980 and to 33,000 the following year. Pontiac responded by dropping the 400 V8, and the short-lived 403. The old straight-six had already been replaced by a Buick V6 in two-barrel and four-barrel forms, and there was a small-block 305 ci V8 Chevy as well. A turbocharged 301 ci V8 replaced the big-cube motors and was almost as powerful, at 210 hp, and became the standard engine in 140 and 155 hp form, alongside the V6.

The old Firebird/Trans Am had been thirteen years in production and showed it. Its 1982 replacement (alongside the similar Camaro) retained a family resemblance: it was still a rear-wheel-drive 2+2 coupe, but there the two cars diverged. The new-generation Firebird weighed only 2,800 lb in basic form, it had good, efficient aerodynamics, and the base power unit was only four cylinders. Quite a culture shock for diehard muscle car fans, but a sign of the times (Ford had long been selling a four-cylinder Mustang) and inevitable if Pontiac was to comply with the CAFE federal fuel consumption regulations. Firebird fanciers need not have worried though, for there was also a 171 ci V6 (soon also available in HO 135 hp form), while the Trans Am came with a 150 hp 305 ci V8 with carburetor or fuel injection.

There were three basic models: base Firebird, S/E, and Trans Am. The latter remained by far the most popular, making up around half of all sales, which fluctuated throughout the 1980s, sometimes climbing up to six figures, sometimes slumping back again. Both S/E and Trans Am were given face-lifts in 1985, with new front and rear

BELOW RIGHT: Pontiac had to pay the Sports Car Club of America (organizers of the Trans Am race series) a five dollar royalty on every car bearing that badge. But it was money well spent, as the name became more closely associated with the car than with the race.

ends. Buyers seeking the most dramatic looks were advised to go for the Trans Am with its optional W62 ground effects body package.

Meanwhile, the Pontiacs were moving back into true muscle car power figures, with the 305 ci V8 available in three versions: base, HO, and TPI (Tuned Port Injection) with 155–205 hp. Cubic inches were making a comeback too, and for 1987 a 350 ci Chevrolet V8 found its way into the series, this one with 210 hp, followed by a 235 hp TPI V8 the following year. Options began to reflect the return of serious performance, with hardware and cosmetic items back on the list. Y99 was a suspension package, consisting of front and rear stabilizer bars with custom shocks. The GTA was a new, upgraded Firebird, slotting in between the Formula (that name had come back too) and the Trans Am. With options like all-wheel disc brakes and performance suspension, it held the promise of a budget Trans Am; over 20,000 were sold.

BELOW: It seems a shame to admit it, but the Trans Am never actually raced in the series it was named after. A team of Firebirds did, powered by Chevy Camaro Z28 engines, but by the time Pontiac's race-ready V8 was finished, the rules had changed. Pontiac decided to launch the Trans Am anyway.

But from 1987, history began to repeat itself. The '82 Firebird appeared to have aged rapidly, and after only four years on the market, sales sank, from a high of over 110,000 in 1986 to around 24,000 by 1990. Even the Trans Am seemed to have lost its shine, with fewer than 2,500 finding buyers that year. A restyle in 1991 helped lift sales temporarily, but what Pontiac really needed was a new pony car.

They got it in 1993, when, once again, a new Camaro and Firebird/Trans Am were launched at around the same time. Maybe after the embarrassment of that delayed launch in '67, Pontiac people with long memories had sworn that the same thing would never happen again! Not that the Firebird was very different. It shared both bodyshell and 350 V8 with its Chevy rival and relative, and the only styling differences were beneath the waistline.

Under the skin, it was a typical high-tech 1990s coupe, with ABS and driver and passenger airbags. Engine options amounted to three: the base 207 ci V6 of 160 hp, the Chevy 350 V8 (280 hp), plus a high-performance version of the V8 with fuel injection. This was the 300 hp LT1, fitted to a performance flagship named Firehawk.

This had actually begun life in the last year of the old Firebird, as a supertuned car to rival the ZR1 Corvette, but now it was an established part of the range. Transmission choices were a four-speed automatic or six-speed manual, and the '93 Firehawk could dispatch the standing quarter mile in 13.5 seconds.

The days of the Firebird as an affordable, good-looking car were long gone, and the emphasis in the nineties was on performance. The WS6 handling package, for example, included larger wheels and tires, stiffer suspension, larger stabilizer bars, and four-wheel disc brakes. Meanwhile, the LT1 had a marginal power boost to 305 hp, and *Motor Trend's* test Trans Am, equipped with this motor, rocketed to 60 mph in 5.7 seconds. Another uprating to 320 hp in 1998 brought that down to 5.1 seconds.

For the Trans Am's thirtieth anniversary in 1999, Pontiac unveiled a limited edition. Both coupe and convertible came in white with blue racing stripes (just like the first Trans Am) and had white leather seats and blue-tinted seventeen-inch wheels. But the Trans Am wasn't the performance flagship any more. That role fell to the Firehawk, now with 345 hp and 350 lb ft. Even the most rabid late-sixties muscle car freak would have been happy with that.

For 2004, muscle fans had a new Pontiac performance flagship. The GTO was back as an all-new V8 coupe, while the Firebird, Trans Am, and Firehawk had gone. One of the great muscle car survivors had finally died, and one had risen phoenix-like from the ashes.

"The kinesthetic ecstasy of the wind in your hair and a 5.0 liter V8 under your throttle foot. It's the Mustang legend come alive, and you feel part of it every time you take the wheel. Only the legend has never been more true, nor the Mustang ever better than it is right now."

Ford: Meet The Boss

In the fifties, Ford was the sluggard in the Detroit V8 power wars. It seems hard to believe now. Ford, the company of "Total Performance" in the sixties; Ford, the winner of countless international rallies, whose Formula One V8 (with a little help from Cosworth) did a similar job in Grand Prix. Certain Ford Mustangs and Galaxies had a muscular reputation too. And it was Ford that came up with the first mass-produced V8, the flat-head, back in 1932, bringing a new level of performance to the man in the street and laying the foundations for a whole generation of hot-rodders. How could this Ford have dropped behind in the horsepower race?

Personalities, for better or worse, often determine the course of the companies they control. It's tempting to believe that big corporations are really controlled by accountants, lawyers, and technocrats of varying function and usefulness. And much of the time, that's probably true, especially in the complex, modern world. But big, strategic decisions are often made by big personalities as well. Just taking Detroit as an example, it was Lee Iacocca's enthusiasm that made the Ford Mustang a reality. Over at Pontiac, the GTO wouldn't have happened had it not been for the "gas heads" in charge—"Bunkie" Knudsen, Pete Estes, and John DeLorean. And much more recently, when Bill Ford tried to clean up Ford's environmental act, it wasn't because a team of advisers thought it would make great publicity, but because he sincerely believed that it was the right thing to do.

This stunning dream-machine is a 1970 Boss Mustang 429. The 429 was built solely to legalize its 375 horsepower "semi-hemi" V8 for NASCAR .

428
428

ABOVE AND RIGHT: ***Was the Ford Thunderbird a muscle car? Well, no, especially in four-seater form as shown here. But as a two-seat "personal car" in the 1950s, it had much in common with the later pony car concept. While the Thunderbird could never go around corners like a Corvette, it could at least match it in a straight line.***

ABOVE: *Strong men wept, or at least wrote letters of complaint, to Ford when the two-seat T-bird was dropped in favor of the bigger four-seater in 1958. It had never been a muscle car, but the original T-bird could be specified with a supercharged 300 hp V8 by the end, so losing it opened up a gap in Ford's range, at least as far as enthusiasts were concerned.*

Let's go back to the fifties. Robert McNamara has achieved a top job at Ford, and he makes for an interesting character among Detroit executives. Most Detroit men had engine oil in their blood: cars were their life. To McNamara, cars were a means of transport, no more, no less. The top motor industry executives were career car people. They joined GM, or Ford, or Chrysler on leaving college, and there they stayed until a comfortable retirement and the golf links beckoned. McNamara had come from the Navy. He was one of the "whiz kids" brought in by Henry Ford II in the late 1940s to save the tottering Ford empire. After doing his stint at Ford (including a brief time as president), he left Detroit to become defense secretary in the Kennedy administration.

Speaking of politics, McNamara was a Democrat—most of his top brass colleagues were staunch Republicans. But despite the differences, Lee Iacocca, who worked under McNamara and typified the cigar-chewing, seat-of-the-pants Detroit executive, had fond memories of him. "A very kind man as well as a loyal friend," he later wrote in his autobiography.

So while McNamara was high up in Ford (he was a vice president and general manager before becoming president), there was less emphasis on road-burning V8s and more on making cars profitably. The back-to-basics Ford Falcon of 1959, just simple, straightforward transportation, was McNamara's baby—and it vindicated his approach, selling in huge numbers. You won't be surprised that Ford's bespectacled chief wasn't a big motor racing fan either. When the AMA (Automobile Manufacturers Association) announced a voluntary ban on factory involvement in racing, Ford agreed, without resorting to the back-door support that GM employed.

That's not to say that Ford in the late fifties was a performance-free zone. One notable hot car was the two-seat Thunderbird, which started out as a boulevard cruiser but ended up with a 300 hp supercharged option. Mind you, a Thunderbird with that sort of power was best exploited on the straight-line interstates, not roads with corners in them.

Thunderbird or no, by 1958, Ford had fallen behind. By then, Chrysler had the first generation Hemi and the 413 ci Max Wedge. Chevrolet had long since broken the

BELOW: It looks tough (the wide wheels are nonstandard), but the four-seat Thunderbird was no muscle car.

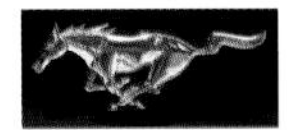

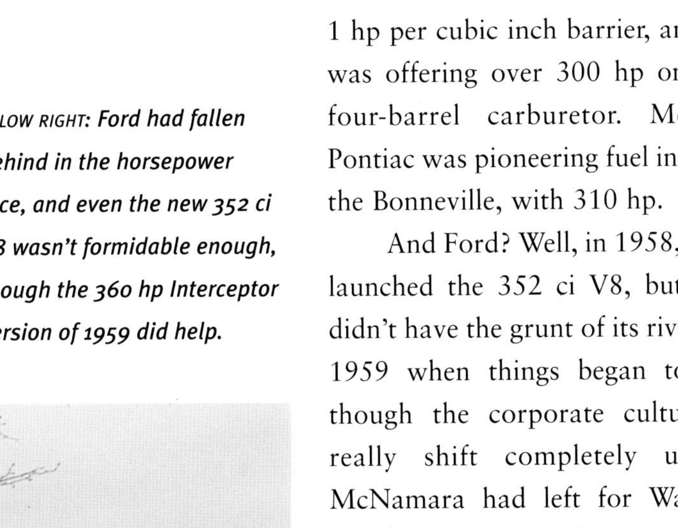

BELOW RIGHT: *Ford had fallen behind in the horsepower race, and even the new 352 ci V8 wasn't formidable enough, though the 360 hp Interceptor version of 1959 did help.*

1 hp per cubic inch barrier, and its 348 was offering over 300 hp on a single four-barrel carburetor. Meanwhile, Pontiac was pioneering fuel injection on the Bonneville, with 310 hp.

"Wherever—whenever—your Thunderbird appears in public, the effect is electric. All eyes turn to its long, low, graceful beauty. All hearts say, 'That's for me!'"

And Ford? Well, in 1958, Ford had launched the 352 ci V8, but this just didn't have the grunt of its rivals. It was 1959 when things began to change, though the corporate culture didn't really shift completely until Bob McNamara had left for Washington. In that year, Ford announced the Interceptor version of the 352, also known as the Super Interceptor and Thunderbird Super. This brought a Holley 540-cfm four-barrel carburetor, 10.6:1 compression ratio, an aluminum intake manifold, plus cast-iron exhaust headers, cast nodular crank, solid valve lifters, and a dual-point ignition system. The result was 360 hp, and Ford's return to serious performance. At first, the Interceptor wasn't even available with an automatic transmission, which indicates its status as a performance engine.

The new engine didn't go into any intermediate Ford (we weren't into the muscle car era yet), but instead was available on any of the full-size models. The big Galaxie was very full-size indeed, 214 inches long, 81 inches wide, and with a wheelbase of 119 inches. It wasn't the obvious choice for a performance car, but Ford would concentrate their hottest, big-cube motors in the Galaxie over the next few years. The car repaid the compliment with a whole host of drag and NASCAR wins, plus

RIGHT: Maybe it's unfair to write off the four-seat Thunderbird as a performance car. After all, the third-generation T-bird shown here (it was launched in 1962) could be had with a 390 cubic-inch engine under the hood, delivering 300 hp. Fins had shrunk back to early 1950s scale, and the new Thunderbird relied on its pointed nose and sharp lines to make an impression.

CLASSIC
YSK659

stunning performance on the road. With the Interceptor under the hood, a slightly modified 1960 Galaxie was capable of 0–60 mph in 7.5 seconds, and a top speed of just over 150 mph.

Encouraged, Ford announced that they were suspending their support of the AMA's ban, and underlined the fact by taking an Interceptor-engined Starliner Galaxie to Daytona, where it proceeded to lap (for 40 laps) at an average of 142 mph. The company won 15 Grand National races in 1960, and once the big V8 was approved by the NHRA, Ford announced they were getting back into drag racing as well.

That was just the start. For 1961, a new 390 ci V8 was announced, starting at 300 hp for the base version. A police-spec 390 made that 330 hp, while the top Thunderbird Super (with four-barrel carburetor) made 375 hp at 6,000 rpm. Later in the year, a triple two-barrel option took that up to 401 hp, enough for quarter-mile times of just over 15 seconds, and 0–60 mph in 7 seconds. Not surprisingly, Thunderbird Super-equipped Galaxies did well in drag racing.

Now there was no stopping Ford's progress up the power escalator—maybe the blue oval thought they had some catching up to do! In early 1962, they announced

RIGHT: This Thunderbird has been customized to turn it into the two-seater that many Ford enthusiasts were clamoring for, though this probably wasn't quite what they had in mind. They wanted a two-seat sports car to rival the Corvette, and Lee Iacocca and his team very nearly gave it to them.

LEFT: Ford might not be in the muscle business just yet, but they turned the full-size Galaxie into a formidable performer by adding their hottest and biggest V8s. From 1961, these included a new 390 ci unit, offering up to 375 hp with a four-barrel carburetor. With this sort of power on tap, even the Galaxie's weight didn't hamper it too much.

BELOW: What would Robert McNamara have said? The successful Falcon was designed as simple, basic transport, but with the right sort of V8 under the hood . . .

another new V8, this time of 406 ci. Its power increase was actually marginal over the 390, and the new Thunderbird Special 406, to give its official designation, carried over the same triple two-barrel carburetor setup of the hottest 390, along with its special camshaft, valve gear, bearings, ignition, and exhaust system.

For the less committed, a single four-barrel version was available, with twenty horsepower less. But despite the carried-over components, the 406 was not a hastily

RIGHT: The Falcon donated many of its components to the lower-powered Mustangs and later acquired its own V8 option. There was never a factory muscle option though.

enlarged 390. The cylinder block was all new, to provide thicker walls and greater strength. There were stronger pistons and con-rods too, while oil pressure was increased from 45 psi to 60, via a modified pressure-relief valve. Dual valve springs helped to control the valves at high revs. Power? With 405 hp at 5,800 rpm, the 406 made barely more peak power than the 390, but it was torquier and made a stronger, more durable basis from which to extract more cubic inches and horsepower.

The option price of $379.70—a relatively modest amount, given what you were getting—also included a Borg Warner four-speed manual transmission, with ratios of 2.36, 1.78, 1.41, and 1.00:1. Ford beefed up the rest of the driveline to suit, with a 3-inch driveshaft, four-pinion differential, and 9-inch diameter ring gear (up from 8.75 inches). The springs and shocks were 20% stiffer, and harder 3-inch brake linings were part of the 406 package too. With all this on board, and the standard 3.56:1 rear axle, Galaxie 406 owners could expect their two-ton car to make 60 mph in just 7 seconds, and top out at around 140 mph.

Of course, all this effort wasn't just directed at the customer on the street. Newly back into both drag racing and NASCAR, Ford was developing big-cube V8s specifically to win races and set record E/Ts. But from the point of view of road-going muscle cars, these motors found their way onto the street as well. That was certainly true of the new 427 ci V8 in 1963: that would be a significant figure for Ford fans, with a 427, along with the 428 and 429 that followed, being Ford's biggest V8 on offer through the sixties.

Right: Big, bold, and brash, and despite their poundage, the Galaxies did well in competition, thanks to sheer horsepower. Some raced in England, dwarfing the Jaguars.

The Galaxie's role as the blue oval's in-house performance car was underlined by the mid-1963 launch of the Galaxie fastback. It was a good-looking car, but the sloping rear pillars weren't just there to impress neighbors from the driveway. Ford also had an eye on NASCAR, where increasingly high racing speeds made aerodynamic efficiency a key factor in winning. This was the beginning of a process that by the end of the sixties would see outrageous NASCAR racers like the Plymouth

Superbird and Dodge Charger Daytona, the "Winged Warriors."

The first Galaxie 427s were actually aimed at the drag strip, and fifty special lightweight versions were built. They were stripped down and basic, leaving out almost everything that didn't contribute to straight-line acceleration. As for the 427, that came with twin Holley 600 cfm four-barrel carburetors, with a rated output of 425 hp at 6,000 rpm, though the true figure was thought to be much higher. This was mated to a special version of Ford's top-loader four-speed manual transmission, with a special aluminum case to cut weight. All the effort paid off, with a weight of less than 3,500 lb. and quarter-mile times in the low 12s, though ultimately, even the lightweight Galaxies proved too heavy to be really competitive on the drag strip. That's when Ford turned its attention to a special lightweight version of the smaller Fairlane.

"One of the quietest—if not THE quietest—cars we've driven in any price class . . . stops, goes and rides easily but not without noticeable acceleration squat and deceleration dive . . . Easy to drive and especially easy to live with.

(MOTOR TREND, *MARCH 1967: GALAXIE 500*)

Meanwhile, it built nearly 5,000 road-going Galaxie 427s in 1963. Many of these were bought by weekend racers, so the distinction between pure road and race cars was often blurred. But these 427s were road-legal cars that could be used every day.

Two versions of the 427 were on offer, one with a single four-barrel and 410 hp, and the full twin carburetor 425 hp setup, which cost an extra $461.60. Both were sold with the Galaxie and Galaxie 500XL.

This was all very well, and the big Galaxie continued to be Ford's weapon of choice in NASCAR racing, as well as the recipient of its big-block 427. But from 1964, the midsize Fairlane was preferred for the drag strip: being lighter, it had a built-in

FORD GALAXIE 500 1967

Engine: *315 hp 390 cubic-inch V8, 427 lb ft*

Transmission: *three-speed automatic*

Steering: *recirculating ball, power assisted*

Tires: *8.45 x 15 tubeless nylon, 4-ply rated*

Brakes: *front 11.87-inch discs, power assisted (optional); rear 11.03-inch drums, power assisted*

Suspension: *front independent, single lateral arm, coil springs; rear rigid axle, three control arms, coil springs*

Wheelbase: *119 inches*

Height: *54.7 inches*

Weight: *4,243 pounds*

DUNLOP

LEFT: No doubt about it, the Galaxie was one full-size automobile, but Ford sought to overcome that with ever-larger V8s to suit. The 1961 390 ci was soon followed by the 427, and Ford started out building a limited number of special lightweight Galaxie 427s for the drag strip. They packed an official 425 hp (unofficially thought to be higher) plus an aluminum four-speed manual transmission and stripped-out interior. That saved on impressive 500 lb. on the road-going Galaxie.

Above: The fastback Galaxie was originally designed with NASCAR in mind, where its superior aerodynamics would count at high speeds. But with the 427 V8 under the hood, it could be formidable on the drag strip as well, and the special lightweight cars assembled by Ford could be depended on for quarter-mile times in the low 12s.

"Quiet, strong, beautiful. A great road car."

advantage to start with, and Ford produced a few stripped-out lightweight cars (the famed Thunderbolts) specifically for competition. Road-going Fairlane customers could also order the car with the top 289 ci V8 from the hottest Mustang. The vital letter to look for was the "K" code, otherwise known as the Hi-Po 289. This came with a 10.5:1 compression ratio, a single four-barrel carburetor, and a claimed 271 hp at 6,000 rpm.

What Ford didn't do was make a real muscle car out of the midsize Fairlane, at least, not yet. It was another two years before the 390-powered Fairlane offered a credible alternative to the GTO. Pontiac, Chevrolet, and Chrysler were all busy squeezing big-block V8s into midsize cars in the mid-sixties, making classic muscle cars in the process. But Ford didn't follow suit immediately. Ford's problem was that these big block V8s were larger externally than the 260 and 289 units, so squeezing them under the hood of a Fairlane or Falcon would probably have involved a substantial redesign. That's what happened to the Mustang, where the need for big-

BELOW: Customer Galaxie 427s weren't so special or so lightweight (or so fast, come to that), but many found their way onto the drag strip. Even as those 427s were rolling off the production line, the Galaxie's days as a top-line drag racer were numbered. In production form, it would soon prove too big and heavy to be competitive.

block performance was so vital, Ford redesigned the whole car to make that possible.

The big-block Fairlane finally arrived in 1966. It wasn't much bigger externally, but Ford had enlarged the engine bay so that a 390 or 427 V8 would slip in as easy as you like. Both were on the options list, and Ford's advertising made it absolutely plain that this beefed-up Fairlane was aimed directly at the GTO: "How to cook a tiger!" In GT form, the Fairlane came with the 390 V8 315 hp. Opting for the more expensive GTA brought a higher-lift cam and bigger carburetor for 335 hp, just enough to be competitive with the GTO.

Other special GTA parts included a three-speed Sport Shift automatic transmission which could be used in either manual or auto mode. There were some dress-up parts too, all aimed at making that big-block look as impressive as possible

BELOW: Fairlane V8 rears off the line. It says much for the 1960s-sourced muscle cars that they can still be drag raced today with good results, albeit with the addition of some modern technology.

ABOVE: Ford soon realized that the drag racing Galaxie was in danger of being outclassed, so for 1964 concentrated its efforts on the smaller (intermediate-size) Fairlane. Just one hundred Fairlane "Thunderbolts" were built that year, with 427 ci V8s pumping out an official 425 hp (unofficially, make that around 500 hp), enough for Gas Ronda to dominate the NHRA '64 World Championship. His Thunderbolt made an E/T of 11.6 seconds at 124 mph.

when you raised the hood at gas stations to give the kids a thrill. Chrome-plated rocker covers, oil filler cap, radiator cap, air cleaner cover, and dipstick were all standard.

Thus powered, the Fairlane GTA had a better power-to-weight ratio than 427 Galaxie, accelerated from rest to 60 mph in 6.8 seconds, and completed the quarter mile in 15.2 seconds. The ultimate 427 was an option too, complete with a big hood scoop, but only sixty of these were ordered in 1966. By contrast, Ford sold over 37,000 Fairlane GTs and GTAs. For 1967, power was actually pegged back a little, and the 390 alternatives were a 270 hp two-barrel and 320 hp four-barrel, though in both cases heavy-duty suspension was standard.

It was back to business as usual the following year, when the new upsized Fairlane came with a 427

FORD FAIRLANE GTA 1967

Engine: *335 hp 390 cubic-inch V8, 427 lb ft*

Transmission: *three-speed automatic*

Steering: *recirculating ball*

Tires: *Goodyear Super Sports 500 7.75 x 14*

Brakes: *10-inch drums front and rear*

Suspension: *front independent, upper wishbone, lower link, antiroll bar, coil springs; rear rigid axle, semi-elliptic leaf springs*

Wheelbase: *116 inches*

Height: *55 inches*

Weight: *3,640 pounds*

option for the first time. At first, it came in relatively mild form, but its place was soon taken by the new 428 ci V8, the Cobra Jet.

BELOW: Probably the most famous muscle car in the world, if a mid-'70s Torino could be described as such. This is a replica of the Torino which starred in the TV cop show Starsky and Hutch.

This was really Ford's FE big block V8 with 427 cylinder heads, and the base "Q" version in the Fairlane (muscle car fans preferred the fastback, for choice) came with 10.7:1 compression, a single Holley four-barrel, and 335 hp at 5,600 rpm. More ambitious drivers could order the Super Cobra Jet "R" version, with a slightly lower compression but Ram Air injection, giving a claimed 360 hp at 5,400 rpm.

It later emerged that Ford was being excessively modest about the CJ's power (a cunning ploy to have it downgraded a class in drag racing), and that the true output

was more like 410 hp. With that figure in mind, the quoted times of 0–60 in just over 6 seconds and a quarter mile of 14.5 seconds became highly credible. Both options were still on offer the following year, though now also in a fairly basic form as the Torino Cobra, the idea being to sell a low-priced muscle car to compete with Plymouth's highly successful Road Runner.

The big-blocks were also available in the Torino GT, which was basically a sportier version of the Fairlane 500. In fact, you could also order either of the Cobra Jets with the basic, plain-Jane Fairlane 500 for as little as $2,674, ready to roll. This really was the era of cheap performance.

Most buyers wanted a slice of image though, and paid extra for the sporty-looking Torino instead of owning a "street sleeper" Fairlane. From 1969 onward, the Torino carried on as Ford's standard midsize (though growing in size, along with the other Ford intermediates) sporty car.

The base power unit was a 302 ci V8 of 220 hp. Next up was a 250 hp 351, then the 320 hp 390 V8 in four-barrel form. The milder 427 option was replaced, so the top engine remained the 428 Cobra Jet, with 335 hp at 5,200 rpm and 440 lb ft at 2,600 rpm. An extra $420 or so brought the Ram Air version of this engine, and that same year (1969) saw the slope-nosed, fastback

BELOW: A popular midsize Ford of the '70s (as owners of full-size Fords downsized), the Torino originated as a sporty version of the Fairlane 500, though with a base 200 ci six, it was hardly a muscle car. That was in 1968, but within a couple of years the Torino fastback (another NASCAR aspirant) could be had with the 428 Cobra Jt Ram Air V8. With 335 hp available, that bought a 0–60 mph of 6.3 seconds, allowing David Starsky's car to credibly tire-squeal its way through city alleyways a few years later.

F O R D
ABM
287B

LEFT: Halfway house between Falcon and Mustang? Well, not quite, but the Falcon Sprint did show the way things were going. It was an attempt by Ford to meet and beat the attractive Corvair Monza, by adding a fastback and some extras to the basic Falcon.

BELOW: The 164 hp 260 ci V8 still didn't turn the Falcon into a muscle car, but it did boost performance considerably. Car and Driver *magazine recorded a top speed of 107 mph, and 0–60 in 12.1 seconds.*

Torino Talladega. This was built purely to make the Torino competitive in NASCAR racing, with great attention paid to aerodynamics. Only 754 were built—a minimum of 500 was needed to qualify it as a production car (homologation). All 754 were powered by the Cobra Jet 428, though they were allowed to race with Ford's latest 429 V8, which had been homologated for racing separately as the engine in the Mustang Boss 429.

Meanwhile, the Galaxies continued to enjoy their status as heavyweight, full-size muscle cars. But the full-power 427, named as "Thunderbird Super-High Performance" from 1965, in 425 hp form endowed even the heavyweight Galaxie with quite startling performance. The lightweight track-bound cars were something else, but even with full road equipment—carpets, sound-deadening, everything—a '65 top-power Galaxie could sprint to 60 mph in just over 6 seconds and run the quarter mile in just over 15.

Sheer power was the secret, though not a very well-kept one—a 425 hp Galaxie was not a subtle car. In 1966, with the 427 available on the Galaxie 500 and sports trim 500XL, it still carried only 9.6 lb. per horsepower, a respectable figure for a big car that weighed over 3,500 lb. It was also reasonably affordable, at $3,233 for the 427-equipped 500XL two-door hardtop, and Ford was now claiming 0–60 mph in less than 6 seconds.

Left: "Sprint V8" sounds sporty, but the hopped-up Falcon was never more than a brisk performer, and Ford never felt the need to make a 289 ci (or 390 ci) V8 available as a dealer fixture, as Chevrolet did with the big-block Chevelle.

For 1966, the Galaxie received the new 428 V8, as well as a "7-Liter" badge. The new engine may have been only one cubic inch bigger than the old 427, but it was a very different engine. With a smaller bore and longer stroke, it was designed more for smoothness than high revs, though in the latest Galaxie it still produced 345 hp with a single four-barrel carburetor as the "Thunderbird Special," or 360 hp in "Police Interceptor" form. However, serious performance enthusiasts could still pay extra for the higher-tuned, harder-revving 427 (which would make its last appearance in the full-size Fords in 1968). The choice was 410 hp "Thunderbird High Performance" and 425 hp "Thunderbird Super-High Performance."

So the Galaxie was Ford's full-size muscle car through the sixties, while the Fairlane/Torino did the same job as its intermediate muscle. But Ford didn't do the same trick with the compact Falcon.

On the face of it, this was an odd decision, since the lightweight Falcon with a big-block 390 or 427 would have given even more exciting performance than the Fairlane. So while Chevrolet was making its big V8s available in the compact Chevy

BELOW: *The Falcon's real significance in the muscle car story was the number of components it lent to the Mustang. It's fair to say that on cost grounds there would simply have been no Mustang without the Falcon to supply those parts.*

II Nova and Chevelle, the Falcon received a mild 260 ci V8 option, with a single two-barrel carburetor and just 164 hp.

After a 1966 facelift, the 289 V8 did join the list, in 200 hp form, but it was still no muscle car in the tire-smoking tradition. Ironically, Falcon GTs actually did well in international rallies, with the 289 in 285 hp form, but that was never on sale in a Ford showroom.

Maybe, with the Fairlane GT/GTA, Ford never felt the need to come up with a direct rival for the Pontiac GTO or Chevelle SS. And, of course, the company already had a compact muscle car—the Mustang.

MUSTANG: THE ORIGINAL PONY

BELOW: Mustang! Ford invented a new class of car with the Mustang, and with deceptively simple ingredients, a mixture of Falcon and Fairlane parts, plus that classic long hood/short deck body shape, the pony car was born.

The Mustang was a phenomenon. It single-handedly created a new class of automobile—the pony car. Its youthful image appealed to young and old alike. It made new sales records, caught all of Ford's rivals on the hop, and turned into a respected muscle car. Yet it nearly never happened at all.

Lee Iacocca is generally acknowledged to be the father of the Mustang, though many talented people were involved in its conception. At age thirty-seven he was Ford's fastest-rising star, already a vice president and general manager of the Ford division. He and a group of other Young Turks would meet regularly to discuss future models—the meetings had started out as social gatherings, but soon became serious brainstorming sessions. Don Frey, Chief Engineer at Ford, was a regular, as was

BELOW RIGHT: ***Take out the sporty three-spoke steering wheel, the bucket seats, and floor-mounted shifter, and the Mustang had a bland interior plucked straight out of the Falcon. But those three items were the magic ingredients, guaranteed to give the Mustang showroom appeal.***

production man Hal Sperlich. Frank Zimmerman from marketing, Walter Murphy from public relations, and a copywriter named Sid Olsen made up the party. They called themselves the Fairlane Committee and would meet at the Fairlane Inn, about a mile down the road from Ford headquarters. Here, relaxed and informal, they could talk and swap ideas more freely than in some committee room back at headquarters. "We were young and cocky," Iacocca later recalled. "We saw ourselves as artists, about to produce the finest masterpieces the world has ever known."

In the very early sixties, one thing occupied the Fairlane Committee more than anything else—the Chevrolet Corvair Monza. The Corvair sedan, a radical piece of rear-engined lateral thinking, had not been a huge success, but the Monza was. This pretty coupe version of the four-door Corvair, with the addition of bucket seats, a floor-mounted stick shift, and sporty trim, was selling like hotcakes. And Ford had nothing to answer it with. Fastback versions of Ford's compact Falcon and full-size Galaxie were on the

FORD MUSTANG PRE-SEPT 1964

Engine: *101-horsepower 170 cubic-inch in-line six; initial top option 210-horsepower 289 cubic-inch Windsor small-block V8*

Transmission: *four-speed manual (convertible automatic)*

Steering: *recirculating ball*

Wheels & tires: *5.5 x 13 inch wheels, 6.50 x 13 inch tires*

Brakes: *four-wheel hydraulic drums*

Suspension: *front short/long-arms and coil springs; rear longitudinal leaf springs and a solid axle*

Wheelbase: *108 inches*

Height: *51.1 inches*

Weight: *High Performance (Hi-Po) 289 V8 3,050 pounds, convertible 2,700 pounds*

RIGHT: Had it not been for Lee Iacocca's brainwave, the Mustang would have been a two-seater selling in small numbers, but the extra pair of seats transformed it from sports car into sporty family car with much wider appeal. Hardtops like this outsold the convertible by a big margin.

ABOVE: ***A simple rear-end treatment for the Mustang, which relied on its basic style to tempt buyers into the showroom. That relatively large trunk was another reason for its strong appeal, equally able to carry a week's groceries or a set of golf clubs. Looking good had never been so practical.***

way, but these looked what they were, mildly modified sedans. Iacocca was convinced that somewhere out there was a market looking for something more radical.

Simple demographics would prove him right, and any market researcher could have pointed to the same trends. During the early sixties, the postwar baby boomers would get into their twenties. Many were college educated, in good jobs, and on a high and rising income. They were ready to buy their first new car, but in tune with the times, they didn't want the same car as their parents. It's become a truism that the sixties was a time of rebellion and social upheaval. Sometimes that just involved buying a Mustang instead of a Fairlane, but then market capitalism has a way of harnessing rebellion to its own ends. As well as this new generation of younger car buyers, some of the older ones were in the market for excitement too. The shine had come off those sensible compacts—the Falcon, Corsair, and Valiant—and now two-car families were starting to look for something interesting to park in their driveway alongside the full-size sedan. "Here," said Lee Iacocca later with hindsight, "was a market in search of a car."

The Fairlane Committee's first thoughts were for a two-seat sports car to compete with the imports. Ever since the Thunderbird had turned into a four-seater in

1958, enthusiasts had been pleading for the return of a two-seat Ford. Drawings were made and a clay mock-up shown to those same enthusiasts—they loved it. But Ford's finance people were horrified, predicting that a two-seat sports car would only sell around 35,000 units a year—cars were always "units" to the finance guys, whom Iacocca contemptuously referred to as "bean counters." So the two-seater was vetoed, and this became a turning point in the whole project. Iacocca ordered the engineers to stretch the sports car into a four-seater, maybe a cramped four-seater, but a four-seater nonetheless. It wouldn't be a sports car, but what he called "small-sporty."

ABOVE: Ford's early advertising centered on straitlaced individuals transformed into fun-loving adventurers the moment they got behind the wheel of their new Mustang. It was the original Walter Mitty car.

RIGHT: *Mustangs always offered a wide choice of engines, and the first cars were no exception. Budget buyers could have a new Mustang in the driveway for less than $2,500, so long as they were happy with the mild, Falcon-derived 170 ci six. The 289 ci V8 was a little more interesting to enthusiasts, preferably in Hi-Po 271 hp form.*

The concept of the pony car had been born. To cut costs and save development time, the small-sporty (soon to be code named "Cougar") would use engines, transmissions, and other parts from existing Ford sedans. It would blend good looks with practicality, have a sporty image, be easy to drive, and have a decent-sized trunk. One visionary described it as, "a car you could drive to the country club on a Friday night, to the drag strip on Saturday and to church on Sunday." Well, OK, said the bean counters, maybe a car like that could sell 100,000 a year. Iacocca disagreed—he reckoned on twice that. In any event, both figures were grossly pessimistic.

Henry Ford II, the ultimate boss, was still skeptical—he and Lee had a difficult relationship at the best of times. But reluctantly he gave his approval, and the Cougar project got the green light. The engineers still had quite a job on their hand, twenty-one months before the projected launch in April 1964, but things moved fast. Three months after that green light, the classic long hood, short deck styling was approved, and the serious engineering work began: within months, "Cougar" prototypes were on the road.

BELOW: So the Mustang looked good, could accommodate the family, and had a wide choice of engines, but other things accounted for its huge sales success. It was light and easy to drive, not at all intimidating, and Ford offered a long list of tempting options to "personalize" the Mustang just how you wanted it.

Except that it wouldn't be called Cougar at all. Countless names were bandied around. Henry Ford favored "T Bird II" to recall Ford's late lamented two-seater, but that was soon rejected. "Torino" was another favorite, but Henry vetoed it. Why? Well, at the time, he was stepping out with an Italian divorcée, and giving the new car an Italianate name could lead to unfortunate rumors. Finally, everyone agreed on "Mustang," which had all the right connotations: "The excitement of wide open spaces," someone said, "and as American as hell."

If anyone at Ford headquarters was worried about the Mustang's public launch, they needn't have been. "Easily the best thing to come out of Dearborn since the 1932 V8 Model B roadster," enthused *Car and Driver* magazine. They predicted that Ford would sell a quarter of a million in the first full year, though this (like those earlier in-house estimates) proved a long way short of reality.

The American public was knocked out by the new Mustang. Their appetite whetted by prime-time TV advertising, not to mention advertisements in 2,600 different newspapers, they swamped Ford showrooms. Ford had been careful to ensure that every single dealer had a Mustang on display on launch day, and over that first weekend, four million people tramped through their local showroom for a closer look. Twenty-two thousand firm orders were placed on the first day alone,

BELOW: ***Shelby Mustang GT500KR, the first factory-built Mustang with a big-block 427 ci V8. Ford soon followed with its own production-line 427 Mustang.***

and after a couple of weeks, it became clear that all sales estimates would be short of the true total.

The waiting list for new Mustangs began to grow, and at one point customers were being asked to wait three months before taking delivery. Ford turned over a second factory to Mustang production, then a third—demand for the Falcon had caught them out before, and they were determined this wouldn't happen again.

BELOW RIGHT: *Though this one isn't much to look at, the big-block 427 endowed the Shelby GT500 with effortless performance—very different from the original GT350.*

The Mustang development team had been given two figures to aim for: a curb weight of 2,500 lb. and a base price of $2,500. They were a little over on the weight (an optioned Mustang with the 289 cast-iron V8 made over 2,800 lb.) but the basic price was a mere $2,368, which looked like a bargain for something so exotic and sporty looking.

Of course, the basic Mustang came with a 170 ci six-cylinder engine, skinny tires, drum brakes, and didn't even have a heater or radio. If every customer had bought one of those, Ford would probably have barely made a profit on the whole project. But they didn't, because Ford's cunning strategy was to price the bare car at the lowest possible price, then offer a whole range of attractive options that few could resist . . . and which carried a higher profit margin. So there were four different engines to choose from, no less than seven transmissions, four braking setups, and so on, not to mention a whole host of interior and exterior bits and pieces. The variations of all these different parts were innumerable, giving the impression (albeit a false one) that every new Mustang had been personalized by its owner and was therefore unique. But every single new Mustang did have that sports-car-like body, plus bucket front seats, a floor-mounted stick shift, and sporty three-spoke steering wheel. The last three did add a few dollars to the cost of each car but gave the Mustang immense showroom appeal and underlined its sporty, special image. But was the first Mustang a true muscle car?

The answer is no, no, maybe, and yes, depending on which engine was specified. First off was the 170 ci six, straight out of the Falcon, mustering a decidedly puny 101 hp. It was, according to one unkind journalist, "about as exciting as a dish of babyfood." That would be a no, then. Next up was the 260 ci V8 from the Fairlane (most of the Mustang's components came from either Falcon or Fairlane, depending on the engine used), and this too was in a mild state of tune, with a single two-barrel carburetor, an 8.8:1 compression ratio and 164 hp. The "maybe muscle" territory began with Ford's 289 ci V8 (an enlarged version of the 260) in warm rather than hot guise, namely a single four-barrel carburetor and 9.0:1 compression. *Car and Driver* tried one of these at Ford's Dearborn proving grounds at the original press launch, and recorded a 0–60 mph time of 8.2 seconds, with a 110-mph top speed.

Two months after that launch, the ultimate Mustang was finally available. Still 289 ci, but in HiPo (High Performance) guise. On paper that meant 35 percent more power than the 260 V8, thanks to all the classic tuning tricks for a North American V8. High compression 10.5:1 pistons, a big four-barrel carburetor, and low-restriction air cleaner. A high-lift camshaft worked with mechanical lifters while the valve stems were chrome plated and the exhaust had individual headers. The whole engine was

RIGHT: Of course, another reason for buying a Shelby Mustang was the personal touch. Three factories churned out stock Mustangs by the hundreds of thousands, but Carroll Shelby's little place in California built just over 3,000 cars in 1967. It was always the most exclusive Mustang.

LEFT: Shelbys were only ever based on fastback or convertible Mustangs, never the basic hardtop. A fastback had joined the stock Mustang lineup in 1965, slightly less practical than the hardtop (with no trunk lid and less room for rear passengers), but it looked sleeker.

COLORADO
365 AYV
COLLECTOR VEHICLE

LEFT: Popular though the Mustang fastback was, it was only a minority seller compared to the mainstream hardtop. More relevant to most buyers was the '67 facelift, which made the Mustang big enough to accept Ford's big-block V8s, the 390 and (when that proved insufficiently muscular) the 428 Cobra Jet.

ABOVE: This Mustang fastback has the popular GT option package, which brought features like front disc brakes, stiffer suspension, dual exhaust, five-dial instrument pack, and front fog lights.

RIGHT: The GT package could be had with any of the hotter V8s, though this is the Cobra Jet 428, the most powerful motor available on a 1968 Mustang. Ford's pony car was being left behind by other muscle cars—the 428 caught it up.

strengthened with high-tensile connecting rods, cross-bolts for the crankcase, and a vibration damper on the crank itself. The result, said Ford, was 271 hp at 6,000 rpm and 312 lb ft at 3,400 rpm, enough to keep up with a Pontiac GTO, which had also been launched that year. That claim sounded a little optimistic, given the GTO's extra cubic inches and horsepower, but according to *Car and Driver*'s first test of a 271 HiPo Mustang, it was true. They published figures of 5.2 seconds to 60 mph, and a 14-second standing quarter—the GTO equivalents were 7.7 seconds, and 15.8. Mind you, that was with a drag race low 4.1:1 rear axle, which made the Mustang a fussy and noisy beast on the highway. The standard ratio was 3.89, which would probably have equaled the Pontiac on acceleration.

No matter, for the arguments would rage on through the sixties as to which made the better muscle car: a pony car, a sedan-based muscle car, or a Corvette (which couldn't be classed as either). At the time, it was the 289 HiPo Mustang that grabbed most of the limelight, especially from the motoring press, but it made up only a tiny fraction of Mustang sales. Just 1.3% of Mustang buyers opted to pay extra for the

ABOVE: That fake air intake, a Mustang styling feature from day one, was joined by a louvered exit on the fastback, which helped to provide through ventilation. Fastbacks also benefited from a split rear seat to help with the luggage stowage.

LEFT: The original Shelby Mustang GT350 was a serious performance car, virtually ready to race. An aluminum-cased four-speed transmission and a thoroughly stripped-out interior (the rear seat was ditched) cut weight substantially. The front suspension was tweaked and the rear setup redesigned. The body shell was stiffened and strengthened, and big front disc brakes hauled the GT350 to a halt.

ABOVE: White with blue racing stripes reflected the character of the car, for the GT350 was a wild beast that was more at home on the racetrack than the road. Compared to a standard Mustang, it was an expensive machine but repaid that with race car behavior: driving it on the road was for the indefatigably enthusiastic only.

BFGoodrich
BFGoodrich

LEFT: *Move on a few years, and the Shelby Mustang has transformed. Ford product planners and accountants took a trip to California and soon pinpointed ways in which the car could be made cheaper and easier to live with. So it lost the limited-slip differential and custom-designed rear suspension. You could have a choice of colors apart from white with blue stripes, and the rear seat made a comeback.*

ABOVE: After a makeover by Ford's head office, the Shelby Mustang lost its racing edge. It was softer and more user-friendly, not to mention cheaper to buy and with greater appeal.

hottest V8, though maybe cost was part of the problem. Ford wouldn't sell the HiPo option without fitting the handling package (stiffer springs and shocks, a thicker front antiroll bar, and quicker steering) as well, plus wider 6.95 x 14 tires, pushing the total option price to $442. For that sort of money, buyers could have the milder 289 V8 (uprated to 225 hp for '65) plus front disc brakes, the handling package, or air conditioning.

In any case, most Mustang buyers weren't interested in (or couldn't afford) high performance. Only 4 percent of them checked the dual exhaust option, and 2 percent went for the limited-slip differential. Comfort/convenience items like air conditioning, windshield washers, and whitewall tires were far more popular. And once the basic six-cylinder engine had been boosted to 200 ci/120 hp, more than a third of buyers

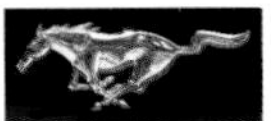

chose that instead of the V8s. An interesting reflection on what the majority of Mustang customers wanted from their "small-sporty"—they certainly didn't want a sports car.

Many were tempted by a sporty image though, and the new GT package for '65 did prove popular. This brought together the handling package (essential for serious drivers, said the magazines) plus other essentials like front disc brakes, that dual exhaust, a five-dial instrument pack (the standard Mustang made do with the Falcon's dour strip speedometer), front fog lights, and assorted stripes and badges.

But down in California, an ex–chicken farmer, racing driver, and Le Mans winner was about to turn the Mustang into a far more committed performance car. Carroll Shelby was a good friend of the Ford Motor Company. He'd done a lot for the corporate image by choosing the 260 V8 for his Cobra, which combined the English AC company's lightweight sports car body/chassis with American muscle.

The Cobra was a hairy machine, but won lots of races and made Shelby famous. So not illogically it was to the Texan that Lee Iacocca turned when he wanted to take the Mustang racing. Shelby agreed to build one hundred specially tuned Mustangs (which the minimum required to qualify for production racing), and the Shelby GT350 was born.

BELOW: There's no doubt that Shelby sold more of the new soft-generation Mustangs than it ever did of the original hard-edged GT350. This is a later shape (post '67) GT500, with the big-block 427 ci V8 and torquey performance. Options now included automatic transmission—and a radio!

Later Shelby Mustangs were increasingly cosmetic and civilized, but the 1965 original was a true racer for the road. To save weight, the rear seat was ditched and the steel hood replaced with a fiberglass item, while the standard exhaust went in favor of a side-mounted muffler. In fact, the Shelby conversion touched almost every part of the car.

Below: Softened it might be, but the Shelby name and cobra logo still carried a lot of (metaphorical) weight, so Shelby Mustangs carried on selling in small but steady numbers right up until 1970, when Carroll Shelby called a halt to production.

The suspension was thoroughly reworked, with a thicker front antiroll bar, longer idler and Pitman arms, lowered upper control arms, traction bars, and Koni adjustable shocks. The body was strengthened with a steel bar braced between the two front shock towers, and 11-inch front discs replaced the standard drums. More weight was saved with an aluminum-cased Borg Warner four-speed transmission; the intake manifold, sump, and valve covers were all of aluminum too. And of course, there was more power,

with 751 cfm Holley carburetor and Tri-Y exhaust headers and low restriction mufflers adding up to a claimed 306 hp at 6,000 rpm

The car was finished off in white with optional blue racing stripes and those instantly recognizable GT350 stripes along the sills. At nearly $4,500 ($1,000 more than a 289 Hi-Po Mustang), the Shelby GT350 was for enthusiasts only. They would need to be committed to drive it, as the car was a wild, noisy beast that leaked water and exhaust fumes into the cockpit through the holes in the floor cut for the new torque arms. Meanwhile, the Detroit Lock differential was great for racing starts, but

***BELOW:* By then, most of the work to create a Shelby Mustang was done on Ford production lines, with the Californians making the finishing touches. It was a cheaper, but less pure way to do the work.**

Right: *Was the Shelby Cobra a muscle car? Not in the classic sense, but it joins that small group of two-seat muscle cars that includes the Corvette. More to the point for the modern muscle car story, it directly inspired the Dodge Viper, which has been the flagship of big-cube power right into the twenty-first century.*

LEFT: The Cobra was a marriage of two distinct traditions—American V8 horsepower and a lightweight English sports car—and the result was explosive. It was none other than Carroll Shelby who approached AC and suggested they ship Ace sports cars over the Atlantic for him to fit a 260 ci Ford V8 in place of the standard 122 ci six. They agreed, and the Cobra was born. In six years (from 1962 to 1968) it became one of the legends of motoring.

ABOVE: Inside, the Cobra was as sparse and businesslike as British sports cars were in those days. Not that owners seemed to care—all that power and torque in the featherweight AC chassis gave startling performance, though it could be a real handful on bumpy corners. Coil-spring suspension and rack-and-pinion steering were fitted later, which made the Cobra a little more composed. Either way, it dominated SCCA racing for a while.

> **"The rear seat leg and head room are best described as marginal. In fact, leg room is almost zero."**
>
> (Car and Driver, *January 1969*)

noisy and clunky in traffic. About 500 GT350s were sold that first year, but Ford was convinced that Shelby could have sold more if the car were toned down.

So a team of cost experts traveled to the Shelby factory, and proceeded to slash over $100 from the car's price by deleting some of the more specialized race-bred parts like that limited-slip differential and the expensive English wood-rimmed steering wheel. They softened the suspension, and put back some soundproofing and the rear seat. A radio and automatic transmission joined the options list! GT350 buyers even had a choice of colors now—white with blue racing stripes wasn't compulsory. The new, sanitized Shelby might not be as race credible as the original, but it was acceptable to a lot more people, and well over 2,000 were sold in 1966. Mind you, that was still chicken feed compared to Mustang sales in general—over 600,000 were sold that year, its best year

BELOW: Always known in the U.S. as the Shelby Cobra, it was the AC Cobra in England, and even the Ford Cobra on occasion. Whatever the name, it remained one of the hairiest sports cars of all time.

ever, and Ford declared that they had built the three fastest-selling cars of all time: Model A, Falcon, and Mustang. One footnote to the early Shelby story is that Ford persuaded Hertz to put one hundred of the original 350s on its rental fleet. It sounded like a recipe for disaster, allowing any young driver with a driving license and the fee of seventeen dollars a day, access to one of the fastest, hardest-to-drive cars on the road. Inevitably, many of those Hertz rental 350s were worn out in drag races, but the

BELOW: Later Cobras were fitted with the 427 ci V8 of 345 hp, giving a racer power-to-weight ratio in a road-legal car.

RIGHT: Perhaps only Carroll Shelby would have contemplated squeezing a Ford V8 into that tiny engine bay, designed for a straight six of less than half the capacity, but it worked.

BELOW: AC strengthened the Ace chassis to suit the V8's torque, and fitted a beefier Salisbury rear axle. That apart, it was much the same as the original Ace, in production since 1953.

BELOW: *Classic sports car interior for the Cobra, which made no concession to creature comforts. It wasn't the only English sports car to make use of American muscle—the Sunbeam Tiger, TVR Griffith, and MGB GT V8 all made use of Detroit-designed cubic inches.*

experiment garnered a huge amount of publicity for both Ford and Hertz, who even ordered another 1,000 Shelbys for its nationwide fleet, though these were toned down compared to the first batch.

For its first eighteen months, the Mustang had the pony car market to itself, but in 1967 it began to face some tough opposition from the Chevrolet Camaro, its Pontiac Firebird cousin, and a new Plymouth Barracuda. The GM pony cars offered more space, power, and performance, and if the Mustang wanted to keep up with the muscle car wars, it would have to change. The trouble was, its small engine bay wouldn't accept Ford's big-block V8, and the only alternative was to redesign the car.

So the '67 Mustang was three inches longer and two inches wider than the old

one, with an engine bay big enough to accept Ford's 390 ci V8. With an easy 320 hp in single four-barrel form, this would surely be enough to see off the critics. Lee Iacocca for one, was not pleased, As he saw it, his "small-sporty" had been adulterated and he later described it as "a fat pig." Indeed, the new Mustang did look plumper than the old one, and weighed significantly more. Still, *Car and Driver* seemed to like it when they tested a 390 fastback.

Despite an extra 400 lb. over the front wheels (thanks to the heavier big-block motor) the latest Mustang handled well, and they also reckoned it was faster than any other pony car, running to 60 mph in 7.3 seconds, and turning in a 14.5-second quarter-mile.

But what a difference a year makes. In early '68, the magazine put a Mustang GT390 up against five main muscle car rivals, and it scored bottom (or close to it) over a whole range of features. With bad understeer and a recalcitrant engine, the 390 was placed last on points, and by some way.

Then Carroll Shelby announced the GT500, the biggest-engined Mustang yet, with Ford's 428 ci V8 offering 355 hp and 420 lb ft; 6.5 seconds to 60 mph, and 15.0 over the quarter mile. A lot had changed since the original GT350 . . .

BELOW AND RIGHT: Last of the Shelbys. By 1969, the Shelby Mustangs were body-kit cars only, mechanically identical to those flowing off the production lines. The differences were limited to a profusion of fiberglass panels and scoops, special wheels, and stripes. So when Carroll Shelby called a halt to production that year, few tears were shed.

SHELBY
BFGoodrich

RIGHT: It might not be any faster than a mass-production Mustang, but the Shelby did stand out. With two million Mustangs on the road by the end of the '60s, that was no bad thing. Shelby himself could see that encroaching safety and emissions legislation would restrict his low-volume cars still further in the near future, hence his decision to stop building Mustangs.

GT 350
BFGoodrich
Radial T/A

Muscle Fatigue

BELOW: Does this Mustang look bigger and fatter than the original? That's because it is—for 1967, the pony car was made wider, longer, and heavier, to accommodate bigger V8s and keep up with the increasingly muscular opposition.

But had Ford fallen behind again? It looked that way. The muscle boom was reaching its height in 1968, when Chevrolet and Chrysler were offering cars with 350 to over 400 hp that anyone could walk into their nearest showroom and buy. Never had such high performance been available to so many people, at such low cost. In this climate, the Mustang 390's 320 hp—even the Shelby GT500's 335—just wasn't enough to be credible. That didn't mean that 400 hp cars were actually being bought in large numbers. But they were being tested by magazines, and their glamor would influence many enthusiasts to buy a cheaper version of the same model. Not everyone could afford to buy and insure a genuine Hemi Dodge Charger, but they might be persuaded to go for the much cheaper 383, and bask in some of that reflected glory. And that was the Mustang's problem in early 1968—everyone knew it was falling behind in the

power race. Veteran dealer Tasca Ford realized this and began offering their own 428 Mustang conversion, which was easy to do as the 428 block was the same external size as the 390 it replaced. Ford soon cottoned on, and announced their own 428 Cobra Jet Mustang. A preproduction 428 was said to have covered the standing-quarter in 13.56 seconds. Ford was back in the performance business.

One might have expected all this to make Carroll Shelby go out of business, as it took away the GT500's status as the biggest-engined Mustang. In any case, the GT500s were now built by Ford, with only some minor finishing work (spotlights, roll cage, and rocker covers) being done at Shelby's California plant. But the spirit of the original GT350 wasn't dead, especially if you ordered a tuned version of the GT350, now upgraded with Ford's 302 ci V8. For just under $700 extra, buyers received a 350 with big valves, a gulpingly large four-barrel carburetor, and a claimed 315 hp. If that wasn't fast enough, Shelby even offered a Paxton supercharger on top, with 335 hp. He also put together a prototype supercharged GT500, which road testers found would squeal its rear tires at 80 mph. It never reached production.

The Mustang was by now leaving its "small-sporty" roots far behind, and grew even more for 1969, four inches longer than Iacocca's 1967 "fat pig." The range grew too, with a choice of no less than nine different V8s, plus two straight sixes. As well as the 302 ci V8 in two- and four-barrel form (220 and 290 hp respectively), there was

BELOW: It was upsized again for '69, and yet again for '71, each additional inch and pound taking the Mustang further from its relatively lightweight roots. All of these cars kept a strong family resemblance though: they could never be mistaken for anything else.

RIGHT: The Boss. New for '69, the two Boss Mustangs were aimed primarily at competition success. The Boss 302 was intended as a Trans Am racer, with its revvy 302 V8 and emphasis on quick handling. But the Boss 429 (seen here) was a natural for the drag strip, with 375 hp and a mountain of torque—actually, that was a byproduct, as the bigger Boss's true purpose was to homologate Ford's special semi-hemi 429 ci V8 for NASCAR.

the 351 ci Windsor engine in 250 or 290 hp form. The 390 was still on offer, albeit for the last time, while the 428 ci Cobra Jet now came in two states of tune: 335 hp or 360 hp. Finally, the most powerful Mustang yet was the Boss 429, with 375 hp.

Two of these new choices came courtesy of the two Boss Mustangs, which were built with quite different aims in mind. The Boss 302 was intended to rival the all-conquering Camaro Z28 as a high-revving small V8 that would be suitable for Trans Am racing. The 302's power unit was highly tuned, with a high-lift camshaft and 780 cfm four-barrel Holley. It was also balanced both statically and dynamically, which allowed it to rev higher than any other Ford V8. Road testers thought it wasn't quite as quick as a Z28 in a straight line, but handled better. As for the Boss 429, its sole purpose was to homologate Ford's 429 hemi-head V8 for NASCAR racing, so it was a limited edition with special parts like aluminum heads with O-ring gaskets. One magazine thought 400 hp was closer to the mark than the quoted 375, and recorded a 14.09-second quarter mile. The Boss twins—302 and 429—certainly grabbed headlines, but most Mustang buyers were steered towards the Mach 1, with the new SportsRoof body and lots of matte black detailing: engine choices covered the two-barrel and four-barrel Windsor, the 390, and 428 Cobra Jet.

But just as Ford finally caught up, providing a huge range of Mustangs, some of which were true muscle cars, the muscle car market was on its way down. In fact, the Mustang seemed to suffer more than most. It had most to lose, having sold in huge numbers in the early days, and led the pony car market from the start. By 1970, its sales had halved in three years. To put that in perspective, Ford still sold 190,000 Mustangs that year, and it was still the best-selling pony car by some way, but the fall from that 1966 sales peak had been steady and unrelenting.

It wasn't just that the original pony car now faced a whole field of tough opposition—American Motors had now got in on the act, as well as Chrysler and GM—but the whole muscle car thing was losing its rumble. As power outputs grew, so did the accident rates, and insurance premiums followed swiftly. The most potent muscle cars were becoming very expensive to insure (almost prohibitively so for young drivers), so buyers

began to shy away. Among the engine options for the road-sporty Mach 1 Mustang, the most popular was the mildest two-barrel 351. Emissions and safety legislation was tightening too. That was partly why Carroll Shelby decided to cease production of the GTs—it looked like the Mustang's wild days were coming to an end.

Not that you would have known it in 1971, when another biannual renewal saw the Mustang grow in size yet again. It was now seven inches wider than the 1964

original, and eight inches longer. The smallest 200 ci six-cylinder engine was dropped, but you could still have a gas-guzzling 351 or 429 V8.

In defense of Ford's strategy, the range was trimmed somewhat, with the two Boss Mustangs being replaced by one Boss 351 and the 390 option dropped altogether. There was still a 429 (not the semi-hemi bound for NASCAR, but a shrunken version of Ford's cooking sedan 460 unit), but it was barely faster than the 351 and far more expensive. Less than 1 percent of Mustang buyers paid extra for this big-cube option, and it was withdrawn before the end of the year. But the 351 gave quite a good account of itself in the Boss, in four-barrel form giving 330 hp and 370 lb ft. It rocketed through the standing quarter in 13.8 seconds with a terminal speed of 104 mph, faster than the Boss 302 "screamer" of the previous year, and as mentioned, nearly as quick as the current 429.

BELOW: Inside, the Boss 429 looked civilized and well-equipped, but that belied its real reason for being, to make the 429 motor race legal. Fitting the big V8, even to the upsized '69 Mustang, involved extensive modification, and the engine compartment had to be widened by two inches to make room. The work was done by Kar Kraft.

When the 1972 Mustangs were announced, the hot 351 had disappeared. Of the engines that remained, all were detuned, with lower compression ratios to suit regular fuel. At first glance, the resulting power cuts looked larger than they were, because Ford began measuring horsepower by the more strict SAE system. Still, the combined effect was to make the 1972 Mustangs look like the puniest ever. The base 250 ci six now claimed 98 hp, and the cheapest V8, the 302, managed 140 hp at 4,000 rpm. The 351 was still available, but only in detuned 168 hp (two-barrel) and 200 hp (four-barrel) guise while the big-cube 429 was dropped altogether. There were few other changes to the Mustangs that year, apart from safety features like the front seat belt

ABOVE: The original Boss 429 was only available for a year, but by then its job was done. You could still order a 429 Mustang for 1970, but this V8 was a very different beast, a regular production engine downsized from Ford's 460 ci V8, and not the NASCAR-bound semi-hemi. Either way, very few buyers ordered one, and it lasted less than a year.

reminder system—if either front occupant failed to belt up, a buzzer buzzed and a warning light flashed. On a more cheerful note, the Sprint Décor package was a patriotic red, white, and blue color scheme for both inside and out. Not mincing, but not muscle.

Hot car freaks could have been forgiven for sinking into gloom—the muscle car's brief golden age looked like it was gone for good. Then halfway through the 1972 model year, Ford reintroduced a hotter 351. It didn't carry Boss badges any more, but the latest 351HO option was only slightly less powerful, with 275 hp at 6,000 rpm, measured on the stricter SAE rating. Under the skin, there were lots of changes to clean up the 351's emissions. Milder cam timing, a different ignition timing, and a modified carburetor all aimed at a less dirty exhaust, while the compression ratio was dropped from 11.2:1 to 8.8:1.

But look beyond the backpedaling, and this was still a big, strong engine, with forged pistons, big valves, and alloy con-rod bolts. It might take a second longer to cover the standing quarter than the previous year's Boss 351, but at 15.1 seconds, it wasn't exactly slow. It still would reach 60 mph in 6.6 seconds, and three figures in 16.4, so the death of the muscle car, like that of Mark Twain, had been greatly exaggerated.

Well, maybe not that greatly. For 1973, the final year for the traditional long hood/short trunk Mustang, the 351HO was dropped, its place taken by a hybrid V8 that toned down the tuning still further, to 266 hp, plus 301 lb ft. Not a disastrous fall, but the Mustang now weighed more than ever before, thanks in part to elaborate new impact-absorbing bumpers. The 1973 Mustang weighed up to 900 lb. more than the 1964 original, and measured a whopping 194 inches from stem to stern. Any pretense it clung to of being true to its "small-sporty" roots, was gone. The last big Mustang was awkward to park and maneuver, worlds away from the original concept.

Road Test magazine tried a top of the range Mach 1, with the four-barrel 266 hp 351, and dryly described it as having "adequate power for most of today's motoring needs." Not exactly the breathless hyperbole we'd become used to from muscle car road testers, and there could be no clearer message that the 1973 Mustang hadn't just lost its small-sporty roots, but it wasn't a muscle car any more either. One thing hadn't

***Above:* Seven inches wider than the original '64 Mustang, and eight inches longer, the '71 car sat 900 lb. heavier on the scales as well. To paraphrase Ford's later advertising slogan, it was the wrong car at the wrong time.**

changed. The Mustang could still be ordered as a convertible, which in 1973 was a rare thing indeed. Safety concerns had eaten away at open-top sales for years, and now there was a rumor that they might be outlawed altogether. So no one was surprised when Ford announced that 1973 was the last year for the fresh-air Mustang. Still, ten years later, it was back—the death of the convertible had also been exaggerated.

Mustang II: Breaking in the Pony

Ford described it as, "the right car at the right time," and the Mustang II was certainly in tune with post–oil crisis America. Seventeen inches shorter than the 1973 Mustang, four inches narrower, and 360 lb. lighter, Lee Iacocca's seriously downsized Mustang for 1974 went back to basics. Sporty looking, convenient, and economical, it must have seemed like 1964 all over again.

But the new Mustang was no muscle car. The base engine had, get this, just four cylinders: 2.3 liters giving a whole 88 hp and 116 lb ft. If that wasn't enough, the "power" option was a 2.8 liter V6 of 105 hp. If you insisted, you could still buy a Mach 1 Mustang, complete with wide tires, rallye stripes, and optional competition suspension and limited-slip differential . . . but no more horsepower. One road test recorded a 0–60 time of 14.2 seconds, and the big surprise was that many testers actually preferred the 2.3 four—the V6, especially in sporty Mach 1 guise, seemed to promise more than it could deliver. To add insult to injury, the new V6 Mach 1 cost over $500 more than the 1973 V8! Muscle car it wasn't, nor was it cheap, but the Mustang II really was the right car at the right time, and Ford sold almost 386,000 of them in the first eighteen months. If the excitement of the magazine writers was

RIGHT: Retreat! The days of unrestricted muscle cars were fast disappearing, as new emissions and safety legislation (not to mention rising insurance premiums) forced Ford to detune every engine option; 275 bhp Boss 351 was now the hottest.

anything to go by, then the V8 option, which arrived the following year, would do even more for sales. It didn't, but then the Mustang II V8 still wasn't a muscle car. It was sprightly enough, with a 0–60 time of 10.5 seconds, but was detuned right down to 122 hp, and came with a compulsory automatic transmission.

Buyers waiting for the return of the muscle car may have had their hearts set racing in 1976, when advertisements started to appear for a "Cobra II" Mustang. Now this really looked the part of a latter-day hot rod. In white with blue stripes, it sought to evoke memories of the original Shelby GT350. As if to underline the heritage, Carroll Shelby himself appeared in the ads, giving Cobra II his official seal of approval. There were big spoilers front and rear, a nonfunctional hood scoop, racing mirrors, and loud graphics. Could the Shelby spirit really have come back?

No, it couldn't. Underneath all the spoilers and stripes, the Cobra II was a fake. It didn't even have the mild-mannered V8 as standard—unless you paid extra, the Cobra II came with, you've guessed it, the 2.3 liter four. Thus powered, it was the

classic sheep in wolf's clothing. Naturally, it was reviled by those who considered themselves true enthusiasts. The general public, on the other hand, loved the Cobra II. They didn't care that it was a fake, and Ford sold 35,000 of the things in 1976. The buyers weren't ready to buy a muscle car again, but they did want a slice of the image.

BELOW: Out of tune with the times it might be, but the early '70s Mustang could still be had as a convertible, though its days were numbered. Ford sold a mere 6,401 of them in 1972. When it announced that '73 would be the final year, sales nearly doubled. There would not be another open-top Mustang for ten years.

Ford tried the same trick in '78, the Mustang I's final year, but the King Cobra was a flop by comparison. It was even more look-at-me than Cobra II, with a giant snake decal on the hood, spoilers, flares, racing mirrors, and all set off by a bright-red paint job. On paper, it looked more serious than its predecessor, with the V8, four-speed manual transmission, and competition suspension all part of the package. Given the success of Cobra II, one might have expected this even louder version to sell even better, but Ford struggled to sell even 4,000 King Cobras in 1978. By contrast, it sold nearly 150,000 plain, basic Mustang I cars that year. A minority of all buyers (one in five) actually paid extra for the V8. The simple truth was that the Mustang II was not a performance car and never would be. That didn't stop it from selling in huge numbers, but hot car freaks could take heart, for in 1979 it was replaced by a new Mustang, one that would form the basis of a muscle car comeback.

At first, it didn't seem that way at all. The third-generation Mustang for 1979 looked clever, high-tech, and efficient—very eighties. And that's exactly what it was. The new Mustang was designed from the outset to be lightweight, with good aerodynamics and fuel consumption to help Ford comply with the new CAFE regulations. Overseen by Lee Iacocca (just before Henry Ford II finally sacked him), the new Mustang was slightly bigger than the old one, but weighed 200 lb. less. It had been designed with the help of a wind tunnel and made great use of thinner glass, lightweight alloys, and plastics.

The base engines were unchanged, the same 88 hp four and 109 hp V6 (though the latter was soon replaced by Ford's ageing 200 ci straight six). The V8 was an option too, now with 140 hp at 3,600 rpm, but the real surprise was a turbocharged version of the little four. Ford evidently saw this as the muscle car of the future, offering it as an option alongside the V8, and with all the same sporty options of wide wheels and stiffer suspension. With a Garrett AiResearch TO turbocharger and two-barrel carburetor, the 2.3 liter four was boosted to 131 hp at 5,500 rpm. Performance was almost identical to that of the V8, said Ford, but the turbo Mustang was 70. lb lighter and used less fuel. At first, it looked as though the company's turbo-vision would come true, and 60,000 Mustang turbos were sold in the first year, outselling the V8 slightly. But the early turbo didn't prove durable, and Ford later dropped it.

Only 14 percent of Mustang buyers chose V8 in the first year, and the most popular engine choice was the basic four. In 1980, things were even more gloomy for V8 fans. A second oil crisis meant rocketing gas prices and lines at gas stations. Overnight, car buyers' priorities shifted, and two-thirds of Mustang buyers opted for the 2.3 four. To try and make the V8 acceptable, Ford downsized it to 4.2 liters, with small valves and ports, plus a high rear-axle ratio to save fuel. Power was down to 117 hp, and the 1980 Mustang came as an automatic only. It didn't convince the public, and only 2.7% of them ordered V8s that year.

ABOVE: *Even in the gloom of 1972, when Mustang sales slumped to an all-time low, it was still possible to order one with all the muscle car accouterments. Truth be told, the low-compression, regular-grade fuel Mach 1 was a pale shadow of earlier hot Mustangs, but it still looked the part.*

THE BOSS IS BACK

"The boss is back!" proclaimed the Mustang advertisements for 1982, and for once, they weren't exaggerating—this was the year when the Mustang muscle car returned, to a delighted press and public. On the face of it, the changes didn't look that radical. The full 5.0 liter V8 was back, with a four-speed manual transmission. A few internal engine tweaks, including a high-lift camshaft, bigger carburetor, and a few other bits and pieces, boosted peak power by 14 percent. But behind that modest increase was a fatter, healthier torque curve, and in the lightweight Mustang with a manual transmission, the effects were quite something.

Motor Trend said it all, with an attention-grabbing headline centered around 0–60 mph in 6.9 seconds. With most tests recording 15/16-second standing-quarter times, this was something to get excited about, the return of muscle car performance.

To back up the Mustang's newfound go, the V8 came with handling suspension as standard, P185/75R-14 tires on cast aluminum wheels, a Traction-Lok differential, power brakes, and power steering. Low profile Michelin TRX tires were an option. And, as icing on the cake, Ford brought back a Mustang GT, with fog lights, spoilers, and lots of black detailing. The buyers loved it, and although overall Mustang sales fell in 1982 (along with the entire US car market), one in four of them were V8s. The boss was back, and how.

In fact, as the 1983 model year rolled around, it became clear that the old days were back for everyone. GM had never stopped making the Camaro, and through the 1980s it would battle the Mustang in a reborn horsepower race. For 1983, Chevrolet announced a 190 hp fuel-injected V8, and Ford responded with a 175 hp version of its lower-tech motor, which, of course, persevered with a carburetor instead of injection, and used no electronic controls. Instead, a traditional four-barrel carburetor did the business, with a big air cleaner and aluminum intake. Despite the power gap, it could still keep up, the Mustang being lighter than the Camaro. There was a five-speed transmission too—a close-ratio Borg Warner T5—and the many magazine tests that pitted these reborn muscle cars against each other found the cheaper, lighter

FORD MUSTANG GT 1982

Engine: *160 bhp 302 ci V8, 247 lb ft*

Transmission: *four-speed manual (automatic not available)*

Steering: *rack and pinion, power assisted*

Wheels & tires: *forged aluminum 15.35 x 5.9 inches, Michelin TRX 190/65R390*

Brakes: *front 9.31-inch discs, power assisted; rear 9-inch drums, power assisted*

Suspension: *front independent, MacPherson struts, coil springs; rear four-link, coil springs*

Wheelbase: *100 inches*

Height: *51.4 inches*

Weight: *3,319 pounds*

Mustang to be a match for the high-tech Chevy in a straight line. It might be a little crude, but the Mustang GT V8 relived the sixties in a way that no other eighties car could.

The Mustang turbo was back, reliability problems figured out, and it now offered 145 hp. But few buyers chose it—the little turbo wasn't as fast as the V8, but actually had a higher price tag. And if it used less fuel, few US drivers cared, now that the second oil crisis was a rapidly receding bad memory. By contrast, one in three Mustang drivers bought a V8 instead.

One knew that the V8 Mustang was really accepted back into the public arena when the police started buying them. The California Highway Patrol (CHP) were attracted to the V8's combination of high performance with relatively low cost. Their purchase criteria stipulated 0–100 mph in thirty seconds, and 120 mph in less than two minutes. The Mustang could do that, and the CHP ordered 400 of them for patrol cars.

Meanwhile, Ford was persevering with the turbo, which now emerged from the company's Special Vehicles Operation (SVO) as a complete car. Now with an intercooler, the 2.3 turbo offered 175 hp, plus a beefed up low-rev performance. It could rival the V8 for performance, with 0–60 mph dispatched in 7.5 seconds, not to mention a top speed of 134 mph. The SVO Turbo was certainly more popular than the early 2.3 turbo Mustangs, and came with every conceivable performance and luxury extra at a price tag of over $15,000. It also had muscle car performance, but did that make it a muscle car? You decide.

For 1985, V8 power was boosted yet again, this time to 210 hp. This was actually the final year of a carburetor for the Mustang, and the following year it would follow the electronic injection route, along with everyone else. But in the meantime, having a gulping four-barrel carb under the hood provided a strong link with the past. Muscle cars had always been this way, and the Mustang's extra 35 hp for 1985 came from a higher-lift camshaft and high-flow headers as well as that four-barrel Holley. It was all good old boy stuff.

> ***"The Ford boys have done it again. Their cars handle impeccably. No rolling, no pitching. Push them as hard as you want."***
>
> ***(Motor Trend, March 1969)***

***Above:** Later Mustang fastbacks were termed "SportsRoof," but the final 1971 version didn't meet with unstinted praise. One magazine likened it to a "bread van," and even if you liked the looks, the visibility through that near-horizontal rear window made parking a nightmare.*

RIGHT: The final long-nose Mustang had grown so big that even full-size V8s were dwarfed by its spacious engine bay. Not that you could order a big-block engine after '71, when the 429 was dropped. The final choices were 200 ci six, 302 ci V8, and 351 ci V8.

> **"*Mach 1 puts Mustang back where it all started—Numero Uno.*"**
>
> (Motor Trend, *March 1969*)

It worked too, with magazine tests recording 0–60 times of 6–7 seconds and 14–15 seconds over the standing quarter mile, which made this reborn muscle Mustang quicker than most of the old ones. Ford still persevered with the SVO Turbo as a high-tech alternative to the V8, now boosted to 205 hp, but only 2,000 people bought them that year, compared to nearly 50,000 V8 customers, who made up one in three of all Mustang buyers.

The Mustang V8 made its name as one of the few good-value performance cars of the 1980s, but even so, the price was now nudging $10,000 in standard form. However, there was a cheaper route to the same sort of modern muscle experience, using that age-old technique of juggling options. The trick was to order a Mustang LX coupe (the cheapest in the range) and add the following options: 5.0 liter V8, 5-speed transmission, 2.73:1 Traction Lok differential, and 15-inch Goodyear Gatorback tires with alloy wheels. The result was nearly $600 cheaper than the fancy GT, but just as quick, or even quicker, as it weighed around 125 lb. less. Ford even made the cheap V8 official, by reintroducing it as the Boss Mustang. No air conditioning or electric windows, but who cared? Another muscle car tradition—the low-spec, top-performance car—was back.

But there was one modern development that Ford couldn't ignore. In 1987, it finally ditched the Mustang's four-barrel carburetor in favor of electronic sequential fuel injection. The result was slightly less power but a healthy 7.5% increase in peak torque (now 285 lb ft) and a much fatter torque curve. This cut acceleration times, and one magazine recorded just six seconds for the 0–60 mph sprint. It was a symbolic change as well, as the four-barrel carburetor had almost iconic status in muscle car culture, and the Mustang had been one of the last performance cars to hold out against fuel injection. But sentiment aside, injection made the Mustang faster, easier to drive at low speeds, and more efficient, so there were no placard-waving protesters outside Dearborn.

Despite injection (and a front-end facelift the same year), *Hot Rod* magazine decided that the latest Camaro IROC Z28 was finally the better car. It had long been more high-tech and competent than the back-to-basics Ford, but a new 230 hp tuned-port injection V8 made it faster as well. Ford couldn't take this lying down, and hit back the following year with its own injected GT boosted to 225 hp—the thinking was that the Mustang's lower weight would be sufficient to make up for the small power deficiency. A bigger air intake, larger 60 mm throttle body, and freer-flowing cylinder heads helped liberate the extra horsepower, and larger ventilated front disc brakes helped to keep it under control.

As the Mustang approached its twenty-fifth anniversary (a fact which Ford acknowledged with a little plaque on the dashboard), top brass at Ford were

BELOW: Mach 1 was always the show-off Mustang, majoring on stripes and spoilers, while the more serious Boss 302 and 429 did without them. It was a popular option though, even with a detuned V8 under the hood.

considering its future. An all-new Mustang, code-named SN8, small and high-tech with stunning performance, was touted, but it would have cost a lot of money and time to develop, so that was that. Another proposal was to rebadge a Mazda coupe as the fourth-generation Mustang—the Japanese company was now Ford's Far East partner. But the news leaked out, and there was such an outcry that Ford rapidly backpedaled, launching its rebadged Mazda as the Probe. To Mustang customers, it seemed, a Mustang must always be rear-wheel drive with a torquey V8 upfront, a modern incarnation of the sixties muscle car. So a rebadged front-wheel-drive Mazda, however good it was, just wouldn't do the job.

Right: ***New for 1994, the fourth-generation Mustang certainly looked the part of a 1990s pony car. Beneath the skin though, many parts were carried over from the old car, including the 302 ci pushrod V8, which would hamper the Mustang's performance vis-à-vis the Camaro/Firebird.***

But for all its rip-roaring muscle, the Mustang would need more power in the next few years—a 5.7 liter (351 ci) factory Mustang had already passed through the rumor mill—and Ford commissioned tuner Jack Roush to come up with a prototype super-Mustang. Roush's car was that all right, powered by a twin-turbo 5.7 liter V8 producing around 400 hp. It would have created quite a stir, but given the practicalities of putting a 400-horsepower car through modern emissions and safety legislation (not to mention the public relations minefield), Ford decided not to go ahead.

Instead, it acknowledged the role of the LX V8 Mustang as a bargain muscle car by making it a model in its own right. The LX 5.0L Sport came with the same 225 hp V8 as the look-at-me GT. The same T-5 manual transmission, sports seats, suspension, and Traction-Lok rear axle. At just $11,410, it cost less than some Japanese four-cylinder coupes, and offered a totally different driving experience, with near-Porsche performance in a straight line. For a while, it would actually outsell the GT. And looking like a standard LX four-cylinder Mustang, the 5.0L Sport proved that the street sleeper muscle car was not dead.

Meanwhile, the tuners and hot rodders were having a field day with the now-aging Mustang. Steve Saleen in particular had turned his special Mustangs, with body kits and hotter V8s, into series production. For 1989 he announced his hottest Mustang,

Ford Mustang GT 2001

Engine: *260 bhp 4.6 liter sohc V8, 302 lb ft*

Transmission: *five-speed manual*

Steering: *rack and pinion, power assisted*

Tires: *245/45ZR-17*

Brakes: *front 10.9 vented discs, power assisted; rear 10.5-inch discs, power assisted*

Suspension: *front independent, coil springs; rear rigid axle, coil springs*

Wheelbase: *103 inches*

Height: *53.1 inches*

Weight: *3,305 pounds*

LEFT: In early 2004, Ford gave a sneak preview of what the '05 Mustang would look like, and it was a clear case of respecting your elders. Everything about the fifth-generation Mustang paid homage to the past.

BELOW: Compare this to the Shelby or the Boss. Ford was clearly going for the nostalgia ticket in 2005, underlining the Mustang's heritage to boost the fortunes of this latest pony car.

yet, the SSC (Saleen Super Car) claiming 292 hp from the familiar V8, thanks to revised cylinder heads and bigger stainless-steel headers. *Car and Driver* thought it was more like 270 hp, recording a 0–60 time of 5.9 seconds and a 14.2-second standing quarter, both faster than the standard car, but not by a great deal. Tall gearing also blunted the SSC's top speed, and it ran out of breath at 149 mph—it was fast all right, but maybe that power claim was a little ambitious.

Turbocharging provided a much more substantial boost in power, and the 5.0 liter V8 responded well to it. Tuning house Cartech thought it had the ultimate tuned Mustang in 1991, utilizing the strong, well-proven V8 to good effect. The engine, of course, was backed up by the tough Borg Warner T-5 transmission, which had also proved its strength and durability over the years. Cartech's fully legal Mustang turbo, complete with catalytic convertors, claimed 392 hp at 5,000 rpm and 550 lb ft at 4,200. But for Cartech, that wasn't enough. Boss Corky Bell was determined to build the first 200 mph street-legal Mustang, and added a Haltech fuel injection system (with a separate injector for each cylinder), bigger valves, high-tension valve springs plus polished intakes and exhausts. Finally, he turned the turbo boost up and took car and stopwatch to a suitable open space.

Before those changes, the Cartech Mustang had been timed at 4.9 seconds for 0–60 (and that on a 2.73:1 rear axle), and the new one produced 371 hp at the rear wheels, so well over 400 at the flywheel. At 6 psi boost, it topped out at 183 mph, but with the boost at 10 psi it later recorded an official 203 mph. This was surely the fastest road-legal Mustang ever.

Fast it might be, but time was running out for the old Mustang. It had been in production for nearly fifteen years, and was starting to look decidedly old-fashioned: especially in 1992, when GM announced a sleek new Camaro/Firebird. Not surprisingly, sales dropped to less than 80,000 that year, a new low for the Mustang—it was an open secret that a new Mustang was on the way. Meanwhile, the convertible personified the Mustang's retro appeal more than any other model. Just as fast as the coupe, but with the added sensory treats of wind in the hair, gear noise, and a sharply defined V8 roar and rumble. "Do you hate computers?" asked Martin Peters of *Road & Track*. The rejoinder was that if you did, you'd love the open top Mustang.

BELOW: An early '70s Mustang SportsRoof, complete with supercharged V8, a vast, gulping air intake, and roll cage. This drag strip beast was photographed in Springfield, Illinois. Stylized flames have been a perennial favorite of drag customizers.

To try and divert attention from the new Camaro/Firebird, Ford announced a mildly tweaked Mustang Cobra. Available as a hatchback only, this was a product of Ford's SVT (Special Vehicle Team) and claimed 235 hp thanks to GT-40 cylinder heads with bigger intake and exhaust ports, larger valves, and modified rocker arms. A 70-mm throttle body, new camshaft, and intake manifold did the business, with smaller, lighter crank and water pump pulleys to help the V8 rev harder. The T-5 transmission was strengthened, and there was a 3.08:1 rear axle and ultra-low profile Goodyear tires mounted on 7.5-inch-wide alloy wheels unique to the Cobra. SVT also did much work on the suspension, using softer springs than was traditional on hot rod Mustangs.

VYG 377

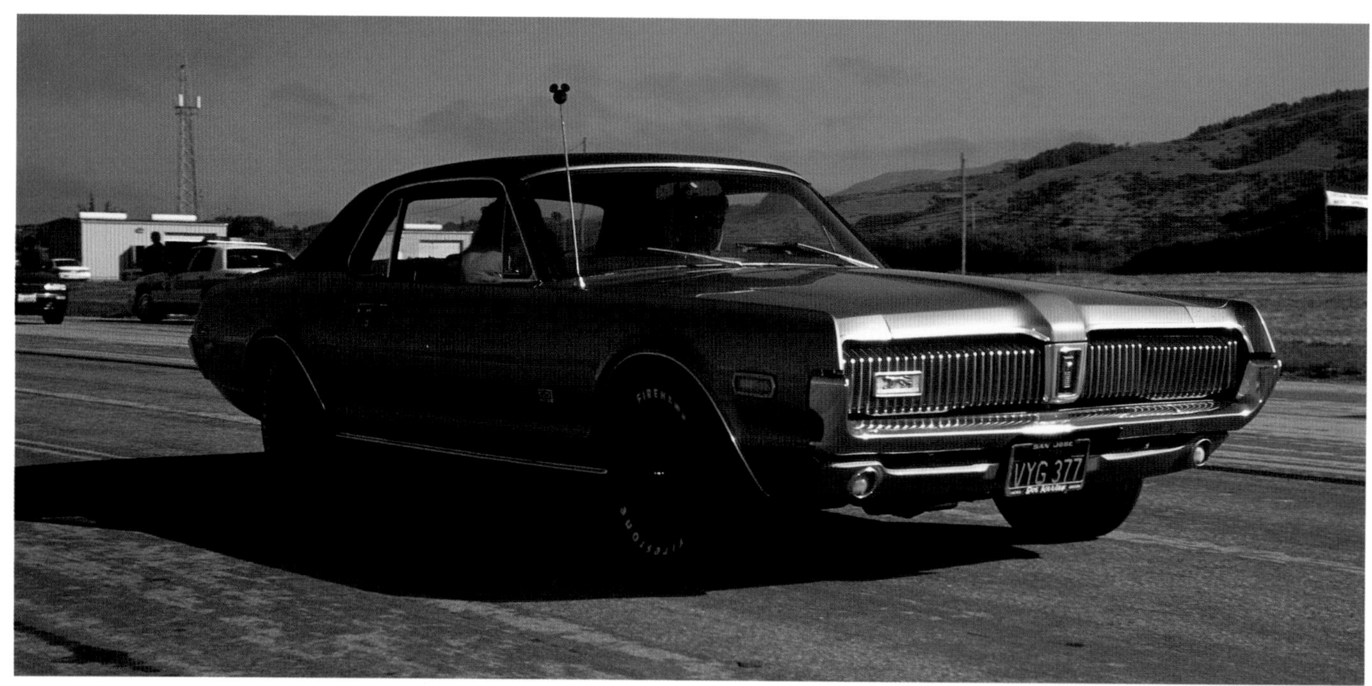

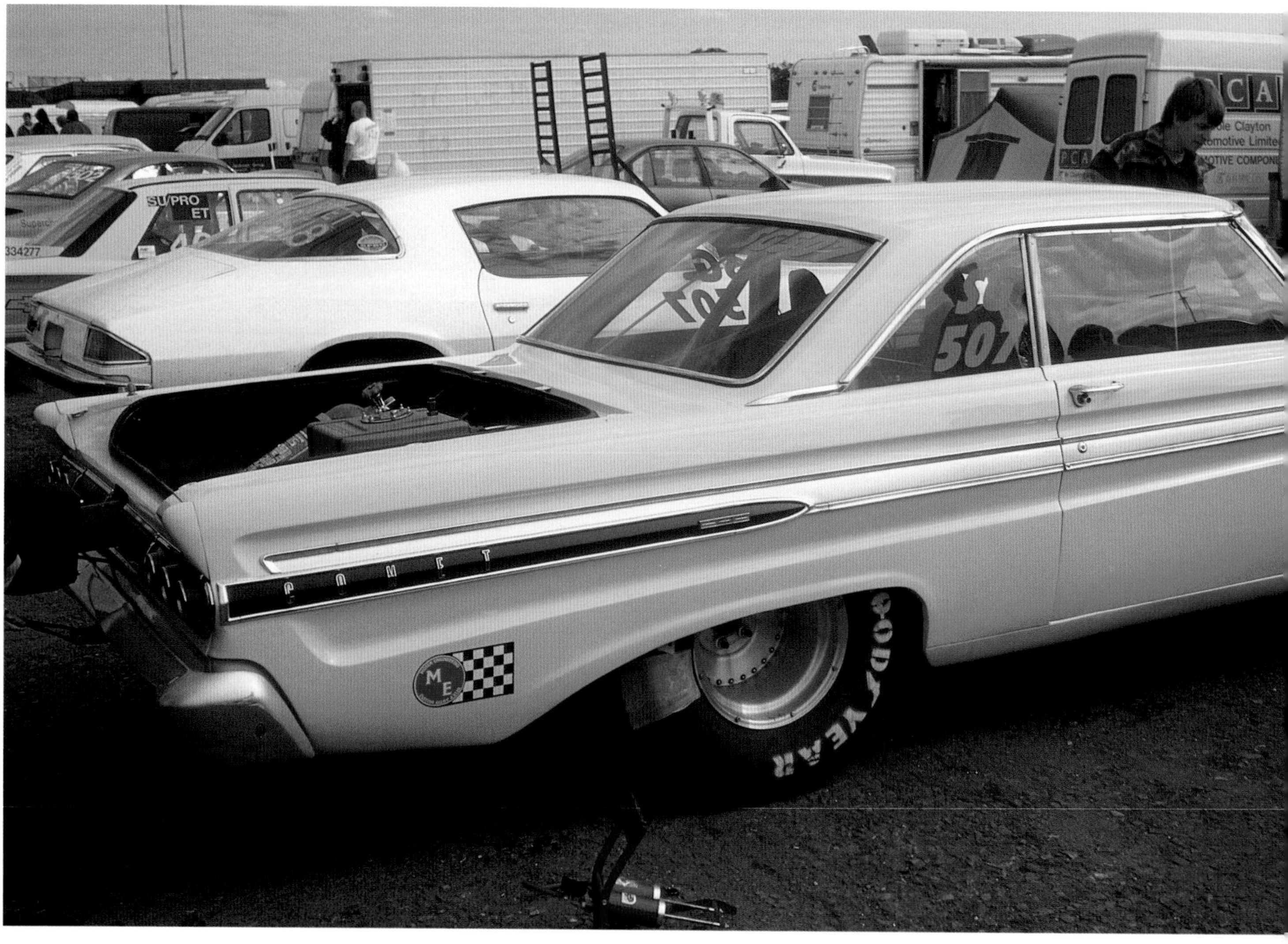
SU/PRO
ET
507
COMET
GOODYEAR

LEFT: Cougar was an upmarket Mustang, sold with Mercury badges and marketed as a luxurious pony car, but there were muscular variants as well, including the big-block 428 V8.

But was all this enough to meet and beat the new F-body Firebird/Camaro? *Car and Driver* put a Cobra up against both in a three-way test, and said they liked the V8 in its latest 235 hp guise. They liked the Goodyear's tenacious road holding and the car's good manners when not being driven hard. But at nine-tenths or more, the Mustang chassis showed its age and needed skill to keep in line. Out of those three American GTs, the Cobra came third.

The Fourth Generation

So when the new Mustang was finally unveiled for 1994, it hadn't come a moment too soon. Not that it was all new; 500 parts were carried over from the old "Fox" Mustang, though most of these were nonmoving parts like brackets and parts of the floorpan. Ford engineers had been given a tough brief in designing the fourth generation Mustang. It was taken as read, by the way, that they couldn't slip in anything radical like front-wheel drive—the new car would be a more sophisticated take on the traditional V8 rear-wheel-drive layout. But it would have to have better ride, handling, and steering than the old car, not to mention more performance, better brakes, and more cossetting comfort.

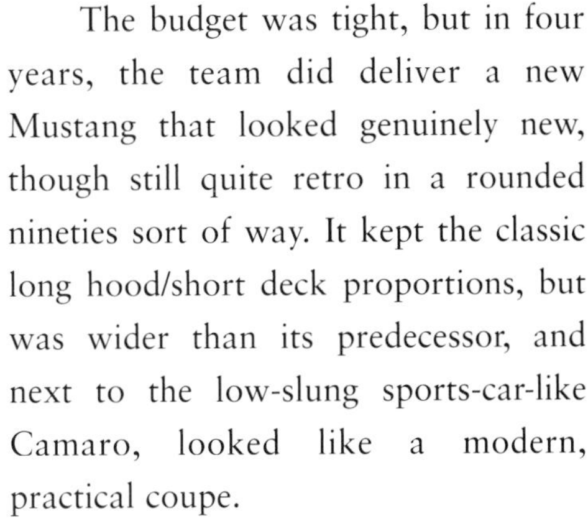

BELOW: The Comet was Mercury's compact (though it later grew to a 116-inch wheelbase, using Fairlane components), and the Cyclone was something of a gentleman's muscle car.

The budget was tight, but in four years, the team did deliver a new Mustang that looked genuinely new, though still quite retro in a rounded nineties sort of way. It kept the classic long hood/short deck proportions, but was wider than its predecessor, and next to the low-slung sports-car-like Camaro, looked like a modern, practical coupe.

But what it lacked was a modern engine. Budget restrictions meant that the overhead cam 4.6 liter V8 slated for the Mustang (and already powering Ford sedans) wasn't ready, so the faithful 5.0 liter, 302, whatever you wanted to call it, was pressed into service yet again. Despite a modest power boost to 215 hp at 4,200 rpm, it was no match for the latest Camaro Z28, which offered 28% more power and rocketlike performance. In other words, the new Mustang had lost its muscle car status. Early road tests

> ***"Captures the spirit of Daytona. Racy, sporty, elegant. That's Cyclone, a just-out model inspired by Comet's incredible Durability Run at Daytona, where four specially equipped Comets each clocked 100,000 miles averaging over 105 mph! In every Cyclone: new Super 289 cu in V8, tach, bucket seats, chrome engine fittings, competition-type wheel covers."***

RIGHT: Mercury Cougar from 1969, the year it got longer, wider, and heavier, just like the Mustang on which it was based. Mercury was Ford's slightly upmarket marque, so the Cougar was intended as a sort of luxury Mustang, with extra soundproofing and equipment, plus a softer ride. It also shared the Mustang's long hood/short trunk concept, though it used its own body. New for '69, this looked sleek, if a little anonymous next door to a genuine Mustang.

RIGHT: Luxurious it might be, but the Cougar still offered most of the standard Mustang's performance options, especially in the hardtop Eliminator launched in early '69. Its standard power unit was the four-barrel Windsor 351, offering 290 hp, but the big-block 390 and 428 Cobra Jet were other options, not to mention the new high-revving 302, in either street or racing guise.

RIGHT: Retractable headlights were standard on the Cougar, and both hardtop and convertible styles were offered. A GT option group added F70 tires, Comfortweave bucket seats, a racing mirror, turbine wheel covers, and various GT badges. Alternatively, the XR-7 pack concentrated on the interior, including a walnut-effect dashboard, tachometer, leather-and-vinyl upholstery and a courtesy light group, among other things.

found it to be softer, calmer, and more sophisticated than the old Mustang, but trailing way behind its archrival on performance. It wasn't slow, with 0–60 in 6.1 seconds, but a Camaro Z28 was a lot quicker. *Car and Driver* also scored the Chevy higher on its brakes, handling, value, styling and even fun-to-drive rating. The muscle-bound Mustang of the eighties appeared to have turned into a leisurely Grand Tourer.

An SVT Cobra Mustang soon followed, with 240 hp and better brakes, with ABS standard. It helped, but it wasn't really enough. Ford also built a limited run of 5.7 liter Mustangs using a block from a Ford marine engine, aluminum alloy pistons added, a special camshaft, forged steel connecting rods, GT-40 heads, and special intake manifolds. This was the Cobra R, and with 300 hp it could match the Z28, but it was a limited production car, and only 250 were made. All were sold before they were even completed. What Ford needed was a mass-produced Mustang with muscle.

It arrived for 1996. Its basis was the new 4.6 liter modular V8, which everyone seemed to know would find its way under the Mustang's hood sooner or later. On paper, it looked decidedly ordinary, with a cast-iron block, single overhead cam per bank, and just two valves per cylinder. Enthusiasts could look closely and note that the engine had plenty of built-in strength for future power hikes, but Ford quoted the same power (215 hp) as for the outgoing 5.0 liter, so in standard form, this wasn't the long-awaited Mustang muscle car for the nineties. For that, you had to order the Cobra.

BELOW: Mercury managed to make the Cougar look quite different from the Mustang, despite using most of the pony car's components. It still looked sporty, in an elegant sort of way, and retractable headlights (hidden behind the grille) further differentiated it from the Mustang

Although based loosely on the same layout as the standard 4.6, the Cobra V8 was radically different. Its aluminum block was cast in Italy and shipped to Ford's Romeo, Michigan, plant for assembly by twelve teams of two workers. They fit double overhead camshaft heads with four valves per cylinder, twin 57 mm throttle bodies, and an 80 mm air sensor, plus a crankshaft, from Germany. Each bearing cap was retained by six bolts. Despite the hand-built nature of the Cobra V8 (and its expense), Ford built 10,000 of them in 1996 to keep up with demand. Ford claimed 305 hp and 300 lb ft, while a fuel cutoff operated at 6,800 rpm.

Despite the 32-valve heads and DOHC, the Cobra hadn't turned into a European sports car. "As American as a John Wayne film festival," said *Road & Track* of a 1997 Cobra convertible. After all, it still had a live rear axle, and could get upset by bumpy surfaces when cornering hard. But who cared? As the magazine writers pointed out, a Cobra might not be as sophisticated as a Euro-sophisticate, but could out-accelerate them and was cheaper. So in a way, even with its electronic trickery and multiple valves, the Mustang still stood for cheap muscle car performance.

So, a happy ending—Camaro and the Europeans finally put in their place? Not a bit of it. In 1998 even the DOHC Mustang Cobra couldn't match the Camaro Z28. As if to rub salt into the wound, the Z28 managed this with a traditional pushrod V8, which offered a fatter torque curve thanks to good old-fashioned cubic inches. Both engines made 305 hp, but the Camaro's torque gave it better acceleration—the difference was slight, but consistent, the Cobra being 0.3 seconds behind, both to 60 mph and over the quarter mile. Admittedly the Z28's pushrod V8 was pretty special—all alloy and fuel-injected—but it was a touch humiliating for the hand-assembled Cobra V8.

RIGHT: Mercury Cyclone fastback, this one dating from 1969. The fastback had proved a far faster seller in 1968, so the basic hardtop was dropped the following year.

BELOW: This Cyclone has come a long way since 1969, but back then, the hottest Cyclone was the CJ, which carried Ford's 428 ci V8 as standard, in 435 hp form. With that on board, owners could expect a 13.9-second quarter mile.

"Mercury Cyclone GT. Fast-backed. 4-stacked. Radial-tracked."

To make things worse, the Z28 had better handling, and one test condemned the Mustang as a "hopeless understeerer." And as if that weren't enough, a Cobra cost $5,000 more than a Camaro. Not that the buyers seemed too bothered. Mustang sales boomed, and the car was easily outselling the Camaro and Firebird combined. Without a cheap four-cylinder option, it would never reach the heights of early Mustangs, but Ford did sell around 120,000 Mustang V6s in 1998—a 3.8 liter V6 had been the entry-level V8 alternative since the fourth-generation Mustang was unveiled. As for the V8 itself, sales of around 46,000 couldn't be dismissed lightly either.

In any case, the following year, Ford finally got the car right. All three of the Mustang's major failings were addressed. First, the styling, which not everyone loved. A little too rounded and organic, thought some, even bland, and certainly not muscular enough. For 1999, the car had New Edge styling, with sharper edges and creases to define its shape, a bigger front grille with a galloping pony emblem, the latter instantly recognizable as the Mustang symbol for thirty-five years. More power was needed, especially on the standard non-Cobra GT. Bigger valves,

BELOW: When new, those late-sixties Cyclones weren't aimed at drag racing at all, but NASCAR. Cale Yarborough had won the 1968 Daytona 500 in a Cyclone, and Ford hoped to repeat the feat with the Cyclone Spoiler II with a rear spoiler and extended nose. Unfortunately, it wasn't legalized for racing in time.

better airflow, a higher-lift camshaft, different combustion chambers, and a new ignition system (now with a separate coil for each cylinder) resulted in 260 hp at 5,250 rpm, plus 300 lb ft. As for the Cobra, that was pushed to 320 hp, and the entry-level V6, the biggest-selling Mustang, got a 25% lift to 190 hp. Maybe the V6 didn't qualify as a full-grown muscle car, but it wasn't far off. Traction control was now an option on all the Mustangs, and maybe it was a good idea with all this extra power and torque fighting its way through.

The Mustang's third big improvement fulfilled a thirty-five-year promise. Back in 1964, when the pony was launched, Ford partially excused the live rear axle and leaf springs by saying that an optional independent rear setup was under development. It never appeared, and the company later said that track tests found it to be no faster around corners than the standard system. But in 1999, an all-independent Mustang finally arrived. It came on the Cobra only, developed by SVT, but it was here. Ford claimed better weight distribution (now 55/45) thanks to less unsprung weight on the back, and *Road & Track*'s first road test seemed to bear this out.

They reported both good ride and good handling—the holy grail for modern coupes—and this was the first road-going Mustang not upset by bumpy corners. Set up for mild understeer, it would power oversteer if you wanted to, and it was decisively faster than a Camaro SS through *R&T*'s standard slalom test (this, of course, was a sweet victory for Ford engineers).

Maybe, knowing that the fourth-generation Mustang had finally come good, that was why Ford was so keen to celebrate the pony car's thirty-fifth birthday. An optional anniversary package brought a spoiler, leather interior, and scoops. Bet now they were glad they hadn't killed the Mustang off in its dark days.

Mercury Cougar 1968

Engine: *325 bhp, 390 cubic-inch cast-iron V8*

Transmission: *four-speed manual*

Steering: *recirculating ball*

Wheels & tires: *14 x 6 in steel rims with Goodyear F70 x 14 tires*

Brakes: *front 11.3 in discs; rear 10 in drums*

Suspension: *front independent, coil springs, upper wishbones, single lower arms and anti-sway bar; rear semi-elliptic leaf springs, rigid axle*

Wheelbase: *111 inches*

Height: *51.7 inches*

Weight: *3,560 pounds*

However, this wouldn't be the Mustang without something not going according to plan and it soon transpired that many of those Cobras weren't producing their claimed 320 hp. It turned out that the exhaust system had been modified late in the design process to clear the rear suspension arms and avoid scraping the road. In the process, it had been pinched, restricting power. Eight thousand cars were affected, and Ford decided to recall them all to fit a freer-flowing intake manifold and exhaust. It was such a lot of work for the relatively small SVT operation that it was decided not to build any new Cobras for 2000.

Besides, SVT had another project to concentrate on that year. The Cobra R really did hark back to the original Shelby GT350s. This was a Mustang virtually ready to race, yet it was street legal and in a pinch could be used as an everyday road car. With a genuine 385 hp and 385 lb ft, it was also the most powerful factory Mustang so far.

Its 5.4 liter V8 was derived from the 4.6, but with a cast-iron block that was usually found in Ford trucks. In the Cobra R, it had an aluminum head with four valves per cylinder and double overhead camshafts. Carillo connecting rods and forged pistons made it strong, and tubular headers and a unique intake manifold took care of the breathing. The

BELOW: "Eliminator" was the Cougar at its most muscular, with front and rear spoilers, plus styled steel wheels, blacked-out grille, tachometer, and clock. Opt for the top 428 Cobra Jet V8, and a hood scoop, locking pins, and competition handling package were all part of the deal.

> **"The Cyclone CJ can best be described as a gentleman's muscle car."**
>
> (Car and Driver, *January 1969*)

Above: For 1970, the Cougar received a new vertical grille and mildly restyled front end, while the Eliminator (shown here) hung on for its final year. The basic Eliminator now offered 300 hp from its four-barrel 351 Windsor V8, while a new option was the Boss 429 V8, with a claimed 375 hp. "Call it the road animal," invited Mercury's brochure.

result was over 70 hp/liter, a high figure for an American-made road-going V8.

Mated to that was the first six-speed transmission fitted to a production Mustang, while both driveshaft and differential case were of aluminum to save weight. Naturally, the R used the Cobra's all-independent suspension setup, but with stiffer Eibach coil springs all around and Bilstein shocks. There were Brembo discs front and rear, while BFGoodrich tires (ultra low-profile 40-section G-Forces) provided contact with the road.

Inside, there was no air conditioning or sound system, though the Cobra R still had power windows, door locks, and trunk release, so it wasn't quite as stripped out as those old Shelbys. But with a huge rear wing, big front spoiler, and skirt extensions, there was no mistaking a Cobra R from the outside, whether it came in Grabber Orange or Performance Red. And finally, was it faster than a Camaro? *Road & Track* recorded 0–60 in 4.8 seconds and the standing quarter in 13.2 seconds. The R would sprint to 100 mph in less than 11 seconds and rev to 6,600 rpm in the gears. Top

ABOVE RIGHT: *"America's most completely equipped sports car," according to Mercury, though the extra weight over a standard Mustang would blunt performance a little.*

speed? *R&T* estimated 160 mph in sixth gear, maybe 170 in fifth. At $54,000, the Cobra R cost ten grand more than a Camaro, but every single one of the limited-edition 300 was presold.

Ford seemed to have gained a taste for special Mustangs, and the Bullitt arrived in late 2001. It was an homage to *Bullitt*, the Steve McQueen movie in which the hard-bitten San Francisco detective takes part in the most famous car chase in the history of celluloid: Dodge Charger chases Mustang chases Charger around the mean streets of San Francisco for a good thirty minutes (or so it seems).

Young kids (and even the not so young) who watched that movie open-mouthed were now of an age to buy a new Mustang, so the new Mustang Bullitt was aimed directly at them. On paper, the Bullitt appeared to be only very slightly stronger than the standard Mustang: five more peak horsepower, 3 lb ft more. But the real story was a fatter, fuller torque curve that delivered 93% of that peak at just 2,200 rpm, delivering even more blinding acceleration than the standard car. Twin 57 mm throttle bodies, an aluminum intake manifold, and freer-flowing exhaust system made the difference, while the Bullitt was supported by stiffer springs and Tokico shocks, giving a lower-than-standard ride height.

Cosmetically, the 2001 Bullitt was carefully designed to suggest the late sixties original: color choices were Highland Green (just like Mr. Frank Bullitt's fastback), black, or dark blue. Five spoke alloy wheels bore a family resemblance to those of a Shelby, and there were hood scoops and side scoops, bright-red brake calipers, and a brushed aluminum gas cap. The Bullitt was a success, and stayed in production for 2003.

Meanwhile, the Cobra was back, now with a guaranteed 320 hp. Traction control was compulsory, but could be switched to "Power Start." In other words, it could be switched off if the driver wanted a muscle car–style, smoking-rubber getaway. If things got out of hand, the traction control would automatically step in again, cutting power and applying a little brake until the car was stabilized. After all, this wasn't 1968 any more.

It might not be 1968 and the height of the muscle car boom, but Ford had a keen understanding of the nostalgia for that era, even among twenty-first century drivers who were too young to remember it. So the Mach 1 Mustang returned for 2003. This was basically a dress-up job, with plenty of references to the classic muscle car era. A Shaker hood scoop quivered in sympathy with the big V8 underneath (though the 4.6 liter unit was actually a minnow by sixties muscle car standards, a mere 280 ci). The scoop was even given the "Ram Air" tag by Ford, just in case you hadn't gotten the muscular reference. Seventeen-inch alloys, a big rear spoiler, and variable-rate sport suspension were part of the package too, as was the DOHC 32-valve V8 in 305 hp form, though the Mach 1 was as much about looks as real-world performance.

For that, and just to underline the fact that the Mustang's muscle days were back, the Cobra got a huge boost, in every sense of the word. Supercharged for 2003, it now offered 390 hp, the most powerful production Mustang ever. At a little under $40,000 (without options), it hardly kept to the original Mustang concept of affordability. But muscle car performance? Of that there was no doubt at all.

Mercury: Upmarket Muscle

RIGHT: 1970 was the final year for the Cougar Eliminator shown here, though some buyers opted for the more luxurious XR-7 option. For '71, the Cougar was upsized and rebodied (along with the Mustang) and lost that elegance that characterized the '67–'68 cars. Engine options remained the 351 to 429 V8s.

Ford's Lincoln-Mercury division wasn't about performance. At least, that was how it started out, but the maker of upscale sedans and convertibles based on Ford parts also got sucked into the muscle car craze. In the sixties, what choice did it have?

The first signs of the division's entry into the sixties power race was in 1964, when the Cyclone arrived as a high performance version of the compact Comet. This was powered by a warm, rather than hot, engine, the 210 hp four-barrel version of Ford's 289 ci V8. Three transmissions were offered—three- or four-speed manual or the Merc-O-Matic auto—the latter allowing a 0–60 sprint of 11.8 seconds and 16.5 seconds over the quarter mile. Oddly, the four-speed manual was over a second quicker to 60 mph but had lost almost all that advantage by the end of the quarter.

For 1965, with everyone else in Detroit clamoring to offer more horsepower, what could Mercury do but follow suit? So the restyled Cyclone, now with an optional twin air scoop fiberglass hood, progressed to the 225 hp version of the 289. A four-speed transmission still cost extra, but thus equipped, the Cyclone's 0–60 time was down to 8.8 seconds—not leading-edge muscle performance, but on the way. It didn't get that until the following year, when the whole Comet range was upsized to a 116-inch wheelbase. Now based on Ford Fairlane components, it had the space to accommodate Ford's big-block 390 ci engine. In the Cyclone GT, this came with a four-barrel carburetor, 10.5:1 compression ratio, and 335 hp.

That cut the 0–60 down to 7 seconds, with a quarter mile in the high 14s. So the optional handling package and front disc brakes were highly recommended. Little wonder that Cyclones would become race winners in NASCAR.

Meanwhile, the Comet Cyclone had left its compact roots far behind, leaving the way open for a new, smaller Mercury to slot in beneath it. They didn't have to look far for a candidate, though—the Mustang was proving a phenomenal success, so why not market a Mercury equivalent, and sell a luxury pony car?

You needed to look closely to spot the family resemblance between a Mercury Cougar and the car it

ABOVE: Ford F-150 SVT Lightning from 1993. This typified the new breed of muscle trucks, with Ford's Special Vehicle Engineering group adding horsepower, handling, and interior equipment. It was a highly successful formula.

was based on. Incidentally, the "Cougar" name was ready and waiting. It had been a code name for the Mustang project, and was one of those shortlisted for the final product. It used the Mustang floorpan, but had its own body, though still based on the same long hood/short deck proportions. Being a Mercury, the Cougar was a more luxurious version of the Mustang, with a higher level of interior trim and more soundproofing. The dashboard, in particular, was quite different; the big slab of wood had a distinctly British look to it, underlined by traditional white on black dials.

As a rule, Cougars were softly sprung boulevard cars, but for the buyer who wanted sporting luxury, they could be upgraded with the same sort of muscle as a

ABOVE: To give the Lightning un-truck-like performance, the 5.8 liter V8 was given GT-40–type cylinder heads, a tuned-length aluminum intake manifold, tubular headers, and 240 bhp, enough for 0–60mph in 7.6 seconds.

Mustang. For 1967, for example, the Cougar GT 390 came with Ford's 390 V8 in 335 hp form. This four-barrel engine, with a 10.5:1 compression, also boasted 427 lb ft, allowing the sort of effortless performance that suited the Cougar's nature. Underlining that, almost half the Cougar buyers of 1967 opted for an automatic transmission. Still, part of the GT package was stiffer springs, bigger shocks, and a beefier antiroll bar, not to mention the power front disc brakes and wide tires.

Mercury was certainly trying hard to give the Cougar a sporting image. A team of cars raced hard in Trans Am, with the legendary Dan Gurney as one of the drivers. Gurney's name was so strong that Mercury applied it to a special edition Cougar. The XR-7G ("G" for "Gurney," of course) sounded quite sporty, but when *Car and Driver* tested one against five other muscle pony cars in early 1968, they found it was anything but. Too soft, too soggy, and not fast enough. "The Dowager of the group," they concluded, "and it didn't like being pitted against such wild brutes."

As time went on, the Cougar grew bigger and heavier, just like the Mustang it was based on. It also came with more muscular power units, such as 370 hp four-barrel 429. With that under the hood, it deserved to be called a muscle car, however tip-top its interior and spongy its suspension.

(As an epilogue to the Ford muscle story, it would be churlish not to mention the machinery on these pages, a success story that just about nobody predicted.)

"Beat it. In the case of Plymouth's Hemi, that's a tall order. Our competitors in organized drag, stock car and unlimited hydroplane racing have been finding out the hard way. Too bad . . . It's gotta be voodoo, baby!"

Chrysler: Winged Warriors

GTO, Shelby, Trans Am. All key words of muscle car culture, all have racing and competition overtones, and all refer to complete cars. But one key word stands head and shoulders above any of the others. It's not the name of a car, or a driver, or a race series. Instead, it derives from the shape of the combustion chamber of a certain Chrysler V8—the Hemi.

This engine—the most powerful road-legal muscle car V8 of them all—was Chrysler's big ticket into the muscle car race. It was an expensive option, both to buy and insure, and the plain fact is that very few customers actually bought them. But that hardly matters. What counts is that for a while the Hemi was the ultimate muscle car engine, looked on with awe on the street, and unbeatable in drag racing.

Just as there were muscular Pontiacs before the GTO, hot Chevys before the 409, and powerful Fords before the Shelbys, Chrysler was building high-horsepower V8s long before the Hemi came on the scene.

Watch the birdy! Plymouth's Road Runner combined rip-roaring muscle car performance with a low purchase price: hence its huge success.

GPF
915J

ABOVE: That "300" badge, with its characteristic checkered flag motif, became the stuff of legends.

Back in 1951, the Firepower V8 actually was a Hemi—it had the same shape hemispherical combustion chambers that would make the later version so effective on street, strip, and race track. With hindsight, it sounds exciting, a 180 hp prototypical Hemi, right there as US manufacturers were just starting to latch on to overhead valve V8s. Except that the big Chrysler saloons of the early fifties weren't exciting at all.

The Saratoga, where the first-generation Hemi found a home, was heavy enough to severely blunt the effectiveness of that 180 hp, while all Chrysler sedans were dull and conservative and their styling hardly altered through the early years of the decade. The move from a split to a full-width windscreen was about as radical as things got, and sales reflected Chrysler's moribund image. However, this was about to change.

Every manufacturer has at least one milestone car, something that didn't just change the fortunes of its maker, but created a new type of market, even persuaded people to look at cars in a different way. In the muscle car story, there are three such cars: the Pontiac GTO, the Ford Mustang, and one that predated them both by nearly

a decade—the Chrysler 300. Today, the big 300 isn't often thought of as a classic muscle car, not in the definitive 1960s sense. But it helped pave the way for the GTOs, Challengers, and Galaxie 427s by creating a new type of car—the sports sedan.

In early 1950s North America, family men bought sedans and station wagons. If you wanted performance, and some sporting image, you bought a sports car: a Thunderbird, a Corvette, or a little European job, in ascending order of commitment, enthusiasm, and (sometimes) mechanical ability. The Chrysler C-300, launched in 1955, changed all that. Not only was it stunningly styled by Virgil Exner, and without the excesses that later became associated with the decade, but the 300 sedan was also stunningly fast. Power came from the Firepower V8, now with 300 hp, which was enough for the car to set speed records at over 127 mph. Suitably modified, it was a race winner in NASCAR. But it could still seat six adults in comfort, and had the "100 Million Dollar Look." Power and style were its not-so-secret ingredients. The 332 ci Firepower V8 was not a cheap or easy engine to make, but its hemispherical combustion chambers allowed for deep

300G 2-door hardtop 1961

Engine: *375 hp 413 ci V8; 495 lb ft*

Transmission: *three-speed automatic (TorqueFlite)*

Steering: *recirculating ball, power assisted*

Tires: *Goodyear Blue Streak Super Sport 8.00 x 15*

Brakes: *front and rear drums, power assisted*

Suspension: *front independent, torsion bars; rear rigid axle, semi-elliptic leaf springs*

Wheelbase: *108 inches*

Height: *not known*

Weight: *3,250 pounds*

Above: A combination of power, style, and performance gave the Chrysler 300 unique appeal in the 1950s. It was really the first high-performance US-built sedan.

Right: We think this is a 300G, at Watkins Glen, New York, 1961. Was anyone there? Four seats, room to stretch. Chrysler muscle cars always had room for four, and the company never attempted to build a Thunderbird or Corvette equivalent.

breathing and efficient burning. They also gave the space for larger valves and encouraged good swirl and therefore combustion. The trouble was, this meant the inlet and exhaust valves were canted at ninety degrees apart, so operating them was quite a headache. On the Firepower Hemi, Chrysler used two rocker shafts, a forest of pushrods, and different-length rocker arms, which was complex indeed compared to the average Detroit V8.

But the results spoke for themselves. For the C-300, Chrysler added twin four-barrel carburetors, a full-race camshaft, and 8.5:1 compression ratio, which added up to 300 hp at 5,200 rpm. That made the C-300 one of the most powerful cars on the market, a status underlined when Tim Flock drove one to victory at Daytona in 1955. At the classic oval that year were four big sensations, according to a well-known journalist for *Mechanix Illustrated*, Tom McCahill: the 1955 Chevy V8, the Ford Thunderbird, Jaguar D-Type, and Chrysler C-300.

The straight-line performance was backed up by stiffer springs and heavy-duty shock absorbers, though, oddly, the C-300 stuck with drum brakes all around, despite the fact that Chrysler already fitted discs to the Imperial. It was a strange omission for such a fast, heavy car, though Chrysler evidently thought that drums were sufficient. They did have power assistance, though.

Below: The closer you look, the more serious the interior of this Plymouth Savoy looks. Three-spoke steering wheel, bucket seats, and add-on tachometer are all period pieces, but the roll-cage and helmet hint at something else.

BELOW: *In the early sixties, Plymouth sales weren't all they should have been, but the name got a substantial image boost when the the big-block Max Wedge V8 was announced in August '62. It would turn cars like the Savoy into formidable dragsters and stock car racers.*

Automatic transmission was standard, though the PowerFlite unit was strengthened to cope with the extra horses. Chrysler engineers also modified it with a higher stall speed, to cut acceleration times, so that the 300 could reach 60 mph in around 10 seconds. For a 1955 sedan, even one so special, that was quick.

So the new 300 series was fast; but its styling would cause a stir as well. Chrysler had traditionally been led by engineering, encouraged by company president K. T. Keller. Keller had retired, and the boss, Lester L. "Tex" Colbert, put a new emphasis on styling. He ditched the aging six-cylinder power units and gave Chrysler's styling department its head. They called it "Forward Look," and for the C-300 it evolved from a long line of concept cars built by Ghia of Italy, though styled by Virgil Exner.

ABOVE: The original 413 ci Max Wedge produced just over 400 hp, but in '63, new NHRA and NASCAR rules permitted up to 427 ci. Within months, Plymouth was offering a 426 ci Max Wedge in 400 hp, 415 hp, and 425 hp versions.

Exner had designed pure two-seaters for the Ghia line, but producing this would have cost too much time and money. Instead, the C-300 took elements from existing Chryslers. Virgil Exner started with the New Yorker two-door hardtop, added rear quarters from the Imperial, and a front grille from the big Imperial. It had impact, but at the same time was relatively restrained, with minimal chrome work and modest tailfins. It also came in a choice of only three single colors, at a time when duotone seemed almost compulsory for US cars. The C-300 customer could choose from plain black, white, or red.

It was less understated on the inside, though. You couldn't have air-conditioning

on the C-300, another odd omission, but a tan leather interior was standard. Options included power steering, power windows, a radio, heater, tinted glass, and even four-way power adjustment for the front bench seat. For those committed to owning a truly distinctive car (and with a sufficiently well-padded wallet) Kelsey-Hayes wire wheels were on offer at a cool $600 a set. In fact, the C-300 was one expensive automobile, costing about twice as much as the average Ford, which is one reason why only 1,725 were built. A long-running dynasty of Chrysler "Letter Cars" was founded by the C-300, but they all remained exclusive—the most prolific of them sold a mere 3,600 in a year.

Hemi-powered 300s followed one another through the late 1950s, until 1959, when the sheer cost of this engine moved Chrysler to drop it in favor of the "Golden Lion" V8, later known as the Max Wedge. Some may have been disappointed to see the unique Hemi disappear, but in truth, the Max Wedge was just as potent, though it relied on sheer cubic inches for its muscle, rather than a complex and clever cylinder-head design.

By 1960, the 300F Letter Car followed the same concept as the original. It was still an exclusive, luxurious, two-door hardtop of fearsome performance, though the styling was less pure than Virgil Exner's original.

Power was still central to the whole experience, and the 300F delivered, with the 413 ci Max Wedge offering 375 hp in standard form, not to mention 495 lb ft at 2,800 rpm. There was a high-lift camshaft, heavy-duty valve springs, low-restriction exhaust system, and air cleaners, a dual-point distributor, and twin four-barrel carburetors. It also had 30-inch intake stacks, which were crisscrossed over each other to squeeze into the engine bay. These boosted performance at low revs, but worked less well over

RIGHT: Only 2,130 Plymouths and Dodges were fitted with a Max Wedge in 1963, but their impact outweighed their numbers, bringing a new dominance to both the drag strip and stock car track.

ABOVE: The Max Wedge wasn't especially innovative, but it used conventional tuning methods to great effect. Sheer cubic capacity was combined with a high 11.0:1 compression (13.5:1 on the ultimate version), single or dual four-barrel carburetors, and a cross-ram intake. In top form, that produced 425 hp at 5,600 rpm and 480 lb ft at 4,400 rpm.

4,000 rpm. So Chrysler also offered a short ram version, by shortening the inner walls of the manifold to create 15-inch rams. The result cost $800 extra (which included a four-speed manual transmission), and delivered 400 hp. And at high revs, the short rams worked. At Daytona in 1960, Greg Ziegler drove one of these cars to a new Flying Mile record, at 144.9 mph.

The following year, the 300F became 300G, with a new inverted grille and canted vertical headlights, while the rear lights migrated from the tailfins to just above the rear bumper. It retained the 375 hp Max Wedge as standard equipment, with its 400 hp short-ram cousin optional. The latter also had solid lifters, larger carburetors, and longer duration cam. But even with the standard engine, the 300G was a seriously fast car, with the modified TorqueFlite auto transmission helping whisk it up to 60 mph in 8.4 seconds, past the quarter mile in 16.2 seconds and on to three-figure speeds in not much over 21 seconds. Not surprisingly, this latest 300 took the Flying Mile at Daytona again, as well as the NASCAR Standing Mile Championship.

Other 300 selling points hadn't changed. Despite the flashier styling, it still came with a choice of sober single colors: black, white, green, or cinnamon for 1961. And the muscular performance was still backed up with stiffer springs all around (torsion

ABOVE: Savoy driver takes a quick breather between rubber-burning demonstrations. The Max Wedge extended high performance beyond the upmarket Chrysler 300.

bars up front, leaf springs to the rear), larger shock absorbers, and 8.00 x 15 Goodyear Bluestreak tires. The brakes were still power-assisted drums, but the four large units did amount to 215 sq. in. of lining area, and the 15-inch wheels helped to keep them cool. Inside, the options covered things like air-conditioning, a six-way power seat, and remote-control exterior mirrors.

So the 300 was still a fast, luxurious sports sedan. Or, as the maker put it, "Chrysler's championship breed of rare motorcars. A limited-edition automobile, precision built for the connoisseur of careful craftsmanship and superb engineering."

RIGHT: Plymouth Belvedere. It sounds like a dainty, refined sort of car, used for gentle trips to church in the leafier outskirts of Boston. If that was ever true, it all changed in 1965, when the midsize Belvedere took over from the Sport Fury as Plymouth's muscle car of choice, especially with top-line Satellite trim.

ABOVE: *Bucket seats and a center console were part of the new package on a 116-inch wheelbase, along with a wide range of engine choices, from a 230 hp 318 ci, right up to the 425 hp Max Wedge.*

LEFT: *A suitably optioned Belvedere was a match for any GTO or 4-4-2, though in truth the top Max Wedge was a pure competition engine, not suited to everyday driving.*

Car Life magazine put it more succinctly. The 300F, they concluded, was "the best road car on the market."

The best perhaps, but far from the best selling, and just 1,617 300Gs were built in 1961, both two-door hardtops and convertibles. Chrysler thought it had found a way to widen the 300's appeal, by basing the 1962 Letter Car on the smaller (but still pretty substantial) 122-inch wheelbase Newport. There was also a budget version, the Sport 300, with a 383 ci two-barrel V8 in place of the Max Wedge.

The omens looked good, especially from a performance point of view, as the new 300H's smaller platform was about 300 lb. lighter than the previous 300G, while the power of the Max Wedge was actually up slightly, to 380 hp. That resulted in an impressive weight-to-power ratio of just 10.6 lb. per horsepower, enough to rocket the 300H to 60 mph in just 7.7 seconds, and a quarter-mile time of 16 seconds. And if that wasn't enough, you could have even more performance, though Chrysler would only supply it to special order. Boring the 413 cylinder block out by 0.06 in. produced a small but useful boost in cubic inches. Chrysler made the most of this, adding forged

***ABOVE:* Most of the visual clues to muscle car status on this Belvedere are later additions, but look closely, and the original badging gives just a hint of what was under the hood—muscle cars were actually pretty subtle machines in those days!**

ABOVE: With its 12.5:1 compression ratio and 320-degree cam, the Max Wedge wasn't a practical engine for street use, and, in fact, Chrysler insisted that the motor was "not recommended for general driving." The milder 365 hp Street Wedge (10.3:1, single four barrel) was a more practical proposition.

12:1 compression pistons, long duration cam, solid lifters, bigger exhaust valves, streamlined exhaust headers, and that short ram induction. With 421 hp at 5,400 rpm, there's no doubt that a 300H thus equipped was a muscle car of the first order.

In keeping with the trends of the early sixties, the H lost the tailfins of earlier Letter Cars, though it retained the distinctive inverted grille and canted vertical lights. But this new-generation Letter Car was no less luxurious than its predecessors, with a tan leather interior, including four bucket seats. The push-button TorqueFlite was still standard. Best of all, it was several hundred dollars cheaper than the 300G, at $5,040 for the hardtop. But the buyers didn't like it. Was the 300H too small to be taken seriously as a Letter Car, too closely associated with the cheaper Newport? Whatever the reason, Chrysler sold only 435 hardtops that year, and 123 convertibles, making this one of the rarest Letter Cars of all.

But the 300J of the following year was rarer still, just 400 being built. Like the 300, this shared much of its styling with cheaper Chryslers, though the J continued the Letter Car tradition. It was a fast, exclusive, two-door sedan with the emphasis on elegance and luxury. Chrysler would probably rather forget the J's square steering wheel, but otherwise it was a subtle performance car, a fact underlined by the color

BELOW: *Dashtop dials (these are much later additions to a Plymouth Savoy) became something of an early muscle car trademark, with their standard speedo and two supplementaries. Tachometers were also mounted atop the steering column or even outside, on the hood.*

choice: formal black, alabaster, Madison gray, oyster white, and claret. The standard 413 ci Max Wedge now offered 390 hp at 4,800 rpm, and 485 lb ft at 3,600 rpm. There was no 400 hp option that year, but it wasn't really needed either. The standard motor included solid lifters, a 10.0:1 compression ratio, twin four-barrel carburetors, and the cross-ram intake manifold. Heavier than the 300H, despite being based on the same 122-inch wheelbase (it weighed over 4,400 lb.), the J wasn't quite as fast to 60 mph, at 8 seconds as tested by *Motor Trend* magazine in April 1963. But it would still cross the quarter mile in 15.8 seconds, and given a long enough straight it could reach top speed of 142 mph. Crossing continents at high speed was a Letter Car forte.

But even Letter Car customers were sensitive to price, and the 300K of 1964, cheapest of the sixties Letter Cars, was also the best selling. To save money, the 413 was de-rated to 360 hp (although the full 390 hp V8 was still available at $375 extra) and the convertible returned to the lineup. But the biggest news was that the two-door hardtop now cost just $4,056, the convertible about $500 more. Over 3,000 hardtops and 600 convertibles were sold, making this the best-selling Letter Car of all.

The extra sales were worth having, but the Letter Car was reaching the end of its life. In the mid-sixties it was still one of the fastest cars on the market, but if performance was your priority, there were far cheaper alternatives. Even the 300K cost over $1,000 more than the hot new Pontiac GTO.

The 1965 300L was the last of the Letter Cars, with the 390 hp Max Wedge standard again, though weight had crept up to nearly 4,700 lb., so the L took 8.8 seconds to reach 60 mph. A Chevrolet Caprice (with a "mere" 325 hp) was actually faster over the quarter mile. But the Letter Cars still hold a special place in muscle car history. Indeed, some people maintain that the original 1955 300, and not the 1964 Pontiac GTO, was the first true muscle car.

The Letter Cars might be gone, but the Chrysler 300 badge lived on in a lesser breed of cars. In 1970, tuner George Hurst sought to transform the latest of these into a modern interpretation of the original. He added a TNT V8 of 375 hp, plus heavy-duty suspension, power front disc brakes, and H60-15 tires. The color scheme, plain white with subtle gold highlights, would have done a Letter Car proud, and transmission was by TorqueFlite. Several hundred were built, and with a 0–60 mph time of 7.1 seconds, the Chrysler Hurst 300 performed like the original as well.

Hemi's Second Coming

The Max Wedge had served Chrysler well. As well as powering the Letter Cars, it proved a formidable competitor on the drag strip, powering both the Dodge Ramcharger and Plymouth Super Stock. Officially, higher-tuned versions of the Max Wedge were intended for "police pursuit work" but Chrysler might as well have changed that to "smoking Ford over the quarter mile," General Motors having pulled out of racing involvement.

The 413 ci Max Wedge responded well to tuning, and typical drag-strip (sorry, police pursuit) tune involved an 11.0:1 compression ratio, twin four-barrel carburetors, and an aluminum short-ram intake manifold. If that wasn't enough, a

Above: Later Belvedere fastback, though without the sporty bits and pieces that marked out the GTX; with a Max Wedge fitted, it was faster than any GTO.

13.5:1 compression version offered 420 hp. By 1963, the Max Wedge had been enlarged to 426 ci, which produced 425 hp in high-compression form.

But this engine was nearing the end of its development. It had always been highly tuned, and there simply wasn't a lot more that could be done for it in the endless quest for more power. It's important to note that drag racing was the main push here. In road form, the Max Wedge offered 380 hp in the later Letter Cars, so it was still one

BELOW: With the GTX, Plymouth finally woke up to the fact that muscle car buyers wanted a bit of show as well as go—scoops, stripes, and bucket seats obliged.

of the most powerful street V8s on the market. Chrysler didn't need yet more power for its showroom cars, but the drag strip was a different matter.

Work began on a new engine in 1962, when management asked Chrysler engineers to design a V8 that would be suitable for oval tracks (i.e., NASCAR) as well as drag racing. So from the start, this new unit was intended primarily as a competition engine, and, of course, it was designed with that in mind. With hindsight,

the route taken by those engineers was obvious. The original Hemi V8, with its efficiency and deep breathing, had been dropped only three years previously, and its impressive performance in the 300 would be a very recent memory for Chrysler's engineering department. Meanwhile, the Max Wedge had shown what a combination of cubic inches and traditional tuning techniques could do. So why not combine the two? Exploit the efficiency of hemispherical combustion chambers with lots of cubic inches and radical tuning. The classic Chrysler Hemi was born.

The arguments in favor of a Hemi head were just as strong in the early sixties as they had been more than ten years earlier, when the original Hemi was just starting out. A hemispherical combustion chamber provides the maximum volume to surface area, and a bigger chamber, of course, allows more fuel/air mixture to be crammed in for burning.

More room also means more space for bigger valves. With the valves canted at ninety degrees, not only can the intake charge flow straight in through the intake valve and out through the exhaust, but there is space to mount the spark plug centrally, thus ensuring a more complete burn.

BELOW: The GTX wasn't just a cosmetic muscle car, with a base power unit of 440 ci and 375 hp. Paying an extra $564 obtained the Street Hemi, with a claimed 425 hp, though even the 440 Super Commando could turn in a 0–60 mph time of less than 7 seconds.

> *"They don't call it King Kong for nothing."*

So despite its greater cost, the Hemi design was the obvious choice for a race engine, where power was paramount. Although it was based on the same principles as the Firepower Hemi of the fifties, and shared its cubic inches with the final Max Wedge, the new-generation Hemi was all new. Designed as a pure racing engine, it came with a 12.5:1 compression ratio and double-roller timing chain. The cylinder block was designed for strength, with cross-bolted main bearings, while the Hemi used the same short cross-ram induction that had proved so effective in the Max Wedge.

A single four-barrel carburetor was used in NASCAR specification, but for drag racing twin four-barrels were fitted, in which form the new V8 was officially rated at 425 hp. In fact, that figure became a sort of mantra, chanted out as the standard Hemi power figure.

Chrysler engineer Tom Hoover, however, once said that this was sandbagging, and that even the street Hemi's true power was more like 500 hp at 6,000 rpm. Not that the top tune was compulsory.

BELOW: Proud owner, classic muscle car. The Belvedere GTX was one of the better intermediate muscle cars, but it had only been on the market a year when the Road Runner came along and stole its thunder. The slightly more upmarket GTX never really recovered.

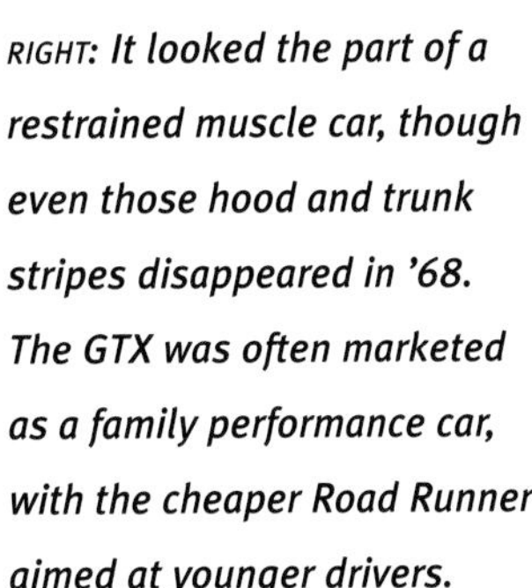

RIGHT: It looked the part of a restrained muscle car, though even those hood and trunk stripes disappeared in '68. The GTX was often marketed as a family performance car, with the cheaper Road Runner aimed at younger drivers.

Alongside the 12.5:1 compression version, Chrysler offered an 11.0:1 version, with a claimed 415 hp. Whatever the true figures, they were enough to impress where it counted. Soon after the Hemi's public unveiling in 1964, it took the first three places at the Daytona 500. As for drag racing, the Hemi just missed the 1964 NHRA Winternationals, but fitted to Chrysler's lightest two-door sedans, the Plymouth Savoy and Dodge 330, it was soon smoking the opposition on quarter miles across the country.

Of course, these Hemis were factory specials, and though the Hemi-powered A990 Plymouth Belvedere and Dodge Coronet were on sale to the public in 1965,

LEFT: Plymouth persevered with the GTX badge, offering it through a couple of Belvedere restyles right up to '71, still with the Super Commando and Hemi V8s.

these were aimed specifically at drag racers, with every possible effort made to shave weight. There was thinner-than-standard sheet metal and acrylic side and rear windows, while all unnecessary interior trim was stripped out. The A990s, with the best will in the world, were not road cars. For drag racing, this wasn't a great problem, but to qualify for NASCAR, Chrysler found that it had to offer street-legal Hemis to the general public, straight off the assembly line.

So that's what they did.

The Hemi was, of course, detuned for its new road role. The lightweight but costly aluminum heads were dropped in favor of cheap and durable cast-iron versions. The trick cross-ram manifold was replaced by a more conventional aluminum item and cast-iron exhaust manifolds replaced the tubular headers. There were still twin four-barrel carburetors—Carter AFBs—but a choke was added for cold starts, along with a manifold heater. To allow the street Hemi to run on premium gas, the compression ratio was dropped to 10.25:1. The official power rating was still 425 hp at 5,000 rpm, but when Tom Hoover talked

BELOW: This vinyl roof hardtop was the most popular body style, but there was a convertible GTX as well, until 1970, when the ragtop was dropped. In '69 it cost a reasonable $260 extra.

ABOVE: Early muscle car interiors (even on better-equipped cars such as the GTX) look sparse by the standards of today, or even those of the late sixties, but those three big-ticket items are all there: floor shifter, bucket seats, and sporty steering wheel. A center console was an increasingly popular addition.

about 500 hp, he was actually referring to this street Hemi, lower compression, cast-iron heads, and all.

When it finally hit the road for 1966, the Hemi was surely the most powerful road engine on the market.

About 11,000 of them were fitted to road-going Dodges and Plymouths up to 1971, a tiny figure in Detroit production terms, but enough to qualify the engine for NASCAR. In practice, most private owners, especially those who weren't contemplating weekend drag racing, found the Hemi option too expensive and specialized to actually buy, and it was always a tiny fraction of production compared to the less fearsome, but of course easier to drive, 383s and 440s.

Still, who cares about the skewed economics? Only the accountants. The Hemi remains the most significant muscle car engine of all time.

> *"GTX. Plymouth's exciting new Supercar. King of the Belvederes. Standard equipment: the biggest GT engine in the world. Our Super Commando 440 V8. Optional equipment: the famous Plymouth Hemi."*

LEFT: *Adding a fastback roofline to the boxy Coronet transformed its appearance, and the Dodge Charger was born. It started out as a last-minute show car, never intended for production.*

DODGE: CHARGING AHEAD

Dodge, along with just about everyone else, was caught out by the Ford Mustang and the Pontiac GTO. Actually, the GTO was less of a problem, because Dodge had access to plenty of meaty Chrysler V8s (of which the Hemi was just one, albeit the strongest) that could easily match its performance. Matching the Mustang would take more effort.

The obvious route (probably the quickest and easiest as well) would be to build something based on the Plymouth Barracuda, and, in fact, Dodge had been invited to share the Barracuda platform to build a joint Chrysler-Mustang competitor. But they decided to go their own way—the Dodge "Mustang," they decided, would have to be distinctively Dodge.

Product planner Burt Bouwkamp and stylist William Brownlie were the men behind this policy, reasoning that the way to build a muscle car was to base it on the bigger Coronet sedan. Everyone agreed that the Barracuda was a pleasant, pretty coupe, but even with its top power option, the 273 ci "Commando" V8, it didn't really have the muscle to compete. The Coronet, on the other hand, had the space to fit far bigger V8s, the Hemi included.

"The hot new car of the Dodge rebellion"

There was just one problem. The Coronet was a plain and boxy sedan that would be unlikely to set pulses

racing, whatever was under the hood and however it was dressed up with red stripes and air scoops. But what about a Coronet-based fastback? The Barracuda had succeeded in transforming the Valiant sedan, after all.

Actually, the Coronet fastback came about as much out of necessity as of any carefully thought out strategy. In 1965, Burt Bouwkamp found Dodge had nothing new or interesting to display at one of the summer auto shows, and asked William Brownlie to come up with something. And what he came up with was a fastback roof on the existing Coronet body shell. (Actually, one source credits Elwood Engle, an ex-Ford designer, for the '66 Charger, and Brownlie with the '68.)

Named the "Charger II" (Dodge had used the name on a show car once already), the new fastback was readied for the show in double-quick time. Normally, show cars like this exist purely to generate "traffic," that is, to attract people to the stand so that they can take a closer look at cars they can actually buy. But the Charger met with

BELOW: Hidden headlights were one of the Charger's key styling features, and gave the car a striking, even sinister, look from the front end. Switching the lights on caused them to rotate into view, though there was an override in case the system iced up.

such an enthusiastic reception that it was decided to slip it into production as soon as possible. Show cars inevitably have some way-out features that are really intended as attention getters and talking points, and the Charger was no exception. However, some of them make it to the showroom.

The dramatic fastback shape, of course, went unchanged, as did the full-width taillights and sharp-edged rear fenders. But the Charger's most radical feature was its front grille. There were no headlights on view at all, just a full-width grille consisting of fine vertical lines. The headlights were actually hidden (a sixties vogue shared with some Camaros and Firebirds), and switching them on made them rotate into view. There was also an override switch, allowing the lights to remain exposed without being turned on, a sensible precaution in case the rotating mechanism froze up in cold weather.

Inside, the production Charger stuck with Brownlie's original vision, with four large, round dials housing a complete set of instruments—many early muscle cars came with just a speedometer and fuel gauge, and you had to pay extra for more information. Nor was this a stripped-out muscle car. There were deep carpets, well-padded bucket seats, and a steering wheel with a fake wood rim. The rear seat even

LEFT: A rare beast, this '66 Hemi-powered Charger—in that year, just over 1 percent of new Charger owners had opted for this ultimate muscle car motor. More popular was the proven big-block 383, which with 325 hp and 481 lb ft was still hefty enough to shoot a Charger through the quarter mile in 15.6 seconds.

RIGHT: Chrysler might not be willing to warranty the full-race Hemi, but a few hundred Charger buyers did pay the extra $500 for the privilege. Most of them would have been bound for the drag strip (a Hemi was nigh-on unbeatable) at the time, but they made up a tiny percentage of total Charger sales.

folded flat to maximize luggage space, though like its Barracuda cousin offering the same feature, the Charger had no tailgate to make the most of that space.

Enginewise, the show car actually came with Dodge's mild 318 ci V8, but most of the production cars were ordered with the more muscular 383, which gave a GTO-rivaling 325 hp. That was enough to shoot the Charger from 0–60 mph in 8 seconds, and over the quarter mile in 16. Top speed was around 120 mph. So that qualified it for muscle car status, but, of course, 1966 was also the year when the Hemi made it into Dodge and Plymouth showrooms. And it was an option on the Charger.

Not that Dodge seemed that keen on the public buying a Hemi Charger to actually drive on the road. There was no factory warranty, and under the hood was a bright yellow sticker that made it absolutely clear where Dodge (and its customer) stood: "This car," it stated, "is fitted with a 426 cu in engine (and other special equipment). This car is intended for supervised acceleration trials and is not intended for highway or general passenger car use. Accordingly, THIS VEHICLE IS SOLD 'AS IS,' and the warranty coverage does not apply." Phew.

But here history becomes confused. Some sources say that the Hemi did come with a warranty, but that it was of a shorter 12-month, 12,000-mile duration, and would be invalidated if the owner made any driveline modifications, or indulged in "extreme operation." In other words, if he fitted a lower rear axle and went drag racing on weekends! Given the Hemi's well-known reputation for domination of the drag strip, this was a sensible precaution on Dodge's part. The Hemi was actually a very strong engine, but that get-out clause helped to forestall a queue of blown motors, burned-out clutches, and mangled rear axles outside the local Dodge dealer come Monday morning.

So if that more stringent "as is" stipulation applied, you'd have to be pretty committed (and rich, and not worried about paying for the odd engine blowup yourself) to use a Hemi Dodge as a day-to-day car. But if you did, the reward was driving one of the fastest cars on the road in 1960s North America. Even in road form, the Hemi still came with twin Carter AFB four-barrel carburetors, and, as we've seen, the official 425 hp power figure was thought to be understating the case by quite a margin. Whatever the true figure, it was enough for a 6-second 0–60 mph time in the Charger, with the

BELOW: *If the Hemi or 383 V8s were too much motor, buyers could always opt for the base 318 ci V8 with 230 hp, or the 265 hp 361, both with two-barrel carburetors and a mild state of tune. And the Charger, fake knockoff wheel trims and all, still looked distinctive.*

quarter-mile figure in the 13s. Part of the Hemi package was stiffened-up suspension, a Dana 60 rear axle, and ventilated front disc brakes with four-pot calipers. And when you think of the power, torque, and speed involved, that was just as well. In all, just 468 Hemi Chargers were ordered in 1966, but over 37,000 Chargers of all types, so maybe most buyers put defense of their wallet before the ultimate road experience, not to mention avoiding that threadbare warranty.

But maybe the new Charger was just a bit too show-off for you. There was a strong tradition in American hot rodding (and indeed among tuners all over the world) for the street sleeper. That is, a car that looked meek, mild, and innocuous, but packed a real punch when the throttle was floored. For this, the Dodge Coronet was

ABOVE: There was no denying that the Charger lost out in the practicality stakes compared to the Coronet sedan. Four bucket seats meant that it would only seat four (sedan buyers expected room for five or six), and the fastback shape restricted trunk space. Fold-down rear seats did help a little, though.

perfect. It was plain and straight and square, the sort of car a librarian or bank clerk might drive. (Except for the many librarians and bank clerks who bought Mustangs, Camaros, and so on.) There were four of these midsize Dodges, the Coronet base, Deluxe, 440, and 500, with two or four doors. As it happened, the plain-Jane Coronet had been offered with a Hemi in '65, though this was the full-race version. "Why not drop a Hemi in the new Coronet 500?" boldly asked an advertisement of the time. So they did, but it was purely aimed at drag racers, not for road use.

For '66, the road Hemi came on stream, with its 10.5:1 compression, hydraulic lifters, and relatively mild manners (compared to the race version, that is). It also cost a fairly reasonable $500 extra—many Chrysler customers had to pay more than that for the privilege of owning a Hemi. There were bucket seats, and a choice of 15 exterior colors for the top-of-the-range Coronet 500 that year, but no hints as to whether or not a Hemi lay under the hood. No badges, no stripes, no decals. Ah, but when the oh-so-conservative Coronet driver put his foot down, the car would pick up its skirts and spring to 60 mph in just 6.1 seconds, and on to complete the quarter mile in 14.5 seconds. Handy for bank clerks late for work.

But let's not get too Hemi-fixated, for Dodge was selling hard-running V8s before

that legendary motor reached the road. Back in 1963, the Polara 500 looked an unlikely muscle car, but the figures told a different story. *Motor Trend* tested a convertible Polara that year, fitted with Chrysler's 383 ci V8, for which the company claimed 330 hp. Hemi or no, the long-running 383 was very well thought of, with a very good balance between performance, cost of ownership, and drivability. It was an oversquare engine, with bore and stroke measuring 4.25 x 3.38 inches, and in the Polara, came with 10.0:1 aluminum pistons and a four-barrel Carter carburetor, not to mention the ability to rev up to 5,500 rpm, well beyond its 4,600 rpm power peak. Torque peak was an impressive 425 lb ft at 2,800 rpm, so even with a 3.23:1 rear axle, the Polara was able to turn in some impressive acceleration times. Jim Wright of *Motor Trend* recorded 7.7 seconds 0–60 mph and 15.8 seconds over the quarter mile.

Considering that the Polara was a full-size convertible weighing almost 4,000 lb, these were highly respectable figures. "Barring the all-out drag-strip engines," Wright concluded, "there aren't many that can stay with the 330 hp 383 in acceleration." Even this sub-Hemi option had to be paid for, and once a few extras had been added to Jim Wright's test car (Sure Grip differential, power steering, power brakes, electric windows, radio, heater, tachometer, and seat belts), it came in at $4,265.79. The basic open-top Polara 500 was more than $1,000 cheaper.

Meanwhile, Dodge decided that the Coronet needed a spruce-up. The street sleeper look was all very well, but not many buyers actually wanted that. As the GTO and Mustang had shown, many buyers wanted the world to know that they were the owners of something a bit special. That was partly what made the GTO such a milestone car—not just the 389 ci V8 squeezed under its intermediate hood, but all the

BELOW: Part of the Charger's attraction was its four-dial instrument pack, a feature of the original show car, when most muscle cars made do with a simple speedometer and fuel gauge. By comparison, the fully carpeted, well-equipped Charger was quite special.

stripes, badges, and wheel trims that made sure that everyone on the street knew that as well.

So for 1967, the Dodge Coronet R/T hit the streets, with a few more visual clues as to what it was capable of. There was a Charger-like front grille (though the quad headlights were permanently exposed, not hidden, which must have saved a good few dollars). Nonfunctional hood scoops suggested something special under the hood, and rear fender air vents looked good, but like the hood scoops, these were just for show. There were red R/T badges too. "R/T" stood for "Road and Track," the implication being that after being driven to work and the mall all week, one's hot Coronet was ready to take to the race circuit or drag strip come the weekend. In the case of the Hemi option, that was true.

BELOW: Equipped with a Hemi or even 383, the Charger could give a good account for itself on the drag strip, though lighter, stripped-out cars like the Road Runner had more potential.

Not that the R/T was a cosmetic pretty-up exercise. Stiff suspension and heavy-duty brakes were part of the package as well, backed up by 7.75 x 14 Red Streak tires. But the most convincing evidence that the R/T was intended as a serious muscle car was that its standard power unit wasn't the 383 V8, let alone any lesser power unit, but Chrysler's full-bore Magnum 440, mated to either a four-speed manual transmission or the ever-present TorqueFlite automatic. Measuring 4.32 x 3.75 inches in bore and stroke, the Magnum had a 10:1 compression ratio in R/T tune, plus a single four-barrel carburetor. So it wasn't super-tuned, but its sheer cubic capacity produced a power figure of 375 hp at 4,600 rpm and 480 lb ft at 3,200 rpm.

Motor Trend magazine tested one, and reported a quarter-mile time of 15.4 seconds and 0–60 mph in 7.2 seconds. Fitting racing slicks (which a super-keen owner might do on drag weekends) cut those times to 14.7 and 6.5 seconds respectively. If that didn't seem fast enough, you could also pay around $900 extra for the Hemi option, which was available to special order on the R/T.

Now it gets interesting. Read the official figures, and the Hemi appears to have a 13 percent power advantage (though if Chrysler engineer Tom Hoover was right, the true figure was more like 30 percent) and only a marginal increase in torque, to 490 lb ft. Furthermore (and assuming all these figures are accurate), that peaked at 4,000 rpm, whereas the beefy 440 delivered its peak 480 lb ft at 3,200 rpm. Now let's look at the acceleration figures. Once again, *Motor*

Trend was on the case, but reported a slightly disappointing 6.8 seconds 0–60 and 15.0 seconds over the quarter. On slicks, this was cut to 6.6 and 14.8 seconds respectively. A Hemi-powered R/T was quicker than the standard 440, but was it $900 quicker? The peakier torque figure meant that its power advantage would only really show up at higher speeds, but then, that's exactly what it was designed for, whereas the Magnum was a road-going engine, pure and simple. Whatever, its advantage on the road, with speed limits, wet tarmac, and lots of other traffic, was marginal to say the least, and if one wasn't planning on weekend racing, then the Hemi option was a pure indulgence. R/T customers certainly seemed to think so, and of the 10,000-odd who bought the cars in 1967, around 1 percent paid extra for the Hemi.

Oddly, the ostensibly more-sporting Charger, with its fastback styling, and now into its second year, offered lower-powered V8s than the R/T. The base engine for 1967 was still the 318 ci unit of 230 hp, offering 0–60 mph in 10.9 seconds. For $119.55 extra, buyers could opt for the nicely balanced 383 V8, cutting the 60 mph time down to 8.9 seconds, and the quarter mile from 18.6 to 16.5 seconds. Still got money to spare? Then $313.60 bought the Magnum 440, the same 375 hp unit that did such a good job in the R/T: expect 0–60 in 8 seconds, and to cover the quarter in 15.5. And this wouldn't be a Mopar muscle car without the Hemi option, though the price was in a different league from the others, at $877.55. With that under the hood, the fastest charging (and highest charging, as someone no doubt said at the time) Charger sprinted to 60 mph in 7.6 seconds, and over the quarter in 14.4 seconds. Just to summarize the neat performance steps of these four options, their quarter-mile terminal speeds were: 76, 86, 93, and 100 mph! Despite the wide range of engines on offer, Dodge sold far fewer Chargers in 1967 than the previous year, less than 16,000. Of these, a mere 118 had the Hemi option.

"What's striped for action, built for comfort and has a lot of dash?" went the full-color advertisement for the '68 Dodge Charger. "Charger R/T . . . the only car that looks as good as it goes." Well, the latest Charger

BELOW: This svelte fastback was a good looker, but just like the smaller Barracuda, was obviously a sedan conversion; for a true Mustang rival, Mopar fans would have to wait a little longer.

BELOW AND LEFT: An evocative name, and this Charger was just the first in a long line of Dodge coupes. With one of the milder V8s on board, it was also relatively affordable.

> *"What's striped for action, built for comfort and has a lot of dash? Charger R/T—the only car that looks as good as it goes."*

did have tail-end wraparound stripes, plush bucket seats, and a full complement of instruments on the dashboard. And it arguably looked better than the '67, too, as Dodge completely restyled it, neatly incorporating the "Coke bottle" flank that was so popular in the late sixties. The R/T version was new, seeking to use the formula that had worked successfully on the Coronet the previous year. Mag wheels, wide red-stripe tires, and that rear end bumblebee stripe were all part of the deal, as well as upgraded suspension and brakes and those essential R/T badges. And despite the restyle, the Charger retained its trademark hidden-lights grille.

The basic power unit was the 440 Magnum, unchanged from the previous year, and emphasizing that Dodge wanted to keep the R/T as a genuine performance option, not just a cosmetic job. According to Dodge's own figures, that made it a whole second and a half quicker to 60 mph than the '67 Charger with the same motor. Surely those R/T badges weren't that potent? Oh, and half a second quicker over the quarter mile, though with the same 93 mph terminal speed.

As ever, there were plenty of options, which included front disc brakes and even power assistance for the stoppers—one might have thought that a car of this weight and horsepower deserved something more than unassisted drums all around. If you specified the discs, they did a good job. *Road Test* magazine tested six muscle cars in

LEFT: Another famous name. "R/T" stood for "Road/Track" and became the hallmark of Dodge muscle cars from the late sixties on. Coronet, Charger, and the later Challenger all wore it.

ABOVE: The Charger retained its distinctive hidden-headlight grille after the 1968 restyle, and kept it right into the early seventies. Look closely, and you can see the gap between real and fake grilles.

June 1967, and found a disc brake–equipped Dodge R/T (not a Charger, but to the same specification) to be the best stopper of them all, though even this was experiencing fade after the third and fourth hard stop. The car with the worst brakes, a Chevy SS396, came to rest another forty-two car lengths down the road!

In fact, brakes were a source of concern with many early muscle cars, since horsepower had progressed far faster than stiffer suspension and stronger brakes. And while these underpinnings were often on the options lists by 1967–68, they weren't yet standard. Just to put things in perspective, *Road Test* took a Rover 2000TC along to those brake tests. This was a yardstick as a decent European sports sedan, with power-

RIGHT: For 1968, the Charger was thoroughly restyled, with a new body incorporating the then-popular "Coke bottle" flank and mildly tunneled rear window. It was a smoother look than the first boxy Charger, though the wheelbase was unchanged at 117 inches.

RIGHT: A Dodge Charger featured in the Steve McQueen film Bullitt, *though it was the bad guys' choice. McQueen, as surely everyone remembers, drove a fastback Mustang. Could he have outrun a Hemi-equipped Charger? Unlikely.*

assisted discs all round. Needless to say, it stopped far, far more quickly than any of the muscle cars, even those with the optional front discs in place. Still, by the standards of the time, the Dodge R/T wasn't too bad, and the company must have been pleased to read that its car also proved the best handling of the nine For the record, the other eight were the Chevy SS, Buick GS 400, Mercury Cyclone GT, Ford GTA, Oldsmobile 4-4-2, Plymouth GTX (closely related to the Dodge), Pontiac GTO, and AMC Rambler Rebel.

Meanwhile, the Coronet was restyled for 1968 as well, and that included the sporty R/T. It now looked quite different from the sober-sides three-box sedan that started life in the mid-sixties, with a wider, lower look. Mechanically, little had changed under the new bodywork. There was still a comprehensive list of equipment as part of the R/T package, including bucket seats, dual exhausts, stiffened suspension, and heavy-duty brakes, though the hood gained a pretend power bulge, and those fake air vents on the rear fenders were still there. The bumblebee stripes on the tail, a new feature the previous year, were still in evidence, and they would become a Dodge

"Join the fun . . . catch Dodge fever."

Above: There was a whole range of Chargers from '68, of which the new R/T was the most muscle orientated, and the only one that could be specified with a Hemi, which cost an extra $600. More popular was the 440 ci Magnum V8, which came with a 10:1 compression ratio and single four-barrel carburetor.

muscle car trademark of the late sixties. If they were a little too subtle, Coronet R/T buyers could also opt for some side stripes at no extra cost.

Motor Trend magazine compared eight state-of-the-art muscle cars that year, and the Coronet came out fairly well. The testers thought it was "easily the best in comfort and room," and also liked its engine and the quality of construction. The 440 V8 was unchanged from '67, but the performance figures had improved for no apparent reason. Its 0–60 mph now came in at 6.9 seconds and the quarter mile in 15.1 seconds, though given the variables (driver, weather conditions, manufacturing tolerances), it was hardly surprising that performance figures for the same model—even the same car—varied from year to year. Some things didn't change, though, and muscle cars were always gas guzzlers. The '68 Coronet R/T varied between 9.6 and 12.1 mpg.

Once again, the Hemi option, at just over $600, didn't have massive appeal, and there were more takers for the more affordable options like front disc brakes ($72.95),

custom wheels ($97.30), limited-slip differential ($42.35), or a center console ($52.85). Air conditioning was another option, but wasn't available with the Hemi.

The year 1968 brought cut-price muscle cars, when manufacturers began to offer muscle performance with a lower level of trim . . . and a lower price. Plymouth's Road Runner was arguably the car that kicked this off, and of course Dodge had to have an equivalent, the Super Bee. For little more than $3,000, the Super Bee was based on the Coronet 440 two-door sedan, and came with the 383 V8 as standard, along with a heavy-duty four-speed manual transmission and Hurst "Competition-Plus" floor shifter. Despite the budget price, a lot of the key muscle car cues were there, notably dual exhausts, heavy-duty suspension, and F40 x 14 tires. There was a bench front seat instead of individual buckets, and the rear windows swung out rather than wound down, but the Super Bee wasn't quite as stripped out as its Road Runner cousin, with door-to-door carpeting, vinyl door panels, and a Charger-style instrument set (though a tachometer cost extra).

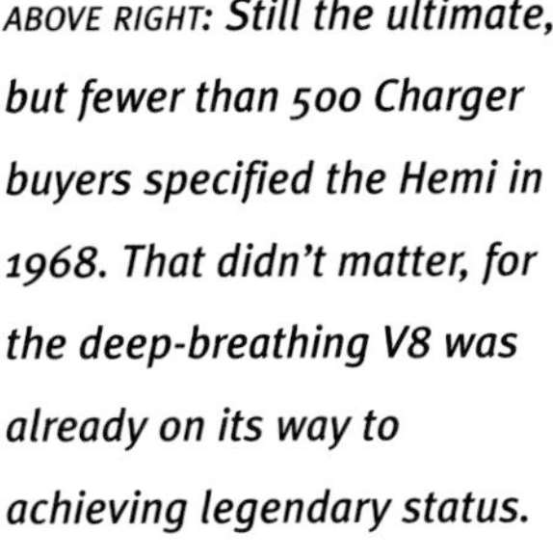

ABOVE RIGHT: ***Still the ultimate, but fewer than 500 Charger buyers specified the Hemi in 1968. That didn't matter, for the deep-breathing V8 was already on its way to achieving legendary status.***

The Coronet and Charger were intermediate cars, but Dodge didn't have a compact muscle car until the Dodge Dart GTS, for GTSport, which was basically the smaller Dart with many of the same go-faster goodies as the R/Ts. And it followed the classic muscle ploy of squeezing a biggish V8 into a smallish car. "When you buy a compact, you get a compact engine, right?" asked the advertisement. "Wrong! Not since Dart GTS. This is a new breed that boasts a 340-cube, 4-barrel V8. That's

BELOW: Lone Star State setting for a '68 Charger R/T, and there's something undeniably Texan about the Charger R/T, a car built for wide open spaces.

standard. There's also an optional 383 4-barrel. Doesn't sound like a kiddy-car, does it? It doesn't look or ride like one either. Bumblebee stripes in back, new air scoop hood design, wide-treads, and a Rallye Suspension that includes heavy-duty shocks, sway bar, and heavy-duty rear springs. And from its roomy bucket-seated interior, it handles beautifully. That's Dart GTS. Why not check your Dodge dealer for details."

The GTS looked to make a lot of sense as a mini-muscle car. Like its Coronet big brother, it wasn't as stripped out as their Plymouth Road Runner cousin (though it wasn't as cheap, either), yet being lighter than the bigger muscle cars, gave excellent performance even from the base 340 ci V8. This was the biggest of the 273/318 ci family of Chrysler V8s, and in GTS form, with a 10.5:1 compression and single four-barrel carburetor, produced 275 hp at 5,000 rpm and 340 lb ft at 3,200. A column-shift three-speed manual transmission was standard, but most owners understandably ordered the optional four-speed with Hurst shifter. There was an automatic, too, the TorqueFlite in competition form.

Another option was the 383 ci big-block V8 with 300 hp, but performance was reportedly so good with the standard 340 that only the keenest drivers need have paid the extra for it. According to *Hot Rod*, the 340 managed a quarter-mile time of 14.38 seconds. Just to underline the GTS's potency, it came with the bumblebee rear end stripe, chrome tips on the dual exhaust, wide wheels, and red stripe tires.

Those bumblebee stripes had become a Dodge muscle car trademark. For 1968, it named the Charger R/T, Coronet R/T, and Dart GTS the "Scat Pack," whose

BELOW: If you couldn't afford a Hemi, 1969 brought a new option, one up on the stock Magnum V8. The "Six Pack" was a set of three two-barrel Holley carburetors atop the 440 Magnum, to replace the single four barrel. Bolted down and ready to go, they helped deliver 390 hp and 490 lb ft. Also available on the Coronet R/T, this offered power not far short of the Hemi itself.

RIGHT: Motor Trend *summed up the look of the late sixties Charger with this observation on the '69 version: "That brute Charger styling, that symbol of masculine virility, was still intact." Not only could journalists write lines like that without a hint of either embarrassment or irony, but the muscle car, too, was in its heyday, with close to 400 hp available to anyone with a medium-sized wallet.*

PEPSI
GOODYEAR
EAGLE GT II

ABOVE: While most eyes were focused on the "masculine" Charger, Dodge still offered hopped-up versions of the Coronet sedan. They weren't quite as eye-catching, but had all the same muscle car credentials. The R/T option brought a Magnum 440 V8 and TorqueFlite transmission.

symbol was a speeding, grinning bumblebee on wheels. *Car Life* magazine decided to test all three of them together: a 340 GTS, 440 Coronet R/T, and Hemi-powered Charger R/T. And guess which came out best? The little Dart. "It was the best handling, most responsive of the trio." Despite having least power, it was actually the quickest over the quarter mile, at 14.68 seconds. That sounds like the 275 hp Dart was defying the laws of physics against a 375 hp Coronet and 425 hp Charger. Except that the compact Dart was a whole 500 lb lighter than the Cornet, and saved 600 lb over the Charger. Plus the Hemi wasn't behaving as it should have.

Car Life's test team also found the Dart plenty big enough for a family of five inside, despite being the smallest car. And its small dimensions also made it the most

ABOVE: *This 440 Coronet carries the standard Magnum, but the Six Pack (a new option for that year) was available, as was the Hemi, at $418, though that remained a specialist option for the serious racers. Of over 7,000 Coronet R/Ts sold in '69, less than a hundred hardtops and just ten convertibles were ordered with a Hemi.*

nimble on twisty going, backed up by neutral, predictable handling: "The Dart permitted all sorts of dumb maneuvers." The disc/drum brakes were rated highly too, and the newest member of Dodge's Scat Pack came out with high marks.

The Coronet convertible didn't start off so well, with a gap between the roof and top of the window glass that let in a lot of rain. They also thought that the body rigidity of this open-top car wasn't all it should have been (although it was still better than some), and weak shock absorbers made it feel softer and more inclined to roll when pressing on through twisty roads. But they loved the 440 V8 ("a *Car Life* favorite") with its lazy, torquey, big-cube feel. It gave fast, effortless acceleration that wasn't far behind that of the Dart, and weighing 150 lb less than the Hemi, the 440 Magnum also gave better weight distribution.

By all normal standards, the Hemi-powered Charger should have walked away with the acceleration honors in this test, but it didn't. It was OK at low speeds and throttle openings, but flooring the loud pedal had it missing and popping "like a Honda that just ate its valves," as the writer colorfully put it. The Hemi was sent back to a Dodge dealer, who cured the full-power problem, only to find that low-speed running had worsened. And even after that, the Hemi couldn't break the 15-second barrier over the quarter mile. A Plymouth Hemi tested by the magazine a few months earlier had zipped through in 13.9 seconds.

Unfortunately, the magazine suggested that this rough-running, poorly performing Hemi wasn't a one-off. "The Hemi is America's most powerful standard engine," they concluded, "but that's only true when it's properly tuned." Many Dodge and Plymouth dealers weren't up to the job, they went on. Consequently many Hemi owners had to put up with poor low-speed or high-speed running, or both. A bitter pill to swallow if you'd paid good money for the most expensive engine option, one that had a superb reputation as the most powerful on the market, but that didn't seem to deliver in practice. Otherwise, *Car Life* liked the Charger, a roomy coupe big enough to carry six adults and with tough, muscular styling.

"It speaks softly, but carries a big kick. Dodge Coronet R/T. Just about the hottest thing going since the cast-iron stove. Witness these credentials: a rampaging 440-cubic-inch Magnum V8 that deals out 375 bhp and 480 lb ft of torque, 4-barrel carb . . . long duration cam . . . chrome engine dress-up . . . low-restriction dual exhaust . . . heavy-duty brakes and suspension . . . high-performance Red Streak tires . . . special air scoop design . . . Check out R/T at your nearby Dodge dealers now."

That styling was even more svelte for 1969, once Chrysler engineers had applied some wind tunnel aerodynamics to the Charger. The changes were subtle, but making the Charger's tunneled-in rear window flush with the fastback, and moving the front grille forward so that it too was flush with the bodywork, cleaned up the Charger's airflow considerably, while the quad headlights were exposed, not hidden by a false grille.

So why this sudden interest in the intricacies of aerodynamics? Had Chrysler decided it was time to improve the highway fuel efficiency of the Charger? The answer, of course, is no. Slipping through the air efficiently was becoming increasingly important in NASCAR as speeds grew ever higher, so manufacturers were constantly seeking ways to improve the aerodynamics of their race cars. But to qualify for NASCAR, any modifications had to be replicated at least 500 times on the production line, so Dodge had to

built at least 500 examples of the new, more slippery Charger. The actual changes were carried out by Creative Industries of Detroit, so they were too expensive to apply to the 20,000-odd Charger R/Ts that rolled off the assembly lines in 1969. So Dodge had just 500 made, and that was the 1969 Dodge Charger 500, with the same options as the standard R/T.

ABOVE: "Speaks softly, but carries a big kick." Dodge sold the Coronet R/T on its mild-mannered looks, Charger R/T performance without the show-off roofline and grille.

BELOW: Exposed headlights show this is a Coronet R/T, not a Charger, though the blacked-out grille confirms that it's far from the stock Coronet sedan.

As for the Charger R/T itself, that was barely changed for 1969, though one new option was the SE (Special Edition) interior, which featured leather bucket seats, extra lighting, and wood-grain trim. As ever, the 440 Magnum was the most popular engine, with only a minority of buyers going for the Hemi option.

The Coronet R/T also got a new option for '69, one aimed at serious

performance freaks, maybe those who aspired to a Hemi but couldn't quite afford one. The standard power unit remained the 375 hp 440 Magnum with single four-barrel carburetor, but buyers could pay extra for a "Six Pack." That is, a triple two-barrel carb setup, which boosted the Magnum's output to 390 hp and 490 lb ft, and came with a fiberglass hood to cover them. Also optional was a Ramcharger air-induction

BELOW LEFT: ***A bluff front end for the R/T Coronet, which didn't go in for any of the wind-cheating tricks of the Winged Warrior Chryslers. In fact, without any fancy body parts at all, the Coronet looked more like a muscle car from the early sixties than from '69.***

BELOW: ***Young men might lust after the unattainable Hemi (cost, tricky insurance, and a flimsy warranty put most of them off), but the plain fact was that a 440 Magnum wasn't far behind in sheer get-up-and-go, and was much cheaper.***

LEFT: Super Bee, trademark of the Dodge Scat Pack of the late sixties. Not only did it create the image of an eager, high-speed, buzzing performance machine, but that bumblebee stripe clinging to the trunk implied the car was moving so fast it almost left its stripes behind!

RIGHT: The idea behind the Coronet Super Bee was to provide a cheaper alternative to the 440 Magnum-powered R/T, and at $3,138 for the two-door hardtop, it was over $300 cheaper. It was a successful formula, and Dodge sold nearly 28,000 of them in '69.

system. Standard on the Hemi-powered Coronets, this fed cold air in from two hood scoops to a fiberglass plenum bolted to the underside of the hood. There were now five different rear axle ratios available: the standard 3.23:1 was most suitable for road use, but those heading for the drag strip could choose from 3.54:1, 3.55:1, 3.91:1, and 4.10:1. Did the Six Pack work? One magazine recorded 6.6 seconds to 60 mph, and a 13.65-second quarter at 105 mph. In other words, it did.

The same Six Pack (mounted on an aluminum Edelbrock manifold) was available on the Coronet Super Bee that year, though this "budget" muscle car came in at $3,138, or about $300 less than the R/T. The cold-air Ramcharger option was available too, and the Super Bee remained a popular member of the Scat Pack, with nearly 28,000 sold in 1969. *Car and Driver* tested one fitted with the base 335 hp 383 V8 against five other budget muscle cars, though the Dodge turned out to be loaded with options, which bumped up the price. It also turned out to be suspiciously fast, with a 0–60 time of 5.6 seconds, and the quarter

"Want to start something? Try a hot-cammed 383-cube mill in a light coupe body. Just for kicks, throw in the heavy-duty suspension, oversized brakes, a brute of a hood, bumblebee strips—the works."

"Beware the hot cammed, four-barrelled 383 mill in the light coupe body. Beware the muscled hood, the snick of close-coupled four-speed, the surefootedness of Red Lines, Rallye-rated springs and shocks, sway bar and competent 11-inch drums. Beware the Super Bee. Proof that you can't tell a runner by the size of his bankroll."

mile dispatched in a touch over 14 seconds. Closer examination revealed that the test car had been tweaked by Chrysler, with a dual-point distributor and bigger than standard exhaust. So that's why, in muscle car comparison tests, the magazines invariably employed someone very thorough and knowledgeable to give each test car a careful inspection, just in case the manufacturer had "accidentally" left some special parts in place!

Meanwhile, the Dart GTS enhanced its reputation as the compact muscle car when the 383 ci option was boosted to 330 hp, which must have been quite something in the lightweight Dart. It was just a pity that the Dart interior (like that of the Coronet) was so dull, with a strip speedometer that wouldn't have looked out of place in a second-rate six-cylinder sedan. The Charger's collection of proper round dials was much more authentically performance car.

If you couldn't afford a GTS, then for '69 Dodge offered something even more affordable. The Dart Swinger 340 was even more of a budget muscle car. No engine options, just the 275 hp 340 ci V8, mated to a four-speed manual transmission with Hurst shifter. Basic it might be, but most of the right ingredients were there: D70 x 14 wide tires, dual exhausts, heavy-duty Rallye suspension, a three-spoke steering wheel, and, of course, those bumblebee tail stripes. At $2,836, the Swinger was a bargain, and was just as fast as the GTS 340.

We left the Charger 500 reveling in its new-found aerodynamic efficiency. Five hundred had been built, and it thus qualified for NASCAR. But no sooner was it racing the ovals than Ford launched the

RIGHT: As stock, the Super Bee came with Dodge's 383 V8, but it could also be specified with the Six Pack 440 (as this car is) to give R/T equaling performance. Even the Hemi could be had as an option, though here again, only a tiny minority of buyers actually bought one.

BELOW AND LEFT: As a Super Bee, the Coronet lost some of its sober-sides subtlety. Quite apart from the bumblebee stripe, just look at the "Six Pack" scoop on that matte-black hood!

598 C

LEFT: Hood scoop agape, a Coronet two-door blasts off the line. That scoop is non-standard, but buyers of new Coronets could specify the optional Ramcharger induction system, which channeled fresh air from twin scoops into a fiberglass plenum on the underside of the hood. It was standard when a Hemi was fitted, and allowed the driver to switch between warm and cold air.

ABOVE: Bumblebee stripe plus 340-inch V8 in the Dodge Dart equals the Swinger 340, an attempt to build a budget muscle car that would be cheaper to insure than the full-size cars, but still fast.

even more slippery Torino Talladega and Mercury Cyclone Spoiler. They soon ran away with the NASCAR title. Dodge had to act fast, and came up with the most outrageous muscle car of all time.

The Charger Daytona was one of Chrysler's two "Winged Warriors." It was designed with just one aim in mind, to improve high-speed aerodynamics so they could win back the title from Ford. At the front, a fiberglass nose cone gave the car its distinctive pointed snout and added 18 inches to overall length. At the back was a dramatic spoiler, standing almost two feet above the rear deck on its dual supports.

The Charger Daytona looked either dramatic, or like something out of a bad science fiction movie. Either way, no one could deny that the nose cone and rear

spoiler actually did their job, reducing drag by 15 percent and allowing the race-tuned version to accelerate to, and maintain, 200 mph. Bobby Isaac drove one to a new closed-circuit record of 201.104 mph, and swept the board at the Daytona 500 in '69.

Of course, to be legally raced in NASCAR, Dodge had to supply 500 Charger Daytonas for general sale. Once again, Creative Industries did the work, and most of the 503 Daytonas built were fitted with the 440 Magnum. You might think that such an icon of speed would have muscle car fans queuing up outside Dodge dealers, but some cars actually remained unsold, and some even had to be converted back to standard Charger specification by dealers before a buyer came forward. The realities of running a Daytona on the road involved general derision from kids and occasional overheating in traffic. Plus, of course, they were a nightmare to park. But then, the Daytona was never intended to ease into a parking slot outside McDonalds. It was intended to lap the ovals at 200 mph, and that it did very well. It was said to have cost Chrysler $1 million in development costs, but given the race wins and the amount of publicity it garnered the corporation, this was probably a million bucks well spent.

ABOVE: One of Dodge's "Scat Pack," the Dart Swinger was really Dodge's answer to the Plymouth Road Runner, which had shown that plenty of muscle car buyers were happy to forsake a little luxury in favor of horsepower per dollar. Weighing less than 3,200 lb, the Swinger made the most of that 340 ci 275 hp V8, with 0–60 mph in around 6.5 seconds, and a quarter mile in the 14s.

RIGHT: All windows apart from the windscreen were of acrylic, not glass, and the door hinges were made of aluminum. The interior was almost completely stripped out (there was carpet, but it had no backing), and even the standard front seats were ditched in favor of smaller, lighter items from the A-100 van. And the engine? What else could a single-minded Mopar performance car use but the Race Hemi, able to push an A-990 through the quarter mile in 11.39 seconds.

BELOW: In 1965, Chrysler built limited numbers of Dodge and Plymouth two-door sedans specifically for drag racing, all known by their code name of A-990. These cars were radically lightened, though NHRA rules now forbade the use of special aluminum or fiberglass parts. Instead, A-990 panels were of steel, but half the standard thickness.

But none of these Chrysler muscle cars were true pony cars to rival the Mustang, Camaro, or Firebird. The Plymouth Barracuda had never had the same level of success, being limited at first to a mild 273 ci V8, then the 383. Meanwhile, the Dodge Charger, though successful on its own terms, was too big and clearly a sedan fastback to seriously rival the big-selling pony cars. But for 1970, the new E-body finally brought Chrysler the pony car it had always needed—compact enough to compete with rival stallions (the E-body was a 2+2, not a full four-seater), but big enough to accept top-performance engines like the Magnum 440 and, of course, the Hemi.

At first, this was a Plymouth project, but it was soon decided that there would be a Dodge version as well—the Challenger—though this was to run slightly upmarket

of the Plymouth, aiming for the Mercury Cougar and Pontiac Firebird. Low and wide, the new Challenger looked quite different from previous Dodges, and every inch the early '70s muscle car.

Three models were available—base, SE, and R/T—but from a muscle car point of view, the real story lay in the engine options. The base engine was the familiar 340 ci V8, but in the R/T, the 383 was standard, with other R/T equipment, including Rallye suspension, heavy-duty brakes (but still drums), F70 x 14 tires, and plenty of striping and badges. The 440 Magnum V8 was a popular option, and actually came in three forms. With a single four-barrel carburetor, it offered 350 hp at 4,000 rpm (and a great mountain of torque—425 lb ft at 3,400). For an extra $113, a hotter camshaft delivered 375 hp. Finally, buyers could order the Six Pack of three two-barrel carbs for 390 hp. But this wouldn't have been a Dodge muscle car without a Hemi option, so that came, too; though, as ever, the actual take-up was very low. The classic muscle car engine remained an option for the rich and committed only.

The existing Dodge muscle cars—the Charger, Coronet, and Dart—continued alongside the new compact. For 1970, the Charger 500 returned, but in name only. The handcrafted aerodynamic improvements were gone, and the base engine options were a straight-six and 318 ci V8, hardly muscle car material. However, the faithful 383 did feature, in two-barrel and four-barrel form, the latter offering 330 hp or 335 hp. Only the Charger R/T came with the beefy 440 Magnum, still in 375 hp guise. Sales dropped in 1970, but Dodge still sold over 10,000 Chargers, forty-two of which were Hemi-powered. As time went on, it seemed that buyers were less inclined than ever to take up the Hemi option, probably thanks to increasing insurance rates, and the fact that the 440 always had good write-ups in the media, and was almost as fast.

The Coronet R/T still came with the four-barrel 440 as well, though continued to offer the triple-carb Six Pack as an option. It was increasingly hard to believe

DODGE CHARGER R/T 1968 (HEMI)

Engine: *425-horsepower 426 cubic-inch V8, 490 lb ft*

Transmission: *three-speed automatic*

Steering: *recirculating ball, power assisted*

Tires: *Goodyear Wide Tread F70-15*

Brakes: *front 11.04 in vented discs, power assisted; rear 10.0 in drums, power assisted*

Suspension: *front independent, torsion bar springs; rear rigid axle, multileaf springs*

Wheelbase: *117 inches*

Height: *53.2 inches*

Weight: *4,310 pounds*

LEFT: Dodge Dart GT at the strip. Small (relatively) but beautifully formed. The '67 ad banner was: "Revolt against kiddy car compacts!" It asked: "How about you? Still smoldering about the size and shape of today's compact cars? Alarmingly small on the inside . . . amazingly dull on the outside . . . now there's another way to go." The unique concave rear window came in for special praise.

ABOVE: This Magnum 440 (without triple-carburetor Six Pack) was the standard engine on Dodge's striking Charger Daytona. The Six Pack was never a factory option on the Winged Warrior, but at least one was installed by the dealer. Seventy had Hemis, but the Magnum, with plenty of power even with a single four-barrel carburetor, remained the engine of choice.

that just a few years earlier, the Coronet had been a conservative sedan. As the 440-powered R/T, it came in a choice of outrageous colors: how does plum crazy (purple), sublime (green), or go-mango (orange) grab you? And if that wasn't loud enough, there were five Scat Pack show-off options as well. Such as the Showboat engine dress-up kit, the Read-Out gauge package, and Bee-Leiver high-rise manifold. Hard to believe that someone got paid for dreaming up those names.

Meanwhile, the Challenger had proved a real success in its first year, with 83,000 sold. That put it right up with the big-league pony cars, but sales slumped in '71, right down to 30,000. In fact, this year would be a turning point for the Dodge muscle cars, with pressures on emissions, safety, and insurance forcing muscle cars in general to retract. So it was the last year for the 426 ci Hemi, though by now it had become a minority interest. Unlike Dodge's other engines, the street Hemi had barely changed since its launch in 1966, but then it had never been intended as a serious road-going

engine—it was in the options list to keep it legal for racing and to bolster the Dodge image in general.

Despite this unpromising climate, in 1971 Dodge chose to restyle the Charger as a model in its own right. It had long been a fastback version of the Coronet, but that now returned to its four-door sedan roots, while the Charger got its own two-door hardtop body with a shorter 115-inch wheelbase. This may have been the last gasp of a long-running muscle car (now into its sixth year on sale), but the Charger went out with a bang, offered in both Super Bee and R/T forms, with a whole range of V8s encompassing the 383, the 440 Magnum (with or without Six Pack), and the ever-present Hemi. But in a sign of the times, demand for Chrysler's top engine sunk to an all-time low: just sixty-three Charger R/Ts were ordered with the Hemi, and twenty-two of the Super Bees.

DODGE CHARGER DAYTONA ***1969***

Engine: *425 bhp, 426 cubic-inch Hemi V8*

Transmission: *four-speed manual*

Steering: *recirculating ball*

Wheels & tires: *15 x 6 steel rims, Goodyear Wide Tread F70-15*

Brakes: *front 11.04 in ventilated discs; rear 10 in drums*

Suspension: *front independent, torsion bars, anti-sway bar; rear multi-leaf springs, rigid rear axle*

Wheelbase: *117 inches*

Height: *53.2 inches*

Weight: *3,940 pounds*

BELOW: Hard to see here, but this Magnum has found a home in a Dodge Charger Daytona, one of the legendary "Winged Warriors." Most of the 500 or so Daytonas built to qualify for NASCAR racing came with the standard Magnum 440, and their aerodynamics was such that a 200 mph top speed was possible in racing trim. The Winged Warriors allegedly cost Chrysler $1 million to develop, a huge sum in 1969.

BELOW AND RIGHT: The Dodge Challenger of 1970 had as many options as its rivals in the pony car wars, the Camaro and the Mustang. R/T Challengers came with heavy-duty suspension, shocks, and brakes, and perhaps not so vital, an electric clock.

However, the muscle car wasn't dead just yet. In the early seventies, manufacturers hurried to offer smaller muscle cars, easier on insurance and gas consumption. Dodge's opportunity came in the form of the Plymouth Valiant Duster, which proved a good seller in 1970. For '71, the Dart Demon 340 was a Dodge-badged version of the same thing. With a 108-inch wheelbase, this was a true compact. The base engine was a 198 ci slant-six; but this, the smallest Dart ever, qualified as a muscle car when fitted with the familiar 340 ci V8, still available in 275 hp form.

It looked the part too, with scoops, stripes, and bright colors, plus Rallye instruments, heavy-duty suspension, E70-14 tires, and dual exhaust. Those who wanted the muscle car look without the expense of a V8 could order all those look-at-me parts as the Demon Sizzler with the slant-six. But the 340 V8 was still a good value, and for $2,721 buyers had a mini-muscle car that could sprint over the quarter mile in 14.49 seconds and to 60 mph in 6.5 seconds. It continued for 1972, albeit with a lower 8.5:1 compression ratio, and the Dart 340 actually stayed in production right up to 1976. By then, the big traditional muscle cars—the Charger, the Challenger, the Coronet R/T—were long gone. As was the Hemi.

BELOW: The 440 Magnum was a $250 option, and the Six Pack was available too. The hotter cam option boosted horsepower to 375. The 1970 Challenger T/A was designed with SCCA Trans Am in mind, with side-exiting exhausts and the Six Pack, plus other improvements, which included jacking up the rear to accommodate big E60-15/ G60-15 tires.

PLYMOUTH: BEEP BEEP!

BELOW: *Plymouth Belvedere GTX convertible. The GTX carried a ragtop option for several years, though the hardtops were always more popular. This is a 1968 example, listed at $3,590 when new.*

Plymouth and Dodge followed parallel paths in the sixties, and unlike the GM divisions, shared engines as well as basic body styles. But there were differences, and the two were in competition. Like Dodge, Plymouth began offering the 413 ci Max Wedge V8, in the early years of the decade, before the Hemi came on stream. The 426 soon followed, but both these motors were intended purely for drag racing, with up to 425 hp from the 426 in its ultimate 13.5:1 compression, twin four-barrel guise.

By 1964, now in Stage III form, the Max Wedge took on a 426 "R" designation, to underline its competition intentions. But that same year, Plymouth announced a 426S. This street version of the Max Wedge claimed 365 hp. That was the official

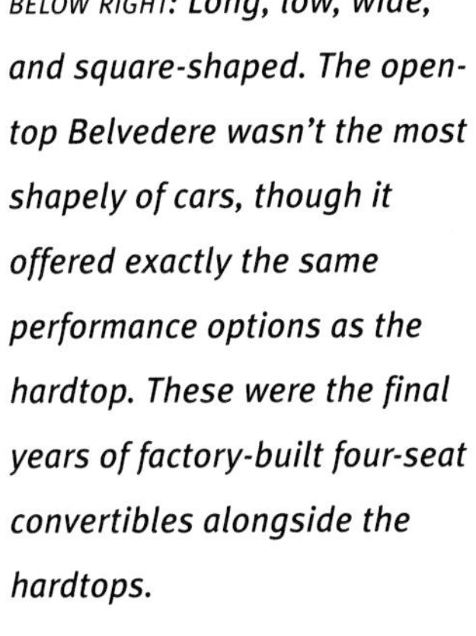

BELOW RIGHT: *Long, low, wide, and square-shaped. The open-top Belvedere wasn't the most shapely of cars, though it offered exactly the same performance options as the hardtop. These were the final years of factory-built four-seat convertibles alongside the hardtops.*

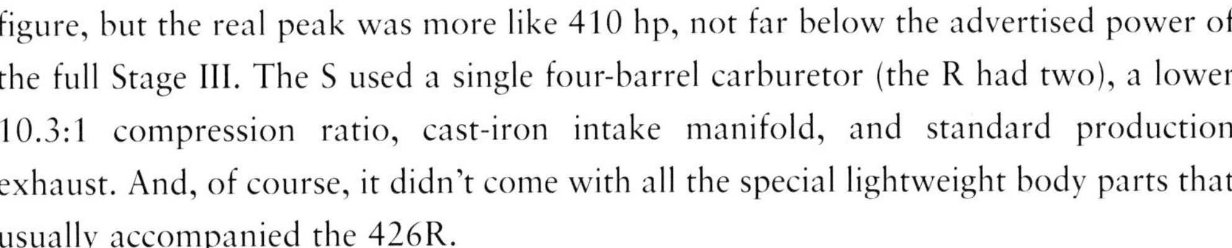

figure, but the real peak was more like 410 hp, not far below the advertised power of the full Stage III. The S used a single four-barrel carburetor (the R had two), a lower 10.3:1 compression ratio, cast-iron intake manifold, and standard production exhaust. And, of course, it didn't come with all the special lightweight body parts that usually accompanied the 426R.

Nevertheless, with 470 lb ft at 3,200 rpm it was still a formidable performer. The 426S V8 was available in any full-size Plymouth, from the Savoy to the Sport Fury hardtop or convertible. In the Sport Fury two-door hardtop, it delivered a weight-to-power ratio of 9.5 lb. per horsepower, enough for a 6.8-second 0–60 time, and 15.2 seconds over the standing quarter. The competition Hemi was an option too, albeit an expensive one, in 415 hp or 425 hp form, both named "Super Commando."

So in 1964, the division was already offering fully fledged muscle cars, albeit of the full-size kind. It didn't yet have a direct competitor to the GTO and it would be a couple of years before there were intermediate Plymouth muscle cars. It did have a rival for the Mustang, though the Barracuda was actually launched a few weeks before Ford's pony car. This should have given Plymouth a head start, but it didn't. The Barracuda failed to hit the spot as a pony car because it was clearly a fastback version of the Valiant. It was neat and good looking, but didn't seem exotic in the way that a Mustang did back in 1964. Once the Ford was launched, Plymouth's pony was completely overshadowed. Not that the Barracuda didn't have its own unique pluses, like a fold-down rear seat, giving "7 feet of fully carpeted 'anything' space," as the advertisement put it.

Spacious and sporty, for less than $2,500, the Barracuda looked like a winner. But it wasn't just lacking the Mustang's aura—it didn't have the Ford pony car's

powerful V8 options. The standard power unit was Chrysler's slant-six, but even the optional V8 only amounted to a 273 ci unit of 180 hp, not really enough to make it a muscle car. The rest of the sixties would see the Barracuda playing catch-up. In 1965, a "Golden Commando" version of the 273 was offered, with higher compression, four-barrel carb, and 235 hp. It was part of the Formula S package, along with heavy-duty suspension, wide tires, and rally stripes. But with a 0–60 of 8.9 seconds, it still wasn't a muscle car.

It wasn't until 1967, when the Barracuda became a model in its own right (and, incidentally, won the SCCA championship national rallying class), that it got the big-block 383. At 280 hp, along with all the Formula S parts, the Barracuda began to look like a real muscle car, though it still wasn't a pack leader. This didn't deter buyers too much, and 1967 was the car's best year ever, with more than 62,500 sold.

The real question was, how did the Barracuda, complete with its optional 383, compare to its pony car archrivals, the Mustang and Camaro? *Motor Trend* compared the three in the spring of 1967, and described the 383 as "a very willing performer; even in standard form, it gives the best economy of the bunch." It wasn't quite as fast as a Mustang 289 (in 271 hp form) or the Camaro 350/396. It didn't quite measure up on handling either, even with the Formula S stiffer suspension, but it did have the best ride. The Barracuda also won out on space ("hands down" according to *Motor Trend*) thanks to its larger size and fold-down rear seat. In notchback form, it boasted

the biggest trunk space as well. And all Formula S Barracudas had a full set of instruments, not something all pony cars offered. In short, the Barracuda was the sensible choice among pony cars, with more space and comfort than its closest rivals, but maybe less of a driver's car.

Even then, the really hot Plymouths weren't to be found in the fastback Barracuda range, but among the straitlaced-looking midsize sedans, the Belvedere and Satellite. There were three basic models—Belvedere I, Belvedere II, and Satellite—the last a little more sporty than the first two, which came with Chrysler's 225 ci six or 273 ci V8 (in the same 180 hp form as in the smaller Barracuda). All three were restyled for 1966, but it was the Satellite that played the role of Plymouth's midsize sporty car, with a huge choice of engines. It had the bucket seats, center console, and the wheel covers with center spinners, plus rear louvers and bright rocker moldings.

BELOW AND LEFT: ***The GTX was nothing if not subtle. This was as big as the engine badges got, indicating (modestly) that this convertible's power plant was the 440 Magnum V8, packing 375 hp at 4,400 rpm, enough for a standing quarter in the 14s and 0–60 mph in less than 7 seconds.***

The Satellite could also be transformed into a true muscle car, and to find out how was just a case of looking down the options list. Unlike its plainer Belvedere brothers, the Satellite (either hardtop or convertible) came with the 273 ci V8 as standard. The options started with the Commando 318 ci V8, with a two-barrel carburetor and 230 hp, and an extra $31 added to the total bill. Then came a 361 ci two-barrel, giving 265 hp. Things began to get interesting with the four-barrel 383, which broke effortlessly through the 300 hp barrier (to be exact, 330 hp). Finally, at an extra $545, you could have the 426S Max Wedge V8, in four-barrel 365 hp form. For 1965, that was the ultimate Satellite power unit. Then a few months into the '66 sales season, Dodge introduced the new street Hemi for its midsize sedans, and the Plymouths weren't far behind. In newly developed street form, it came with a lower 10.25:1 compression ratio, cast-iron cylinder heads, and a few other changes. Cost? Well, the Hemi was never a cheap option, and at $1,100 was twice the price of the old Max Wedge. The race Hemi cost even more, as it was retrofitted at the factory, along with a four-speed manual transmission. So if your original Satellite was an automatic, you could end up paying $1,800 for the complete conversion. A base Satellite two-door hardtop was listed at $2,696 in 1966, so even the street Hemi added about 40 percent to the total bill. Many muscle cars were sold on the basis of cheap, affordable performance, but no one could accuse the Hemi of that.

You weren't just paying for an engine, though, as the Hemi package included compulsory heavy-duty suspension, larger than standard drum brakes, wide wheels, and 7.75 x 14 Goodyear tires. The standard (column-mounted) three-speed couldn't

BELOW: No hidden headlights for the GTX, which made no pretense of hiding its sedan origins. But it was made to look like a poor value by the '68 Road Runner, which outsold it by more than two to one that year.

ABOVE: *Belvedere GTXs could be had with either manual or automatic transmission, the latter in this case, with a neat center console, bucket seats, and sports steering wheel. But add a Hemi and an optional low rear axle (4.10:1 was just one of those available), and it turned into a potent drag strip performer.*

cope with the torque of a Hemi, so a four-speed (floor shift, of course) or (for street-bound Hemis) a TorqueFlite came too. The axle ratio was unchanged at 3.23:1, but manual four-speeds had that in a Dana 60 truck-type axle. There was an alternative 2.93:1 rear end, as well as a limited-slip differential.

What you didn't get was stripes, scoops, and loud colors, just a couple of subtle "HP2" badges on the front fenders. There was no hint of what lay under the hood, and those early Satellites and Belvederes were true street sleepers. They might look like very ordinary sedans, but could turn in a 0–60 time of 7.4 seconds, with a 14.5-second quarter mile. *Car and Driver* soon had a Hemi Satellite in for testing, and did far better than that. Their Hemi rocketed to 60 mph in 5.3 seconds, going on to a 13.8-second quarter mile with a terminal speed of 104 mph. That energetic test car just missed taking part in a six-way muscle car test. Had it been there, *Car and Driver* was in no doubt that it would have won. "Without cheating, without expensive NASCAR mechanics, without towing or trailing the Plymouth to the test track," went the glowing conclusion, "it went faster, rode better, stopped better and caused fewer problems than all six of the cars tested last month." *Car and Driver* staffers also used

ABOVE: *For 1970–71, the Plymouth Barracuda shared the new Chrysler E-body with the Dodge Challenger, which transformed its appearance from sixties fastback sedan into true seventies muscle car. Just as important, it was several inches wider, making the engine bay big enough to accept any Chrysler V8.*

the Satellite for commuting in traffic for a week, proof that a well-tuned Hemi really was a gem of an engine.

That was all very well, but not everyone could afford a Hemi. And just as important when it came to selling muscle cars, most buyers didn't want modest street sleepers, they yearned for a car that not only was fast, but looked fast. The Satellite and Belvedere, however much horsepower lurked under their respective hoods, didn't look fast. That all changed for 1967, with the Belvedere GTX. This gained all the other visual cues that were making other muscle cars so popular. Available as a two-door hardtop or convertible, the GTX had twin hood scoops (they didn't actually do any useful work, but looked the part) with optional racing stripes and chrome wheels. There was a quick-fill racing-style gas cap as well, while inside, the GTX offered bucket seats with a leather insert. Underneath there was heavy-duty suspension.

ABOVE: And here was the result. For the first time, it was possible to buy a Hemi-equipped Barracuda direct from the factory. If you did, the hood scoop carried that "hemicuda" script. There was a base Barracuda, an upmarket Gran Coupe, as well as the sporty 'Cuda.

But it wasn't all about looks. Chrysler's Super Commando 440 ci V8 was squeezed under the hood for the first time on a midsize car. This was the standard GTX power unit, and came in its usual 375 hp form, at $3,178 for the two-door hardtop, and $3,418 as a convertible. For an extra $564 on top of those prices, you could have the full street Hemi, with its pair of Carter AFB four-barrel carbs. But the 440 was pretty potent in standard form. Magazine testers loved its big-cube, torquey nature, and this was after all the biggest muscle car V8 on the US market in 1967.

Better still, the GTX was a relative lightweight, which allowed the 440 its full potential. *Road Test* magazine held a mammoth nine-car test in June 1967, pitting a GTX against a Pontiac GTO, Chevy SS396, Dodge R/T, Oldsmobile 4-4-2, Ford GTA, Mercury Cyclone GT, Buick GS400, and AMC Rambler Rebel. The power, weight, and acceleration tables made interesting reading. The GTX tied for top power with two other cars, the Chevy and the Dodge (the latter was no surprise, as it used the same engine). But at 3,545 lb. it was lighter than every car in the test apart from the GTO and much lower-powered Rambler. Most of the cars tipped the scales at a good 300–500 lb. more. So the GTX was a clear winner on weight-to-power ratio, with just 9.49 lb. per hp. Next best was that original muscle car, the GTO, at 9.67 lb. per hp, while the Dodge R/T languished at 10.8 lb, thanks to its fat-boy 4,075 lb. weight.

This showed up in acceleration. A 440 Super Commando–engined GTX might expect a 7-second 0–60 time, and *Road Test* recorded 14.96 seconds over the quarter mile. That made the Plymouth the fastest accelerating of the nine, followed by the

RIGHT: A Hemi powered the ultimate 'Cuda for 1970, and that iconic 425 hp V8 gave as blistering a performance as ever, with a "shaker" hood scoop to tell the world that something special lurked underneath. Owners could expect a quarter mile of 14.1 seconds and 0–60 mph in 5.8 seconds. All very impressive, but too much so for insurance companies, making the Hemi 'Cuda tricky to get covered.

Below: It came late in the day, but a Hemi-powered 'Cuda remains the ultimate Barracuda for collectors. Very few were built.

Cyclone, GTO, Chevy, Dodge, the 4-4-2, Buick, Ford GTA, and Rambler Rebel. Actually, the test was a bit unfair for the Rambler, which mustered a mere 200 hp and struggled to cover the quarter in 17.94 seconds. As for the GTX, it didn't do so well in the handling test, thanks to soft suspension allowing plenty of body roll, and skinnier tires than some of the other cars. It also guzzled gas at the rate of 11.9 mpg, but that was about average. Gas was so cheap it came free with corn flakes in those far-off days.

So it had its flaws, but the strength of that 440 Super Commando made the GTX a highly competitive muscle car in 1967, and one of the fastest around in a straight

line. The public liked them too, and Plymouth sold 12,500 GTXs in the 1967 model year, all but a few with the 440 and TorqueFlite automatic transmission. The following year it did better, selling over 20,000, most of which were hardtops. The more serious muscle car crowd preferred solid-roofed cars to convertibles, for their extra rigidity. Plymouth might have sold more, had it not been for the highly successful Road Runner (see below), which shared the same bodyshell.

But the GTX proved a durable part of the Plymouth range, hanging on right up to the early seventies. Slightly fewer were sold in 1969 (including a mere 1,026 convertibles), but Bill Sanders of *Motor Trend*, who tested a GTX in January of that year, was in no doubt as to the car's strongest point. "No matter how you may try to camouflage it by loading a car with power and comfort options," he wrote, "when you get down to the nitty gritty of a supercar existence, an inescapable basic fact always remains on the surface. One primary purpose of a super car is to get from here to there, from this light to the next, in the shortest elapsed time. To this end, the Plymouth GTX is the flat out, best qualifier of all."

Bill's test car (with the Super Commando V8 in place, not a Hemi) was helped in that light-to-light dash with an optional 4.10:1 rear axle. With that transferring

BELOW: Fortunately, there were less wild alternatives, and the 'Cuda could be had with the 340 ci V8. This was still meaty enough to provide exciting performance, with a 10.5:1 compression and single four-barrel carburetor producing 275 hp and 340 lb ft. It would accelerate to 60 mph in 6.4 seconds, only half a second behind a 440-powered 'Cuda, which in turn was just one-tenth adrift of a Hemi.

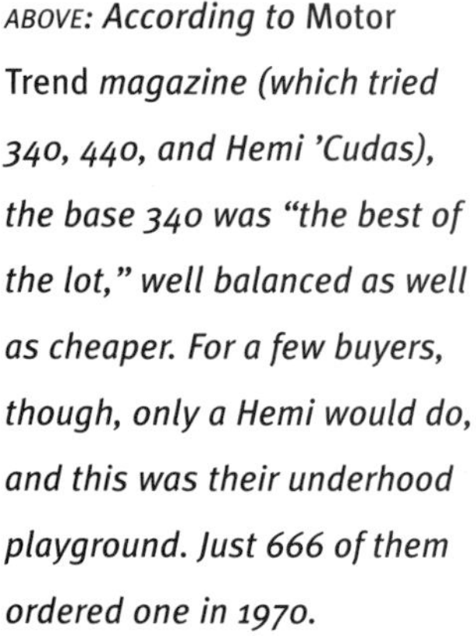
Above: According to Motor Trend *magazine (which tried 340, 440, and Hemi 'Cudas), the base 340 was "the best of the lot," well balanced as well as cheaper. For a few buyers, though, only a Hemi would do, and this was their underhood playground. Just 666 of them ordered one in 1970.*

torque to tarmac, he recorded a 0–60 mph time of just 5.8 seconds, and dashed through the standing quarter in 13.7 seconds, at a terminal speed of 102.8 mph.

The GTX wasn't an expensive muscle car, at a basic $3,329 for the hardtop, but it cost around $300 more than a Road Runner, which comprehensively outsold it (to the tune of over 80,000 cars in 1969). Still, the GTX had a decent level of standard equipment, and could also be optioned up to the eyeballs, if the buyer so chose, or could afford to. The 4.1:1 Super Performance axle fitted to Bill Sanders's test car, for example, added $271.50 to the price. Want a street Hemi? That'll be $604.75. There were countless other less serious options too, such as the famous "Air Grabber" hood scoop ($55.30), three-speed windshield wipers ($5.30), and an AM solid-state radio ($63.35). In fact, to order a car to exactly the same specification as Sanders, the buyer

would have faced a total bill for $4,231.48 delivered. That was with the 440 Super Commando. Specify a Hemi and a few other bits and pieces, and you wouldn't get much change from five grand . . .

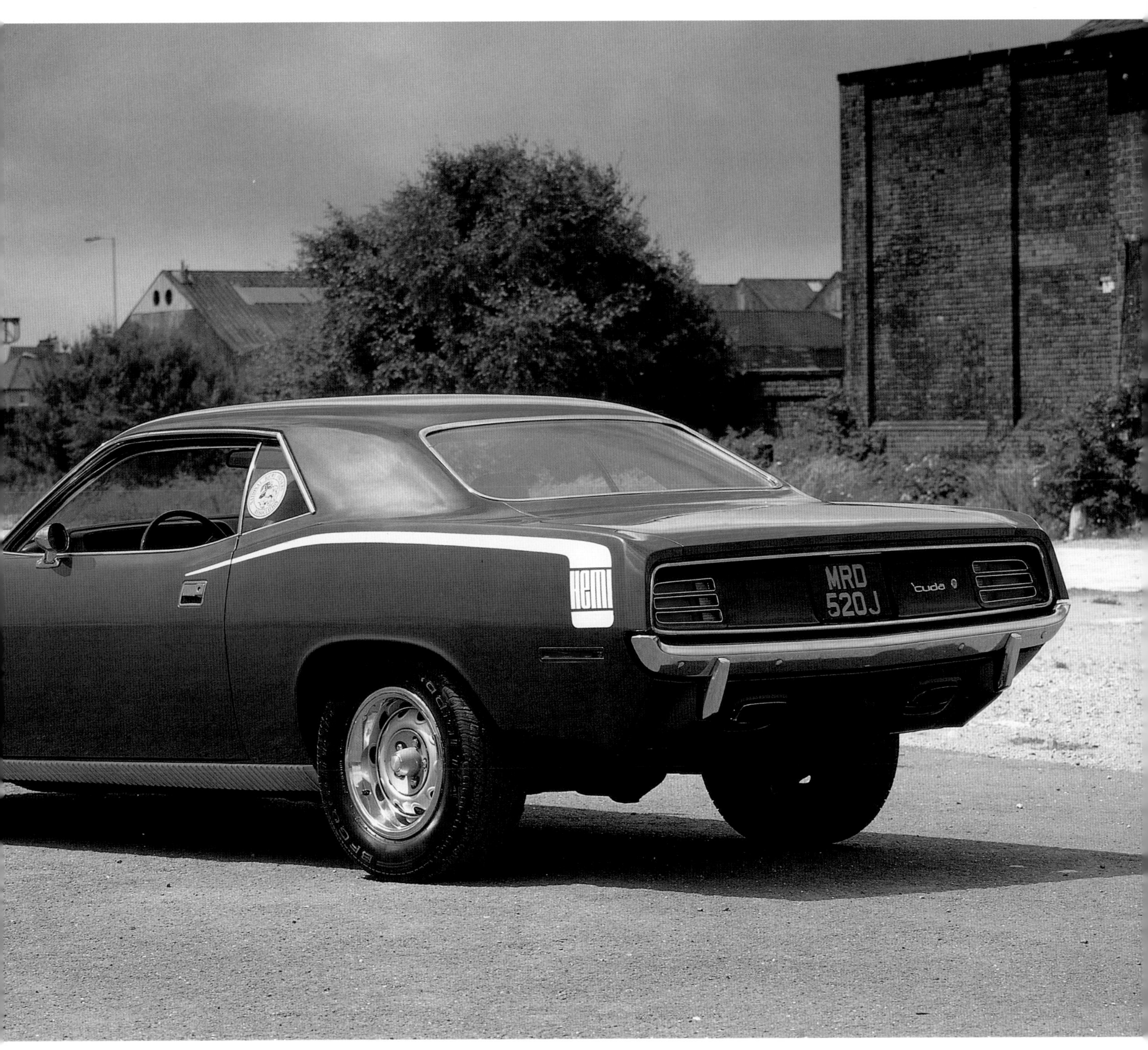

For 1970, the GTX got a few positive changes, such as a new hood and restyled front fenders and grille (along with all the midsize Plymouths). There were high-back front bucket seats, reflective side stripes, and a two-tone horn. And that Air Grabber hood scoop was fitted as standard.

ABOVE: Motor Trend *complained in '67 that the 'Cuda did not have enough engine options, and that buyers of the 383 engine could not order power steering or air conditioning.*

Left: The new E-body Barracuda came in convertible as well as hardtop guise, though by 1970–71 ragtops made up only a small proportion of the total. Just as able to drag race, though . . .

The convertible was dropped, but GTX buyers could opt for the Six Pack 440, with three two-barrel carburetors in place of a single four-barrel. Unusually for a muscle car, automatic transmission was standard (it was the TorqueFlite, of course) though a four-speed manual was a no-cost option. If you were thinking of indulging in some weekend drag racing, then the Super Trak Pak was a must: heavy-duty 9.75-inch Dana Sure-Grip 4.10:1 rear axle, dual-breaker ignition, power front disc brakes, and (essential for good ETs, this one) a wood-grain gearshift knob.

While the intermediates like the GTX and pony cars of the Mustang class were making all the muscle car news in the late sixties, the full-size muscle cars were soldiering on. They weren't as quick of course, but with over 300 hp on tap, acceleration was still pretty brisk, especially considering the weight they were hauling around.

Take Plymouth's Sport Fury. In 1967 spec it weighed 4,319 lb, and its standard power unit was the 325

Barracuda Formula S 1964

Engine: *235 hp 273 ci V8; 280 lb ft*

Transmission: *four-speed manual*

Steering: *recirculating ball*

Tires: *7.00 x 13*

Brakes: *front and rear 9.00 inch drums*

Suspension: *front independent, torsion bars, antiroll bar; rear rigid axle, semi-elliptic leaf springs*

Wheelbase: *106 inches*

Height: *54.5 inches*

Weight: *2,820 pounds*

BELOW: *Lack of a Shaker hood indicates that this was one of the lesser powered 'Cudas, not one of the rare Hemis. As well as the Hemi and that "little" 340 that the* Motor Trend *road testers liked so much, the 'Cuda could come with a big-block 383.*

hp 383 V8—not a promising combination by more compact muscle car standards, but there was still a ready market in North America for full-size cars like these. Some Americans remained wedded to the feel and sheer presence of a big automobile, the sort of feel they'd become used to through the fifties and early sixties. Forget those tearaway kids in their GTOs and Mustangs, this was real American motoring: comfort, a large V8 under the hood, and sufficient performance. That was why Ford kept on selling Galaxie 500s and Chevrolet the Impala SS: plenty of people still wanted cars like this in the late sixties. *Motor Trend* put a Galaxie, Impala, and Sport Fury together in March 1967, and was struck by how similar all three were, in power,

ABOVE AND RIGHT: *Chrysler promoted the 'Cuda as part of its "Rapid Transit System," whatever engine was specified, though there's no doubt that the big-block 383 and 440 laid a good claim to that title, whether or not one opted for the Six Pack.*

ABOVE: Whichever big-block 'Cuda was ordered (this is a 440), it came with the same choice of transmissions. The manual option was a New Process A-833 four-speed, with a 727 TorqueFlite providing the automatic alternative. Both came with a Dana 9.75-inch differential, the axle located by a six-leaf spring on the right, and a five plus two-half leaf spring on the left.

performance, and behavior. There were differences though. The Plymouth rode more stiffly than the other two, and "the Sport Fury reacted to the road as if they two were old friends, steering and braking with the greatest of ease." Like its competitors, the big Plymouth was comfortable, quiet, and reasonably well equipped. Its standing start acceleration times were nothing to write home about (9.6 seconds to 60 mph, 17.4 over the quarter mile), but the sort of driver who bought a Sport Fury in preference to a GTX knew that the 50–70 mph passing time of 5.4 seconds had a lot more relevance in the real world. Leave traffic-light drag racing to the kids.

Sport Fury, GTX, and Barracuda: Plymouth had its muscle cars, but none was really in the top rank. The Barracuda lacked real muscle, and while the GTX looked the part, it cost a lot more than a GTO. It had been late on the scene too, trailing the Pontiac original by a good three years. The Hemi had become an icon already, but it sold in tiny numbers. What Plymouth needed was a muscle car to make everyone—rivals, customers, dealers—sit up and take notice, and to sell by the thousands. The 1968 Road Runner did just that.

It might be one of the standout muscle cars of the sixties, but there was nothing new about the Road Runner. It was simply a crafty mix of existing Chrysler

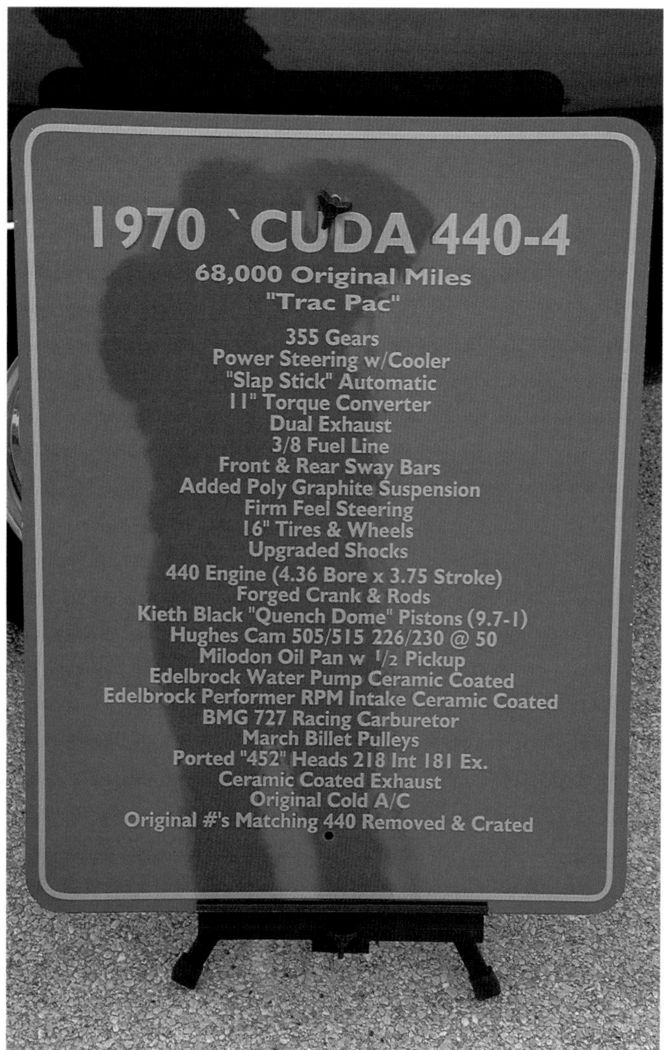

ABOVE: This 'Cuda 440 looks fairly stock, but carries a whole host of modifications under the skin, to the transmission, engine, suspension, and ancillaries. The 440-4 tag, incidentally, differentiates this single four-barrel car from the 440-6 Six Pack.

components, and it's fair to say that little was new except the badges (and the horn, but we'll come to that). To create the Road Runner, Plymouth went back to basics, slotting a big V8 into the cheapest, lightest bodyshell available. Then instead of loading on standard equipment or options, it offered the whole setup at a rock-bottom price. The 1968 Road Runner was all about maximum horsepower for minimum dollars.

So they took the basic Belvedere two-door coupe and fitted the well-proven 383 ci V8, here in 335 hp form. The extra five horsepower than the regular 383 came from modified cylinder heads, manifolds, and a camshaft borrowed from the big 440. (Plymouth was being modest: that level of tuning probably yielded a little more than 5 hp extra.) Along with the 383 came the bare basics to produce a usable muscle car: heavy-duty suspension, four-speed manual transmission, 11-inch drum brakes, and wide Red Stripe tires.

And that was it. No sports stripes and graphics, no gaping hood scoop or fancy wheels. Inside, there was the standard Belvedere instrument set, rubber mats, and

RIGHT: Enough to make the heart of any Mopar enthusiast beat just that little bit faster, and an indication of genuine performance parts inside. This particular 440 benefits from a Hughes cam, BMG 727 carburetor, a forged crank, and ported cylinder heads.

bench front seat: bucket front seats weren't even an option. In fact, the only way to tell the Road Runner from an economy-class Belvedere were little Road Runner badges on the doors and trunk lid. Using that cartoon character name was a masterstroke, and well worth the royalties paid to Warner Bros. Nothing summed up the image of Plymouth's bargain basement muscle car more than that dust-trailing little bird—small, sassy, and above all, fast. Plymouth even proved it had a sense of humor by equipping the Road Runner with an authentic "beep beep" horn!

Best of all, the Road Runner came with a price tag of just $2,870, ready to roll. That made it one of the most affordable muscle cars of the sixties, and over 45,000

BELOW: Beep beep! Plymouth had a serious hit on its hands with the Road Runner, which stripped out surplus equipment to offer muscle car performance at a genuine bargain price.

BELOW RIGHT: *Plain and unadorned, the Road Runner forsook many muscle car look-at-me parts to keep that all-important list price as low as possible. It inspired a whole wave of budget muscle cars.*

were sold in its first year. Nearly two-thirds of those were coupes, though a hardtop was added later in the year. Sales nearly doubled the following year, though for '69 the Road Runner's back-to-basics approach was diluted somewhat. At $2,945 for the coupe, the price had risen only slightly, but a whole range of options were added, so a loaded Road Runner with a price tag to match was now available. Things like power windows, bucket seats, and a center console joined the list of extra costs, while a convertible joined the hardtop and coupe, though it was an unpopular choice. Plymouth sold just over 2,100 of them in 1969.

Plymouth Road Runner Hemi 1969

Engine: *425 hp 426 ci V8; 490 lb ft*

Transmission: *four-speed manual*

Steering: *recirculating ball, power assisted*

Tires: *Goodyear F70 x 15*

Brakes: *front 11.0 inch vented discs, power assisted; rear 10.0 inch drums, power assisted*

Suspension: *front independent, torsion bars, antiroll bar; rear rigid axle, semi-elliptic leaf springs*

Wheelbase: *116 inches*

Height: *54.1 inches*

Weight: *3,938 pounds*

There was a new engine option too, the 440 Six Pack, which came with a scoop black hood and endowed the lightweight Road Runner (it still weighed 3,435 lb. in basic form) with true muscle car performance. But, of course, for the serious aficionados, there could only be one choice: the Hemi. This had been a $700 option on the Road Runner from the start. Along with a few extra options, this added around 500 lb. to the curb weight, but the result was still storming performance. The street

LEFT: Chrysler had to pay a royalty to Warner Bros. to make use of that other well-known Road Runner, not to mention Wile E. Coyote, but it was well worth the payout, giving the car an instant recognition factor.

BELOW: The original Road Runner came with just two engine choices. Chrysler's 383 was the base unit, here with 440 cylinder heads, manifold, and camshaft. A 425 hp Street Hemi cost just over $700 extra.

Hemi, remember, was quoted at 425 hp, but the true figure was probably more than that.

Car and Driver tested six examples of what they termed "Econo-Racers" in early 1969, though the Hemi Road Runner test car was so loaded with options that it would have cost over $4,300 to replicate. Anyway, it was still the fastest car of the six, turning in a 0–60 time of just 5.1 seconds, and streaked through the quarter at 13.54 seconds, a good half-second quicker than most of its rivals. *Car and Driver* also gave this Road Runner the highest estimated top speed (142 mph), and as icing on the cake it had the best brakes as well. On points, it was a close second in driver controls (scoring 17 points out of a possible 18), and a clear winner in performance.

The Hemi Road Runner wasn't for the fainthearted, thanks to its race-bred engine and the extrastiff suspension that came with it, but *Car and Driver* came to an unequivocal conclusion: "The Hemi-powered Road Runner is one hell of an Econo-Racer. It goes about its intended purpose with a sort of well-prepared confidence not found in the others. It probably has zero appeal to the fainthearted but that is the least of our worries—and it should be the least of yours." No doubt about it. In early 1969, a Hemi Road Runner was the quintessential muscle car.

Now a huge success story—at one point it actually made up one in five of all Plymouth intermediate sales—the Road Runner continued for 1970, restyled along

BELOW: A back-to-basics muscle car, the Road Runner was based on the simplest, lightest Belvedere two-door, with minimal creature comforts, but had a peppy 383 V8, four-speed manual transmission, heavy-duty suspension, 11-inch drum brakes, and Red Stripe tires.

Below: The '68 Road Runner looked what it was, a plain-Jane sedan, but for '69 it came in three body styles, with a convertible and hardtop, as well as the original coupe. The basic price went up and the options list grew, though engine choices were still 383 or the Street Hemi.

with the other Belvedere-based cars. It now faced some more serious competition. Never to miss a trick, Ford, GM, and even Chrysler-cousin Dodge had launched their own stripped-down muscle cars to match the Road Runner. In some ways, the 1970 Runner strayed further from its roots. The plain hood made way for a black one, and to save money, the four-speed standard transmission was dropped in favor of a three-speed, losing a lot of muscle car kudos in the process. In its place came convenience items like armrests, a cigar lighter, and glove-compartment light.

Any fears that the Road Runner was going soft would have been allayed by the presence of the 383 V8, heavy-duty suspension, and F70-14 white-line tires. In any case, Plymouth's stripped-down muscle car was still a good value, starting at just

BELOW RIGHT: *It kept the sassy image, but a '69 Road Runner didn't need to be stripped-out anymore. This negated its original concept, but that's life. Power steering was one of the options now, along with power front disc brakes ($91.65), AM radio ($61.55), and a tachometer ($50.15).*

under $2,900 for the basic coupe. An extra $249.55 added the 440 Six Pack, though you had to add a compulsory four-speed or automatic transmission to that. As ever, the Hemi was the most expensive option of them all, at over $800. Race-bred it might be, and (as that *Car and Driver* test had demonstrated) faster, and probably more powerful than everything else into the bargain, but fewer and fewer buyers could afford it. Just over 1,000 Road Runner buyers paid for a factory Hemi in 1968, but only 152 in 1970.

The first Road Runner had been a true Q-car: that is, inoffensive looking but with fearsome performance. The same could hardly be said of the Superbird. Plymouth's most outrageous muscle car of all, this was the company's take on the Dodge Charger Daytona, the original Winged Warrior. Chrysler encouraged competition between its two main divisions, so after Dodge's success with the Daytona in NASCAR in 1969, it was inevitable that Plymouth would soon come up with something similar. Plymouth wanted NASCAR wins too, but its own Winged Warrior would have to qualify separately from the Daytona Charger, and for 1970 the

"The Hemi Road Runner has more mechanical presence than any other American automobile . . . it has an impatient, surging idle that causes the whole car to quiver . . . The exhaust explodes like Krakatau and the wailing howl of surprised air being sucked into the intakes turns heads for blocks. Baby, you know you're in the presence."

(CAR AND DRIVER, *JANUARY 1969)*

minimum production quota was increased from 500 to 1,500. In the event, Plymouth built 1,920 Superbirds (one source says 1,971), so it qualified easily.

Unveiled for 1970, the Superbird looked superficially identical to the previous year's Daytona, as if leftover parts had been bolted onto a Road Runner. In fact it was quite different, with every component, including that dramatic nose cone and massive rear spoiler, being unique to the car. Nor was it a case of just bolting these parts in place. The standard Road Runner front end had to be extended forward to meet the nose cone while the flush rear window was also unique to the car. That's why every Superbird sold to the public came with a vinyl roof: it saved expensive refinishing of the modified metalwork around the rear window.

BELOW: This is a 440-6 'Cuda from 1970, but a rarer option was the AAR. This was aimed at Trans Am racing, whose rules now stated that race engines didn't have to be exactly the same size as the road units they were derived from. So 1,900 AARs were built (named after Dan Gurney's All-American Racers) with the 340 ci small-block V8 providing the power.

You might think that the Hemi would be standard on such a wild-looking machine, but not a bit of it. The most popular option was the Super Commando 440 V8, in single four-barrel guise, offering 375 hp, and 1,120 Superbirds were delivered with this power unit. A further 716 customers opted for the 390 hp Six Pack version of the same engine, and just 135 paid extra for the full-house street Hemi, with twin four-barrel carbs and the claimed 425 hp. The racing Superbirds, of course, which dominated NASCAR that year and even managed to tempt Richard Petty back to the Plymouth fold, used nothing but the full-race Hemi.

Chrysler's Winged Warriors are often seen as the

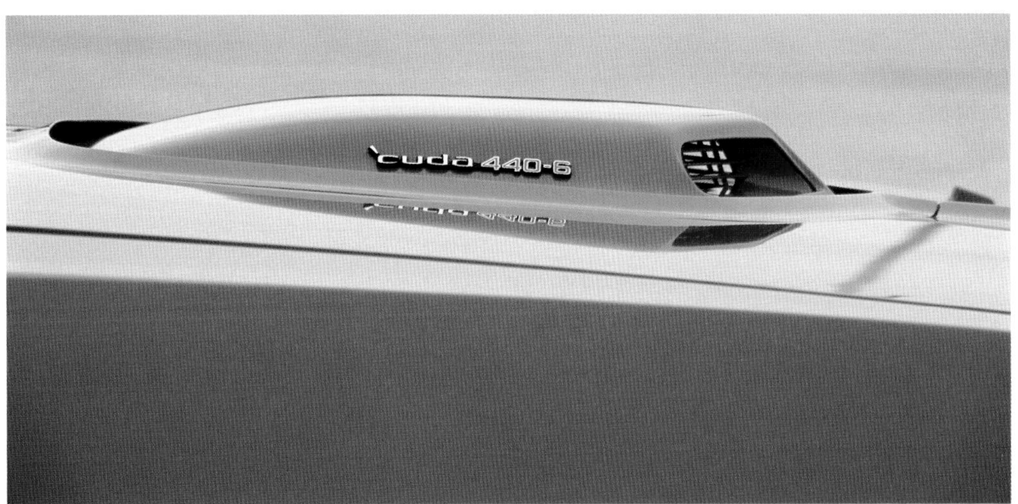

BELOW AND RIGHT: ***More subtle badging and the "440-6" script on this Shaker hood indicate that the 'Cuda in question is fitted with the Six Pack option, a set of three two-barrel carburetors in place of the standard single four-barrel. The Six Pack was in its final years though.***

Below and left: *Muscle cars had certainly progressed from the days when a three-spoke steering wheel and a couple of bucket seats would keep muscle car drivers happy. Many now expected a cosseting interior that wrapped around them like a fighter plane cockpit. The 'Cuda provided that.*

last fling for the flamboyant muscle car. Certainly 1971 saw a change of mood, with fewer buyers than ever paying for the Hemi option. Maybe more relevant to most was the Duster, a sort of mini-muscle car based on the compact 108-inch wheelbase Valiant. *Car and Driver* had long been a champion of compact muscle cars, arguing that they could give better results than heavier intermediates like the Road Runner and GTO. In early 1970 they compared four very different approaches to the muscle car concept: a Chevelle SS454 (traditional intermediate), Mustang Boss 302 (pony car), Shelby AC Cobra (sports car), and a Duster 340 (the compact).

> ***"A gentle hand is not what the Barracuda thrives on; it demands forceful inputs to realize its potential"***
>
> (CAR AND DRIVER, *MARCH 1968*)

Car and Driver paid the Duster the compliment of "mini-Road Runner." Naturally, it trailed behind the featherweight Cobra and big-cube Chevelle in a straight line, though with a 0–60 time of 5.9 seconds and 14.39 seconds over the quarter, it was actually quicker than the Mustang. It was lighter than the pony car too, making up for a power deficiency, which supported *Car and Driver*'s theory that lighter weight equaled more performance. It was a bit of a handful on the handling course (*Car and Driver* thrashed the four cars around

BELOW RIGHT: ***For 1971, the Barracuda buyer could choose from a wide range of seven engines. The Hemi was still there, just, but was more of a minority fitment than ever, with just 115 cars so fitted that year. More popular were the 198 and 225 ci sixes and the 230 hp 318 ci V8. Muscular options started with the familiar 275 hp 340, followed by the 300 hp 383, and 385 hp 440 Six Pack.***

440+6
GPF
915J

LEFT: *The Barracuda wasn't the only Plymouth to offer a 440-6 in 1971. The Belvedere GTX and Road Runner, now both using the sporty Chrysler B-body shared with the Sebring coupe, did the same. This is a Road Runner, and at $3,120, it didn't cost much more than the '68 original, and it had a higher level of equipment. Sales had slumped though—well over 80,000 Road Runners had been sold in the peak year of 1969, but just a couple of years later that had fallen to little more than 14,000. The traditional muscle car, even a budget one like this, was on its way out.*

ABOVE: The '71 Road Runner was a little plusher than the original, with deep-pile carpeting and rallye cluster instrumentation coming as part of the package. Though the base engine was still that 300 hp 383, for just $242 extra you could have the 440-6, now offering 385 hp at 4,700 rpm and 490 lb ft at 3,200 rpm. Add the Air Grabber pop-up hood scoop ($67) and a bolt-on rear deck spoiler to maximize the effect.

the Lime Rock Park circuit) and proved the slowest through corners, though it was still fun. "The Duster," they concluded, "though not the fastest, is certainly the most amusing. It's whimsical and has a kind of disposable air about it." It had its flaws, the writer went on, but "the Duster is a good start toward a compact super car."

Meanwhile, other Plymouth muscle cars were completely restyled in 1970–71. The new E-body, similar for both Dodge Challenger and Plymouth Barracuda, looked far more muscle-bound and aggressive than the sixties Barracuda. Longer, lower, and five inches wider, it was a pure 1970s car, finally leaving behind the Barracuda's mid-sixties roots. Available as a convertible or notchback, the new Barracuda came in base, Gran Coupe, or (sportiest of all) the 'Cuda.

The 'Cuda in particular looked the part of a muscle car, especially when equipped with the optional Shaker hood scoop, which burst through the hood itself, and quivered and shook in sympathy with the big V8 underneath it. The Shaker was actually standard if buyers opted for a Hemi (and 666 did, making this Barracuda the second most popular Plymouth Hemi muscle car, after the 1968 Road Runner), and optional on the 340, 383 or 440 V8s. Plymouth sold over 50,000 Barracudas of all types in 1970, but that slumped to a little over 16,000 the following year. The

BELOW: Road Runner interior for '71. The car was still offered the following year, as the world changed around it. Muscle cars were rapidly losing favor, and sales slumped again, this time to less than 8,000 cars, though the base engine was now a 400 ci V8, and the 440 was still available, albeit in single four-barrel carburetor guise. Standard equipment still included the "beep beep" horn—good to see the car hadn't lost its sense of humor, even if the accountants were fast losing theirs.

Barracuda might have become a truly credible muscle car at last, but it was too late, arriving just as new legislation on safety and emissions began to really bite, and spiraling insurance premiums put the final nail in the classic muscle car's coffin. For 1972, just two years after its launch, the Barracuda lost its Hemi option, as well as the 383 and 440 V8s. The convertible was dropped too, and power options were limited to 318 ci or 340 ci V8s.

Despite falling sales, both GTX and Road Runner soldiered on in 1971, now with the latest intermediate B-body styling. Both had been transformed from plain sedans, with a few stripes and scoops, into sporty-looking coupes. It was the last year for the GTX, which still offered the 375 hp 440 Super Commando V8 as standard equipment, along with TorqueFlite automatic transmission and high-back front bucket seats. You could still have a Hemi for an extra $746, but just thirty GTX customers checked that box on the order form. Times were changing, and 1971 saw Chrysler sell less than 400 street Hemi–powered cars.

And the Road Runner? Slotting in under the GTX, it still fulfilled the role of budget muscle car, starting at $3,120 with the base 383 ci 300 hp V8. As ever, performance could be boosted to GTX levels with an optional 440 or Hemi, but with an eye on insurance

BELOW: Muscle car names to remember. Road Runner and 440-6 might not be quite as evocative as "Hemi," but they're right up there in the top league.

costs, few buyers took that route. Plymouth's budget muscle car was still offered in 1972 (though the Hemi option had gone), but sales slumped by 50 percent. It actually struggled on into 1974, albeit with a new base 318 ci V8 and (for the first time on a Road Runner) a two-barrel carburetor. For 1975, the Road Runner name was used on a small Fury, and then became an option package on the Polara. And so the classic Plymouth muscle cars just quietly faded away.

ABOVE: Road Runner 440-6 gets attention, but in the early seventies, no manufacturer could justify hot V8s like this: the golden age was over.

The '90s Revival: Prowler, Dakota, 300M

These were not happy times for the Chrysler Corporation. It almost collapsed altogether in the 1970s, and only an injection of federal aid kept it going. By then it was losing millions of dollars every quarter, and a complete close-down was in the cards. That's when Lee Iacocca was brought in to turn things around, which he did. Forget the various Mustangs that he championed—saving Chrysler was the biggest achievement of Iacocca's career. Of course, it wasn't just Lee's business sense that turned the company round. It couldn't have been done without that public money, or without sacking thousands of Chrysler employees, or without the front-wheel-drive four-cylinder K-car. Saving Chrysler came about for a variety of reasons, and by 1983, it was back in profit.

Let's fast-forward a decade or so. Chrysler's had its ups and downs, but it's still here. In the 1990s, it will gain a patchy reputation for designing a series of exciting cars that result from lateral thinking, out-of-the-box, some with strong muscle car overtones. Unfortunately, these one-off design coups become isolated, as if they're not part of an overall plan.

The Plymouth Prowler was one of these. It began as a quick sketch for a retro hot rod at a management

Below: Plymouth Prowler, a 1990s interpretation of a 1950s hot rod that made the transformation from impractical show car to something that was drivable every day and usable (as long as you didn't expect to carry too much).

BELOW: A clever mix of authentic hot rod looks and existing Chrysler parts to make the thing affordable, the Prowler could certainly turn heads at Daytona Bike Week. For some, it was probably a choice between one of these and a Harley.

brainstorming session in 1990, at Chrysler's Pacifica West Coast design operation. Chrysler president Bob Lutz noticed it, liked it, and had the immediate and enthusiastic support of the design vice president, who happened to be building his own hot rod at the time. That was one of the driving forces behind Chrysler's left-field cars of the nineties—there were plenty of engineers and designers in the corporation who were car nuts, whether hot rodders, classic car nuts, sports car people, even muscle car types. It was that enthusiasm (and a management open to radical ideas) that allowed cars like the Prowler to get beyond the back of an envelope stage. With top-management support, the Prowler got the green light, not for production, but as a

concept show car. When the covers were flicked off at the International Auto Show in Detroit in January 1993, the public reaction was overwhelming, and in the year that followed, Chrysler received over 130,000 inquiries. That was enough to make the Prowler a production car, though it was another three years before it was finally on sale. It looked remarkably similar to the original concept. There were bumpers now (aluminum extrusions covered in urethane), and the car was three inches wider to make room for side impact protection. The shape of the hood was changed slightly to accommodate a larger radiator, and the windshield had to be altered so that wipers could be fitted. Most under-the-skin parts were sourced from Chrysler's own parts bin (the minivan, Cirrus, Viper, and Grand Cherokee all contributed parts), but as most of these were hidden, they didn't detract from the impact.

That was about it. Otherwise, the production Prowler looked every inch the modern interpretation of a classic hot rod. There had been remarkably few

compromises. It came only with a soft top, for example (early proposals for a retractable hardtop were vetoed by Tom Gale on the grounds that proper hot rods were open tops). If you wanted to take the Prowler to the mall, forget it, as the trunk was a minuscule thing that would have trouble swallowing a six-pack, let alone the weekly groceries. Chrysler's answer to the trunk problem was a matching trailer to bob along behind, though not a cheap option at around $5,000 in 2001.

None of that mattered. Chrysler had produced an outrageous show car, and taken the bold step of putting it into production—it was like 1969 all over again, and the Winged Warriors! Even at $40,000, there were plenty of takers. If there was one criticism, it was that the Prowler wasn't fast enough to deserve its hot rod looks. Power came from a 3.5 liter SOHC V6. With fuel injection and four valves per cylinder, the engine looked up-to-the-minute, but some thought that its 214 hp wasn't enough for a car that looked like the Prowler. Certainly not enough to smoke the huge 20-inch rear tires. The tires, incidentally, were essential to the overall look, in the hot rod tradition of small front/large rear wheels. The car ran 225/45 17-inch tires on the front, the rears were massive 295/40 VR20s. All four were run-flat types: it didn't have room for a spare!

Not fast enough? Chrysler retorted that a V8 wouldn't have fitted, not without intruding into the passenger compartment, or making the car much longer and thus spoiling the look. In any case, the Prowler weighed less than 3,000 lb, so even a 214 hp V6 was sufficient to give sprightly performance. Zero to 60 mph in just over 7 seconds might not be the stuff of hot rod dreams, but it was quick enough to make the Prowler fun. That low weight, by the way (the actual figure was only 2,850 lb), was down to extensive use of aluminum for the body tub, frame, sheet metal, and the wheels, with magnesium used for the instrument panel. Chrysler said about 900 lb of each Prowler consisted of aluminum, making it North America's most aluminum-intensive vehicle.

ABOVE: Some thought that the Prowler didn't live up to its aggressive looks, with a mere 215 ci (3.5 liter) V6 under the hood, but it could still manage 0–60 mph in just over 7 seconds.

Much later, the Prowler was given a boost, up to 253 hp from the same 3.5 liter V6. That was enough for 0–60 mph in 6.3 seconds, and a quarter-mile time of 14.9—authentically hot rod. By this time, Chrysler was also building the P/T Cruiser, which successfully aped 1940s sedans in the same way that the Prowler did with hot rods. Not even the Cruiser's best friends, however, would describe it as a muscle car.

Meanwhile, the Dodge Dakota R/T wasn't a muscle car either, more of a muscle truck. Remember how the US government imposed ever-stricter emissions and safety legislation on cars from the late sixties onward? Detroit found a way around them, and that included the CAFE fuel consumption regulations. The regulations were less strict (or didn't apply at all) to light trucks—in other words, pickups. After intensive lobbying, Detroit also managed to have four-wheel-drive passenger vehicles—SUVs—classed as light trucks. In the early twenty-first century, legislation began to tighten for light trucks as well. In the meantime pickup sales soared, and by the late 1990s "light trucks" accounted for over half of the new-car market. So there was clearly a market for pickups aimed at the purely private buyer.

Into this world, Dodge launched the Dakota R/T pickup in 1986. This has been described as the first compact pickup, aimed to fill the gap between small imported pickups and the full-size all-American variety. It was a success, but the Dakota R/T didn't really enter its muscle truck period until it was redesigned in 1998. Now it had a 250 hp 5.9 liter Magnum V8, enough to spin the rear tires into smoking starts—that was with no weight on the bed, invariably the case with these privately owned trucks.

The R/T (and yes, the "Road/Track" tag was a direct reference to those Chargers and Challengers of the sixties) was an option pack on the Dakota, and a popular one. The Magnum V8 wasn't highly tuned (a dual inlet exhaust was the main change) but did offer 345 lb ft, while a four-speed electronic automatic transmission and 17-inch aluminum wheels with low profile tires were part of the package as well, along with lowered sport suspension and a limited-slip differential. With all this kit on board, R/T owners could expect 0–60 mph in 7 seconds, and a standing quarter of 15.4, enough to make the compact Dakota highly competitive in the NHRA's Pro Stock Truck class.

The same basic Magnum V8 was also available in the full-size Dodge Ram SS/T from 1996. This started life as the limited edition Indy Ram truck, complete with white body with blue stripes to match the Indy 500 Viper GTS pace car. It sold well, but not because of the paint job. It sold because the Magnum V8 offered a new level of performance to buyers of full-size trucks. At 4,216 lb. (as much as a heavyweight muscle car of the sixties), the Ram SS/T wasn't as fast as a performance car, but 0–60 in 7.9 seconds was still quick by truck standards. And if that wasn't enough, a dealer-fitted kit

RIGHT: The Prowler was later given a boost to 253 hp from the same 3.5 liter V6, cutting the 0–60 mph time down to 6.3 seconds, and the quarter mile to just under 15. No one was claiming the Prowler to be a muscle car, but it certainly wasn't slow, and it looked ready to burn. If you want to take the purist view that looks have nothing to do with muscle car performance, then what was that "Super Bee," Trans Am striping, and hood chicken all about?

of engine ECU, camshaft, intake, and exhaust headers was said to take power up to around 290 hp.

Heavy and not really that fast, these muscle trucks only really qualify for their "muscle" tags by virtue of a big, thirsty V8. Where did that leave the Chrysler 300M sedan in 1999? Remember how Chrysler's Letter Cars ended with the 300L back in 1965? Three and a half decades later, the corporation sought to reinvent the concept of a fast and luxurious sedan in the same tradition. But with a few changes. The latest 300M had front-wheel drive and a slippery, aerodynamic shape. It had four doors (instead of two) and was powered, not by a Hemi or Max Wedge V8 of vast size, but by an aluminum V6 of 3.5 liters and 253 hp.

That was a long way short of the 300–400 hp of the old Letter Cars (though their power was measured under the more optimistic gross system) and enough for a 0–60 time of 7.8 seconds. So does it qualify as a muscle car?

Well, maybe a front-wheel-drive V6 sedan never will, but the 1999 300 accelerated as quickly as any of the old ones, and would streak on to a top speed of 145 mph, thanks to its slippery shape.

Still not a muscle car in spirit, but it's not too fanciful to think that a twentysomething driver in the late sixties, proud owner of a Mustang Boss or a Hemi Road Runner, would, thirty years later (with shorter hair and smarter suits), find the 300M the very thing.

***BELOW:* A Shelby Cobra for the 1990s, the Dodge Viper followed the same spirit as the AC/Carroll Shelby sports car of thirty years earlier: big engine, two seats, no frills.**

Dodge Viper: Back to Basics

Prowler, Dakota, and 300M—each in their own way a modern interpretation of the muscle car. But one 1990s Chrysler was not so sophisticated—it *was* a sixties muscle car that happened to be on sale. It was the Viper.

Nothing sums up the muscle car revival—and that of Chrysler—better than the Dodge Viper. Hugely fast and powerful, it could smoke any of those sixties muscle cars, even the AC Cobra that inspired it. Massive 8.0 liter V-10 engine, mountainous torque, and a top speed of 166 mph. This is the sort of car that, in 1973, most enthusiasts thought they would never see again.

But it wasn't affordable muscle, and at $50,000 plus taxes when it was launched in 1992, the Viper underlined the fact that the days of cheap performance in production cars were long gone. In the early twenty-first century, it's still possible to buy a new car that will sprint to 60 mph in less than five seconds, but you need to be one of the richer people on the planet to do so.

The Viper story began in early 1988, and arose out of a series of meetings at which some of the following key people were always present: car nut Bob Lutz (who also happened to be a Chrysler chief); French-born Francois Castaing (VP of Vehicle Engineering); Tom Gale (VP of Product Design, who would help kickstart the Prowler project); Lee Iacocca (who needs no

***BELOW:** Looks quite cozy from here, doesn't it? But despite the $50,000+ price tag, Dodge Vipers (especially the early convertibles) were quite basic, even crude, in the comfort and convenience department. The cockpit was cramped, and entry could be awkward through the narrow doors. Weather protection (a ragtop and sidescreens) reminded some of a sixties MG.*

ABOVE: Even on paper, the Viper looked awesome. Eight-liter V-10 engine, six-speed transmission, and vented disc brakes with four-piston calipers all round. Vital statistics: 400 hp, 465 lb ft, 166 mph—the Viper was faster and more powerful than any sixties production muscle car.

RIGHT: Even at its high price, the Viper created huge interest after the 1992 launch, and, soon afterward, an impatient waiting list. A dozen years later, tweaked here and there but with no major changes, it was still selling, on course to become one of motoring's all-time legends.

introduction); and none other than Carroll Shelby, the man behind the original AC Cobra, as well as all those hot Mustangs. Not all of these men were present at all the meetings, but Shelby's name is significant, for from the start, the Viper was clearly intended to be a Cobra for the nineties, a no-holds-barred two-seat sports car that basically said, "Yeah, so?" to the oil crises and all the environmental concerns that followed. If anyone had been in doubt that the pursuit of horsepower was back, then the Viper surely convinced them otherwise.

While Tom Gale's original sketches were transforming into full drawings, then a clay mock-up, the Viper's legendary V-10 was also taking shape. It's almost become an urban myth that the Dodge Viper uses a truck engine. This is almost true, but not quite. The V-10's origins lay in late 1987, when Chrysler took over Jeep. A new Jeep & Truck Engineering Department was formed, and one of its first jobs was to revamp the Dodge Ram pickup, which needed more power to compete with the big-block V8s coming out of Ford and Chevy. Chrysler's existing 5.9 liter V8 couldn't be stretched any further, but adding two extra cylinders might give the required cubic inches, and be far quicker and cheaper than designing a whole new engine. Skeptics said that such a big V-10 would suffer terrible vibration, but the prototypes worked fine. Meanwhile, Tom Gale's new show-stopping sports car was shaping up nicely, so it made sense to bring the two together.

So when it was launched at the Detroit International Auto Show in January 1989, the Dodge Viper had one of these prototype truck engines under the hood. And

that's partly why it caused such a sensation. Not only was this a two-seat sports car in the classic mold, but it was powered by an 8.0 liter V-10 engine! In no time, countless inquiries and not a few deposit checks were finding their way to Chrysler headquarters, and it didn't take long for Lee Iacocca to announce that the Viper would go into production in early 1992. This was no easy task, and that prototype power unit had to be completely redesigned to make it usable for a road-going sports car. To save weight, a new cylinder-block was cast out of aluminum. Lamborghini (with long experience of building such exotic engines) helped with development and supplied the first five blocks. Almost everything else was changed too: lighter pistons, higher compression ratio, different valves, stronger rods and crank, higher revs. All this was essential to produce the projected 400 hp, and to squeeze under the Viper's long, low hood the manifolds, oil pan, and accessory drive had to be redesigned too.

For nearly three years, a team of one hundred engineers and managers worked to turn the Viper show car into a production reality—all had volunteered for the task. When the result of their labors finally arrived, it didn't disappoint. The V-10 produced 400 hp at 4,600 rpm and 465 lb ft at 3,600, so it clearly wasn't a peaky, high-revving engine. Transmission was a six-speed manual and the brakes were vented discs all around with four-piston calipers. It needed those brakes, with a top speed (despite poor aerodynamics on the convertible) of 166 mph. It reached 60 mph in just 4.6 seconds, so here, finally, was an American-made road car that could accelerate faster than Shelby's '66 AC Cobra. It had taken a quarter of a century, but they'd made it.

***Above:* No one would accuse the Viper of looking beautiful—it was too brutal for that. It was less curvaceous, more lumpen than the original Shelby Cobra, but no one seemed to mind. Here in the 1990s was a car that re-created the golden age of muscle. Anyway, brutish looks somehow suited the concept of an 8.0 liter V-10 sports car.**

Mind you, some things hadn't moved on very far. The Viper RT/10 was quite crude in some ways, with a cramped cockpit and narrow doors. The fabric top was decidedly skimpy and the side curtains came with plastic zips—they didn't fit too well either. And the color choice was limited. In fact, there was no choice at all: red was it. In 1993, you could have black, and a few other hues gradually followed. Did the public care? They did not. Even at a price of $55,000, a waiting list soon backed up.

In 1996, the Viper GTS was launched (though it had been shown publicly three years earlier) with a composite fastback body transforming it from roadster to coupe. Chrysler said the car was more than 90 percent new, with a stronger, stiffer frame, and aluminum suspension parts. New heads, block, and cooling system made the latest V-10 eighty pounds lighter than the old one. The coupe had other advantages. The lift-up glass hatch gave access to a luggage compartment 70 percent larger than the roadster's (still not exactly generous, though), and naturally the coupe had far better

aerodynamics, with the drag coefficient cut to 0.39. The latter was still nothing special by 1990s standards, but a big improvement on the roadster's 0.50.

Through the late 1990s and early 2000s, the Viper became increasingly iconic. There was still nothing else quite like it, and though it gradually acquired more luxury features, including air-conditioning and power windows, it essentially remained an uncompromised performance car. In 2004, the Viper SRT-10 offered a claimed 500 hp and 525 lb ft, and was still one of the fastest-accelerating cars in the world.

So the muscle car might have survived, but Chrysler had changed. In 1999, the world was astonished to hear that it had merged with the German giant Daimler-Benz. Mercedes cars were the result of high-tech, thorough engineering . . . and they were undeniably conservative. Could the new Daimler-Chrysler Corporation be expected to carry on producing cars like the Viper and Prowler? It didn't look that way, and as time went on it was clear that Daimler-Chrysler would be controlled from Germany, not Detroit. Many of the engineers who had produced those radical cars left for General Motors. In 2001, it was announced the Plymouth brand was to go. But the new management had no intention of killing off the Viper, and for 2005 planned to launch the Dodge Magnum, a sporty-looking five-door fastback/station wagon that would reintroduce a famous Chrysler name: "Take charge of the streets . . . Everything about the new 2005 Dodge Magnum says, 'Get Out of My Way' . . . And yes, it's got a Hemi." Arrogant and aggressive? No doubt about it, the Hemi was on its way back.

BELOW: Loosely based on a truck engine it might be, but in practice the Viper's V-10 was completely different, with an aluminum block, different heads, pistons, valves, and countless other details. Plus there was more redesigning to squeeze it all under the Viper's hood.

"Not as fast on the getaway as a 427 Corvette or a Hemi, but it is faster on the getaway than a Volkswagen, a slow freight train, and your old man's Cadillac."

AMC & Studebaker

So much for the Big Three of Detroit, but what about the little guys of the American motor industry? Did AMC and Studebaker build muscle cars worthy of the name? In AMC's case, the answer is yes, but they were a late developer.

In trying to make a muscle car, the little American Motors Corporation was hampered in two ways. First and most obvious, they just didn't have the resources of GM, Ford, or Chrysler. Less money to invest, fewer engineers, and a more limited range of engines—the Big Three had an extensive range of big-block V8s to choose from, which made perfect muscle car motors, but AMC's biggest was an aging 327 ci, producing just 270 hp. The 327's power had actually not increased since the late 1950s.

AMC's second big problem vis-à-vis muscle cars was their image. AMC cars were seen as competent, sensible, and a bit dull. It was an image that AMC seemed reluctant to let go of. Even when the fastback Marlin was launched, one advertising line described it as "Newest of the Sensible Spectaculars." In other words, the sportiest AMC yet was quite a car, but sensible at the same time. It was probably true, but not the way to attract the 1960s muscle car drivers.

More Grand Tourer than muscle car? Maybe, but the elegant Studebaker Super Hawk could be ordered with a supercharged V8.

Studebaker
XSV
377

ABOVE: AMC worked hard to energize its image in the late sixties, both with the Javelin/AMX and re-engined sedans like the Hornet SC/360.

The Marlin fastback was a start at least, a recognition that Ford might really be on to something with that newfangled Mustang. (It certainly was—by the time the Marlin appeared, Lee Iaccoca and his boys had sold over half a million of them.) The Marlin's fastback roof first appeared on the Tarpon, a 1964 show car based on AMC's compact 106-inch wheelbase Rambler American. As such, it would have been a fine compact competitor for the Mustang or Barracuda. But AMC management didn't want a compact pony car, and decreed that the fastback shape be based on the 112-inch wheelbase Rambler Classic instead. By 1965, when the Marlin fastback was finally announced, the Classic had grown by another five inches in length.

However, despite the sporty-looking fastback and black roof, AMC emphasized the Marlin's comfort and roominess—this was a roomy, classy coupe for the buyer who wanted something a little different. "It's got too much luxury," went the advertisement, "to be just another sporty car."

That was a sensible move, as the base engine was a 155 hp 232 six (named "Torque Command"), while the optional V8s were fairly mild too, a 198 hp 287 and the 270 hp 327. You did get power front discs as part of the package (unusual on any

RIGHT: All Javelins and AMXs came with a full set of instruments, which not all their competitors did. With these two, AMC was making a determined attempt to break into the large (and lucrative) pony car market.

BELOW: Halfway between a true sports car and a four-seat pony car, the AMX was basically a short-wheelbase Javelin with two seats. It was a brave piece of lateral thinking, but sold poorly.

US-built car in 1965) and an interesting "Twin-Stick" transmission, which offered five speeds by adding overdrive to the standard three-speed. Still, even with the 327, the Marlin was no muscle car, and *Mechanix Illustrated* recorded a 0–60 mph time of 9.7 seconds on a car equipped with the optional Shift Command Flash-O-Matic (as in automatic, but manually shiftable) transmission. AMC sold just over 10,000 Marlins in '65, which was a decent figure, but less than half that the following year—fastback buyers seemed to prefer the new Dodge Charger.

Things began to get more interesting in '66 though. For one thing, AMC launched their new V8 engine, the Typhoon. Initially available as a 290, this was eventually stretched right up to 401 ci, with no loss of reliability. Strong and dependable, the Typhoon finally made AMC muscle cars a distinct possibility. In its first year, the 290 Typhoon was squeezed under the hood of the compact

AMC AMX 390 1968

Engine: *315 hp, 390 ci; 425 lb ft*

Transmission: *four-speed manual*

Steering: *recirculating ball, power assisted*

Tires: *Goodyear E70 x 14*

Brakes: *front 11.2 inch discs, power assisted; rear 10.0 inch drums, power assisted*

Suspension: *front independent, coil springs, antiroll bar; rear rigid axle, semi-elliptic leaf springs*

Wheelbase: *97 inches*

Height: *52.0 inches*

Weight: *3,205 pounds*

Rambler American, to create the Rogue. Still not at the frontline muscle car class, but with the 290 in 200 hp two-barrel or 225 hp four-barrel form, the Rogue was powerful enough to be taken seriously. It also came with a four-speed manual transmission, a first for American Motors. Less than 1,500 Rogues were actually built that year, but it was at least a statement of intent.

BELOW: Equipped with AMC's latest and biggest 390 V8, the AMX also became the fastest AMC car ever, with a quarter mile in the 14s and 0–60 mph in 6.6 seconds. No other US manufacturer attempted to make a two-seat sports car from pony car components.

For 1967, the next stage of the Typhoon program was revealed with a new 343 ci version, obtained by boring out the 290. With a single four-barrel carburetor, power was up substantially, to 280 hp at 4,800 rpm, and 365 lb ft at 3,000. It immediately became an affordable $91 option on the Marlin, so things were looking up—the Marlin now held the promise of sporty fastback with a bigger V8 and room for all the family. And all for a little over $3,000. Surely just the thing for family men who liked the look of a Mustang but found it too cramped.

Unfortunately, it didn't work out like that. That year, the Marlin's wheelbase was up 6 inches (to 118 inches) and overall length by even more. This intermediate was rapidly becoming a big car, and weight ballooned by 350 lb. Although the 343 Marlin had a lot more power than the 1965 original, it was barely any faster, at 9.6 seconds 0–60. A Charger 383 by contrast, the Marlin's closest competitor, had an extra 45 hp and could sprint to 60 mph in less than nine seconds. Not only that, but the Marlin's attractive price meant it missed out on some vital sporty-car accoutrements. Bucket seats, for example (standard on the most basic Mustang) cost an extra $177, and a center console another $113 on top of that. So it's hardly surprising that a mere 2,545 Marlins were sold in 1967, with only a few hundred customers opting for the Typhoon 343 V8. The Marlin was dropped at the end of the year.

For 1968, AMC finally produced some real muscle cars. The Javelin was the company's long-awaited response to the Mustang and Camaro, and by all accounts it had done a good job. Dick Teague's fastback shape was handsome, even graceful, compared to the pony car opposition, and somehow fitted with the "Javelin" name. That was inspired too, and AMC seemed to have finally woken up to the fact that car names were a vital part of creating the right image. A "Rambler" trudged along, but a "Javelin" flew at speed.

Unlike some pony cars, the Javelin was intended as a full four-seater, not just a 2+2, and AMC was able to point out it was the same size as a Mercury Cougar, but had more rear legroom. In one way though, it was a classic pony car, with a full range of engine options. These started with the 232 ci six, followed by the Typhoon in a range of sizes: the original 290 in its 200 hp and 225 hp guises, plus the increasingly well-regarded 343. This had been hampered by the weighty, upsized 1967 Marlin, but in the lighter Javelin performed well. Order the "Go Package" along with the 343 (which brought a four-speed manual) and your Javelin would accelerate to 60 mph in 8.1 seconds and turn in a 15.4-second standing quarter. Those figures were posted by *Motor Trend*, which proclaimed it the winner of its sports-personal class that year, "The most significant achievement for an all-new car and the most notable new entry in [its] class."

ABOVE: A luggage rack adds to the carrying capacity of this AMX 390. The AMX was roomy and pleasant transport for two, but as AMC was to find, the US market for two-seaters was strictly limited.

Car and Driver singled out the Javelin's handling for particular praise. "Its long suit was its handling," said this stalwart of American motoring journalism. "It felt very much like a British sports car." (Praise indeed for a US-built muscle car.)

Car and Driver's test car had the top 390 ci V8, though it was a very early example, and not quite up to scratch, so it was the slowest in the six-way test with a Camaro SS, Mustang GT, Cougar XR-7, Barracuda Formula S, and Firebird 400 HO. It was also hampered by a Borg Warner three-speed manual transmission, though a four-speed was optional. It's unlikely that many Javelin 390 buyers, having ordered the most expensive, most powerful V8 on the list, would skimp on the transmission.

In any case, there was a whole host of other options to sporty-up your new Javelin, like the SST option and the "Go Package." Front disc brakes, handling

ABOVE RIGHT: *A new V8 named Typhoon saved AMC's skin, in performance terms. It started out as a 290, was bored out as the well-thought-of 343, and finally produced 315 hp in ultimate 390 ci form.*

suspension (with heavy-duty springs and shocks plus a thicker sway bar), wide wheels, and traction bars were other extra-cost options. With all that on board, plus the four-speed transmission and 315 hp 390, the Javelin was a true muscle car. Four years after the Mustang and GTO, maybe, but they'd got there in the end.

The 390 only became a Javelin option halfway through the model year, once the AMX had been launched. Now this was the most muscle-bound AMC of them all. The AMX was unique, being no more nor less than a short-wheelbase two-seat version of the Javelin. No other American manufacturer had tried this trick, using an existing pony car floorpan, engines, transmissions—in fact, just about every part—as the basis for a sports car.

"They just haven't got the message at American Motors when it comes to building performers. Safety features, yes. Economy and worth, yes. Guts and handling, zilch. Somebody at American Motors needs to get out and live with the kids for a while."

(ROAD TEST, *JUNE 1967*)

Different though it was, the AMX (American Motors Experimental) was not a total surprise, having appeared as a show car back in 1966. But who would have thought then that conservative, safe American Motors would actually go ahead and offer it for sale? The AMX was proof positive that AMC realized they had to change their spots and take on a more dynamic image if they were to survive. It wasn't just a case of appealing to younger drivers: many middle-aged Americans, both men and women, were happily buying Camaros, Firebirds, and Mustangs, and AMC had to keep up.

Although it was clearly derived from the Javelin, the little AMX was a whole foot shorter in the wheelbase. AMC sensibly decided to make it a roomy two-seater instead of a squeezed 2+2. Best of all, this shaved a few hundred pounds of the curb weight, and even with the big 390 V8, an AMX tipped the scales at 3,205 lb, so the 390's 315 hp endowed it with startling performance. *Car and Driver* lost no time in getting hold of an AMX 390 for testing, and recorded 14.8 seconds over the quarter mile, at 95 mph, plus a 0–60 mph time of just 6.6 seconds.

> ***"There's no pseudo façade with the Javelin. From the minute you slide behind the wheel and look at that wood steering wheel and the giant speedometer and tachometer staring back at you, you know this is all man's car."***
>
> **(MOTOR TREND, *MARCH 1969*)**

To back up the go, there were all the usual sporty-car cues: reclining bucket seats, four-speed transmission, the heavy-duty suspension, E70 x 14 Goodyear Polyglas tires, and so on. All of these were available on the smaller-engined AMXs as well, the 290 or 343. AMC also hired race driver Craig Breedlove to set a few speed records with the AMX 390. He more than fulfilled his contract, setting up 106 new records on a Texas test track. This again had the effect of boosting AMC's image, and they made the most of it by building fifty red, white, and blue Craig Breedlove special edition AMXs. AMC went racing too, entering a team of Javelins in the Trans Am series. Two cars, joined by Peter Revson and George Follmer, came second and fourth on their second outing.

The AMX and Javelin had certainly done wonders for AMC's image, but 1969 was the year of

AMC JAVELIN SST 390 1968

Engine: *315hp, 390 ci V8; 425 lb ft*

Transmission: *four-speed manual*

Steering: *recirculating ball, power assisted*

Tires: *Goodyear E70 x 14*

Brakes: *front 11.2 inch discs, power assisted; rear 10.0 inch drums, power assisted*

Suspension: *front independent, coil springs, antiroll bar; rear rigid axle, semi-elliptic leaf springs*

Wheelbase: *109 inches*

Height: *52.0 inches*

Weight: *3,430 pounds*

***ABOVE:** The thinking man's muscle car? The Javelin was a breed apart from the GTOs, Mustangs, and Chargers, lacking their brute force, but it was perhaps all the better for it. Whatever, it succeeded in boosting AMC's image.*

loud colors and wild graphics. AMC responded with the "Big Bad" options, which included brash colors like Big Bad Green and Big Bad Orange. Oddly, not many AMX owners paid $34 extra to drive a Big Bad car—maybe AMC customers, even the ones who bought an AMX, were still conservatives at heart! Mechanically, the AMX and Javelin for '69 were little changed, with the 315 hp 390 V8 remaining the hottest option, though if that wasn't enough, a new pair of fiberglass hood scoops was offered (to be installed by the owner), which claimed an extra 12 hp thanks to better breathing.

Things changed for 1970, which would turn out to be the final year for the two-seat AMX. It was face-lifted that year, slightly longer and heavier than the '69 car, but a new base V8 of 360 ci more than made up for any performance deficit. At 290 hp, that was significantly more powerful than the old 343. The 390 option was still there, now boosted to 325 hp, and came with a close-ratio four-speed transmission. Both engines were available with the Go Package, which added power front disc brakes, F70 x 14 white-letter tires, a handling package, heavy-duty cooling system, and Ram-Air hood scoop. With all that equipment, the final AMX looked like a muscle car, and performed like one. Eric Dahlquist wrote about a 390 AMX for *Motor Trend*, and liked its quality. He might also have added that at 6.56 seconds to 60 mph, and 14.68 seconds over the quarter, this AMX was the fastest production car AMC had ever built. Sadly, the AMX remained something of a minority interest, and only just over 4,000 were built. In its best year (1969) the figure was less than 8,300. Maybe it fell between two classifications: too big and American for fans of imported sports cars, and not enough seats for the mainstream buyer. Its name lived on as a badge on other AMCs, but in its short life, the two-seat AMX had succeeded in transforming AMC's staid image.

The Javelin always sold in bigger numbers, never enough to frighten Ford, but respectable for AMC. Around 55,000 Javelins found homes in the first year, and interestingly, nearly half of those had the sporty SST option. So the AMC pony car was clearly viewed as a sports item, not just a cosmetic coupe. The figure was down to around 40,000 in '69, with over half being SSTs.

For 1970, there were no changes to the mechanical options, though AMC capitalized on their Trans Am racing involvement, with a "Mark Donohue" special

BELOW: Studebaker's secret weapon was a supercharged 289 ci V8 that made up what it lacked in cubic inches with sheer get-up-and-go.

edition. In a determined attempt to win the Trans Am Championship (which would boost the company's muscle car street credibility), AMC recruited the dream team of race car builder Roger Penske and driver Mark Donohue. Together, these two had won the championship in both '68 and '69, and now they'd signed a three-year deal to work their race-winning magic with the Javelin. They did make a few changes to the Javelin for racing, the most noticeable of which was a small rear spoiler. To be legal for Trans Am, the spoiler had to be sold on 2,500 production cars, so AMC took the opportunity to create a special edition, complete with a replica of Mr. Donohue's signature on the spoiler. It was restrained in comparison with Mopar's "Winged Warriors," but looked good nonetheless. The Donohue Javelins (all SSTs) also came with dual exhausts, power front discs, E70 x 14 low-profile tires, a handling package, and Ram-Air induction on an AMX-style hood. Buyers could choose from either 360 or 390 V8s, and an automatic or four-speed manual transmission.

Another Trans Am special edition followed, just 100 replicas of Ronnie Kaplan's race Javelin, in red, white, and blue. But the Javelin, like all muscle cars, was suffering from the more difficult climate, and sales slumped by over 30 percent to 28,210. Once again, more than half were SSTs.

BELOW: Doesn't look like a muscle car, does it? In standard form, the Studebaker Hawk was more an elegant, upmarket GT than any sort of muscle car. Tick the "Super Hawk" box, however, and that blown V8 came as part of the package.

BELOW: *The Hawk was looking dated by the early 1960s, and though Brooks Stevens did a superb update, it wasn't enough to secure big sales or save Studebaker from commercial oblivion—the Hawk and Avanti were the final two cars they built.*

While all this was going on, AMC wasn't pinning all their muscle car hopes on the Javelin and AMX. Hurst, the famed tuning parts company, approached the company with an idea for the ultimate Rambler muscle car, by combining the full-power 390 ci V8 with the compact Rambler Rogue sedan. AMC liked the idea—a classic muscle car combination of big engine/small car—and gave the green light.

Based on the two-door Rogue hardtop, the SC/Rambler was powered by the latest 325 hp version of the 390, but weighed only around 3,000 lb, so it was actually lighter than the little AMX. The result was a weight-to-power ratio of 10.03 lb/hp and stunning performance. The factory claimed a low 14-second quarter mile, which was confirmed by *Road Test*, which achieved a 14.4 with a terminal 100.44 mph.

The SC/Rambler (or "Scrambler," as some people insisted on calling it) looked like the hot rod it was, with a massive hood scoop for Ram-Air induction and dual

RIGHT: The Avanti was exotic, individualistic, and quite unlike anything out of Detroit. Fast, too, in supercharged R2 form, but like the Hawk its appeal was too limited to ensure survival.

exhaust pipes. A column-mounted Sun tachometer added to the hot rod image, as did the five-spoke six-inch mag wheels and the red, white, and blue paint job. Over 1,500 SC/Ramblers were built in all, in three batches.

Not a huge seller, but quite an image booster, so for 1970 the SC/Rambler returned. Well, not quite, as the Rebel "Machine" of that year was based on the much weightier Rebel, with 114-inch wheelbase and an all-up weight of 3,650 lb. However, it still came with the 390 ci V8, offering 340 hp at 5,100 rpm, not to mention a close-ratio four-speed transmission with Hurst shifter, Ram-Air, and an 8,000 rpm hood-mounted tachometer. Buyers had a choice of 3.54:1 or 3.91:1 rear axles, as AMC was hoping to attract the drag racing crowd with this car—it was actually launched at the NHRA World Championship event in late 1969.

Heavy-duty springs and shocks, a low back pressure dual exhaust, front and rear sway bars, power front disc brakes, and high-back bucket seats were all standard as well, not to mention the white with red and blue stripes paint job pioneered by the SC/Rambler. There was still a Hurst connection too, though a purely symbolic one—they applied the stripes. Oddly, little was made of it.

Despite carrying several hundred pounds more than the SC/Rambler, with only slightly more power, AMC claimed around the same acceleration times, notably a 14.4-second quarter mile, at 98 mph. On the other hand, AMC's advertising copy for the Machine was downbeat to the point of negativity: "If you have delusions of entering the Daytona 500 with the Machine, or challenging people at random," it went, "the Machine is not fast. You should know that. For instance, it is not as fast on the getaway as a 427 Corvette, or Hemi, but it is faster on the getaway than a Volkswagen, a slow freight train, and your old man's Cadillac." Despite this, AMC managed to sell over 2,300 Machines in 1970.

But the hot rods fell away in 1971, when AMC's sole muscle car offerings were the restyled Javelin and AMX, which now shared the same bodyshell, longer and wider than the old ones, but slightly lower. Alongside it was a muscle version of the all-new Hornet, this aiming at being a low-insurance alternative to traditional muscle cars. It was small enough to avoid the 25 percent insurance surcharge imposed on bigger muscle cars and could return 17 mpg on the highway.

The combination of the 245 hp 360 and compact Hornet body also made it quite fast, with a hot rod recording a 14.8-second quarter mile. Just the thing for straitened times? Well, you'd think so, and AMC talked of selling as many as 10,000 Hornet

SC/360s. Full marks for optimism, but they actually sold fewer than 800.

Meanwhile, the AMX became no more than a slightly more sporting Javelin, with a package of items to differentiate the two, including a rear-facing wide and low hood scoop, extra spoilers, and trims. It also came with a base V8 of 360 ci and 245 hp, with a four-barrel 285 hp version optional. The plain Javelin was also available with a 304 ci two-barrel unit of 210 hp. But the new top-line muscle V8 was a 401, introduced to replace the 390, the most powerful production engine ever offered by AMC.

This produced 330 hp at 5,200 rpm and 430 lb ft at 3,300, with a single four-barrel carburetor. In the final Javelin, it wasn't quite as quick as the 1969–70 390, but it did have the extra weight of that bigger 1971 body to haul around. Performance was still respectable though, with a 0–60 mph time of 7.7 seconds and a standing quarter of 15.5. In this form, the Javelin and AMX survived up until 1974, when they too finally succumbed to the oil crisis.

ABOVE: A rare beast, but rarer still in England, where this Hawk is registered. Studebaker's 289 ci V8 put out 289 hp with a Paxton supercharger on board, giving the Super Hawk brisk (though not Avanti-like) performance.

STUDEBAKER: SUPERCHARGED RARITIES

Studebaker is not a name normally associated with muscle cars. Not only that, but by the early sixties, this little guy of American motor manufacture was struggling to survive. They actually gave up altogether in 1966, a couple of years after closing their South Bend, Indiana, factory and moving to Canada. But in 1963–64, as they were on the final slippery slope to oblivion and the Big Three were just waking up to the concept of a muscle car, Studebaker did build bona fide muscle cars itself. They may not have looked like conventional muscle cars, and didn't have an excess of cubic inches, but they were fast—very fast.

The Avanti certainly didn't look the part of a sedan-based muscle car, because it wasn't. Instead, this Raymond Loewy–designed four-seat sports car was intended to look as Italian as its name suggested it was. Fresh and original in American terms, the Avanti was Studebaker's last desperate throw of the dice. The company was already in deep trouble, and the Avanti was its last chance. It looked sporty, but with a V8 limited to 289 ci, it sounded like a poor excuse for a muscle car, except for one thing: supercharging.

Adding a Paxton SN-60 centrifugal supercharger boosted the 289's output from 240 hp to 289 hp at 5,200 rpm, backed up by 330 lb ft at 3,600. Despite humbler

origins (it started out in 1951 as a 232 ci unit), the Studebaker V8 was strong enough to take this power, using a lower 9.0:1 compression (taken down from the standard 10.25:1) and a sealed Carter AFB four-barrel carburetor.

On top of all that, the Avanti weighed only 3,400 lb, so there wasn't too much to hamper that 289 hp. It also had fine aerodynamics, as top speed trials would demonstrate. In early 1963, an R2 Avanti (R1 was the unsupercharged base car), completely stock apart from its exhaust system, clocked 158.15 mph through a measured mile. There was an R3 as well, which took the supercharged V8 out to 304 ci, though this was only fitted to ten cars. One of those ten established a new two-way Flying Mile American record, at 168.15 mph. Mind you, you had to be quite well off to purchase one of the rare R3s, all of which were hand built at Paxton.

Nor was the Avanti only a top speed specialist. *Road & Track* tested a standard four-speed manual R2 in October 1962 and recorded a 0–60 mph time of 7.3 seconds. That made it quicker than a Pontiac GTO, which at that point was hardly a gleam in

Jim Wangers's eye. The unsupercharged Avanti wasn't in the picture, performance-wise (0–60 in around 9 seconds was typical, with a quarter mile of about 17 seconds), and came with a standard three-speed transmission. But R2 buyers had the choice of that four-speed or a three-speed Power Shift automatic. The Borg Warner unit was modified to allow manual shifting of the gears, and a manual downchange was possible up to 80 mph. According to *Motor Trend*, the Power Shift took an Avanti R2 to 60 mph in 8 seconds.

Better still, the supercharged Avanti backed up its impressive performance with good brakes and fine handling, something that many early muscle cars lacked. It was in fact the first full-size American car to come with front disc brakes, made by Bendix under license from Dunlop.

Just over 3,300 Avantis were built in the 1963 model year, and it returned for 1964, though time was fast running out for the company. Once again, the 240 hp R1, 289 hp R2, and 335 hp R3 were on offer. One new option (perhaps designed for customers suspicious of supercharging) was the R4, which used twin four-barrel carburetors in place of the R2's blower. It didn't give away much in power, at 280 hp, though only one car was fitted with this motor. The R3 remained the performance leader, and one of these was timed at 14.3 seconds over the quarter mile, with a 6.7-second 0–60.

BELOW: Turning a Hawk into a Super Hawk brought power disc brakes, upgraded suspension, wider tires, and full carpeting, as well as the supercharged V8. Supercharging was the only option open to Studebaker, as it didn't have a suitable big-cube V8.

And this wouldn't have been the Avanti without some top speed records. Andy Granatelli, who had set those records the previous year, returned to the Bonneville Salt Flats for another go. He broke his own record, with 170.78 mph in an R3. Even Studebaker President Sherwood H. Egbert couldn't resist a pass, and wasn't far behind Granatelli at 168 mph. All very heroic, and quite an achievement, but it didn't save the company, and the Avanti was dropped after only 809 cars had been built for its final year.

The Avanti wasn't the only actor in Studebaker's admittedly short muscle car story. Remember how the Buick Gran Sports were often described as the "gentleman's muscle car"? The Studebaker Super Hawk was there several years before them. The Hawk had a long and varied history, starting out as a Raymond Loewy design in 1953 with a thorough restyle in 1956. By 1962, it looked near the end of its life, but Studebaker commissioned designer Brooks Stevens (the well-known and prolific stylist) to give it a quick restyling. Quick was the word. In a matter of weeks, Stevens had come up with an elegant four-seat coupe that deserved its Grand Tourismo tag.

Although clearly an update of the original Hawk, this final incarnation looked modern, svelte, and classy. Brooks Stevens did away with the outdated tailfins, squared off the roofline, and gave the car a Mercedes-like front grille. The result looked as if it really was ready to cross the United States or Europe, in fine style, and in the true GT tradition.

None of which made it a muscle car, unless the buyer happened to tick the "Super Hawk" box on the order form. For a very reasonable $581.70, this brought power disc brakes, heavy-duty springs and shocks, traction bars, a rear antiroll bar, and twin-traction rear axle, as well as 6.70-15 four-ply tires, full carpeting, and a 160 mph speedometer. Oh, and the R2 Avanti's supercharged V8!

Naturally, the results were not quite as spectacular as in the lighter Avanti, but 289 hp was still enough to turn the Super Hawk into a reasonably quick car. *Motor Trend* tested one, and recorded 16.8 seconds over the quarter mile and 0–60 in 8.5 seconds, plus a top speed of 118 mph at 5,700 rpm. Transmission choices were a four-speed manual or that Borg Warner Power Shift. Fast, well braked, and roomy, the Super Hawk fulfilled its promise of Grand Touring. But maybe it was just too elegant to be a true muscle car.

"GTX. Plymouth's exciting new Supercar. King of the Belvederes. Standard equipment: the biggest GT engine in the world. Our Super Commando 440 V8. Optional equipment: the famous Plymouth Hemi."

Drag Racing

Racing played a vital role in the muscle car story. The old adage of "win on Sunday, sell on Monday" was never more true than here. Most muscle car buyers were young, male, and enthusiastic race goers. And nothing impressed them more, nothing gained more bragging rights or street kudos outside the drive-in, than the car that dominated the drag strip, or NASCAR, or the Trans Am series.

Of course, the muscle car on offer in the local showroom was often just a distant cousin of its race-winning counterpart. Cars that won races or were fastest down the strip had body parts in aluminum or wafer-thin steel; their ultra-high-compression V8s used solid lifters, peaky cams, and twin four-barrel carburetors. And that was just in Super Stock, ostensibly the class for production cars.

But that hardly mattered, because these super-tuned muscle machines looked almost identical to the showroom car, and clearly came from the same stable. The glamor of race wins trickled down, allowing pure road muscle cars to bask in reflected glory. That created showroom traffic, and sold more cars, which was why the manufacturers put so much time, effort, and money into racing. Those top managers who pushed racing involvement—men like Bunkie Knudsen and John DeLorean—were car enthusiasts who loved being part of the racing scene, but they could only justify it if the bottom line was higher sales on Monday.

Drag racing inspired muscle cars, and vice versa: couldn't have one without the other. Come to the Plymouth meet over the following pages.

PLYMOUTH
TEXAS
FF·5189

ABOVE: *A '68 Plymouth Road Runner lays some rubber down prior to another quick run up the strip. This is a highly modified Runner, but Plymouth's bargain-basement muscle car was a good choice for drag racing, being lighter and less burdened with luxury equipment than some.*

In the Beginning

Muscle cars and drag racing. The two are inextricably linked, and they really play out the chicken and egg conundrum. Did muscle cars grow out of drag racing, or was it the other way round? If you're in any doubt about this close connection, look at the road test figures quoted, not just in this book but in any literature about muscle cars. Outright acceleration, measured over the standing quarter mile, and 0–60 mph time, are the most significant figures for any muscle car, and the key to muscle car kudos. Prospective buyers weren't that interested in cornering ability, or braking, or even top speed. Still less the gas mileage. Standing start acceleration was the key.

This acceleration obsession explains a great deal. It sheds light on why early muscle cars had (by European sports car standards) soft suspension and floppy handling. It explains why these heavy, fast machines stuck with inadequate drum brakes for years after discs had become standard on other high-performance cars. And why so many muscle cars offered a wide range of optional rear axle ratios—it wasn't to allow more restful freeway cruising, or to squeeze a few more miles out of a gallon of gas. It was to give the car an edge on standing-start acceleration. And many muscle car owners really did take their cars drag racing on weekends, whether officially on the strip or unofficially in Saturday night red-light showdowns. So the muscle car really did rise out of drag race culture, which answers that chicken-egg question. Drag racing came first. The first organized race was held back in 1948. No doubt there were plenty of "unofficial" races before then, but the official format of two cars, side by side, both timed over an exact quarter mile, quickly took hold. The sport spread rapidly across the country, with the first dedicated drag strips being built. At first, as is usually the case in "young" sports, it was barely organized, with few rules, if any.

That changed. In 1951 Wally Parks, editor of *Hot Rod* magazine, was instrumental in setting up the National Hot Rod Association (NHRA), which began to set up rules and regulations for official drag racing. Safety standards improved and distinct competition classes were drawn up. Drag racing was becoming more respectable, but there were still horror stories in the mainstream media of reckless kids being inspired to race on the street after watching an official drag meeting. *Life* magazine ran a cover story to that effect as late as April 1957: "Safety groups and some police officers feel that the glorification of speed on the strips infects teenagers with a fatal spirit of derring-do on the highways."

It was debatable whether kids were really inspired to reckless driving after watching a drag race, or whether they would have done it anyway. Either way, the manufacturers couldn't be seen to condone any such behavior, and in 1957 the Automobile Manufacturers Association imposed a ban on factory-sponsored racing. In practice, GM and Chrysler found backdoor routes to helping out favored racers, and only Ford stuck to the letter of the ban. AMC, of course, was far too sensible to go racing, until 1968, when it made a determined bid for the youth market.

BELOW: Drag racing remains and active and thriving sport, and one of its strengths is that classic muscle cars can still be seen competing on weekends all over the United States. Somehow, it seems more fitting than gathering dust in an air-conditioned museum!

In fact, the AMA might as well not have bothered with a ban. At first, the manufacturers sold special parts over the counter for customers to fit themselves. The NHRA found a constant battle on its hands, trying to keep the Super Stock class for standard production cars. That was the original intention, but as ever more exotic parts became available, the average Super Stock drag racer (aided by a well-funded or well-connected owner) moved farther and farther away from its showroom cousin.

So the NHRA changed the rules: those special parts had to be fitted to standard production cars, on the production line. No problem, the manufacturers simply built drag-race specials at the factory themselves, in tiny numbers, and sold or lent them to favorite drivers and teams. Eventually, the NHRA gave up trying to keep all racers stock, and set up the FX (Factory Experimental) class. Now the radically lightened Super Duty Pontiacs, the cut-and-shut AWB Plymouths and Dodges, and (later) the overhead cam Mustangs could fight it out among themselves, leaving amateurs with stock cars a chance to compete in Super Stock.

BELOW: Another good choice. The Plymouth Duster married a midsize V8 with the relatively compact and lightweight Valiant coupe. What was true in 1969 is still true on twenty-first-century drag strips.

Right: The beauty of the quarter mile was that almost anyone could have a go, in almost any car. It didn't have to be trick, exotic, or expensive to have a couple of runs.

Below right: At the other end of the scale, superficially stock bodyshells could hide one-off masterpieces that were hand-built machines with just one aim in mind: E/T slicing.

That still allowed the man in the street to order a showroom muscle car with some trick drag options. The Oldsmobile 4-4-2 was a case in point. A direct response to the Pontiac GTO, it was a typical intermediate muscle car of the mid-sixties, not especially fearsome but with a good reputation for handling. In 1966, the new W30 option package turned the 4-4-2 into a drag racer. This brought stronger pistons, a high-lift cam, a beefier valve train, and high-capacity air intake. There were fiberglass inner wings, to trim off some of the road car's excess weight, and the battery was

remounted in the trunk—the last feature was a dead giveaway as to the W30's intended use. A trunk-mounted battery placed a few more pounds over the rear wheels, aiding traction a little.

The W30 was a popular option, and by 1970 with a 455 ci V8 on board, it could cover the standing quarter in the mid-14s, and rocket to 60 mph in less than 6 seconds. Other manufacturers offered drag options too, often stripped down to save weight, with street essentials like a heater or radio unceremoniously ditched. In theory, any of these strippers could be driven to work or the mall—they were still street legal, after all—but as author Steve Statham pointed out in his book, *Maximum Muscle:* "It was hard to picture any other function for the car (a stripped-down Chevy II) but racing, despite official protestation otherwise."

Some manufacturers were more transparent, offering only limited or even nonexistent warranties on street-legal cars intended for the strip. The Chrysler street Hemi was one such, and Pontiac inserted a clause into the handbook for its 1962 Super Duty, to make the situation crystal clear: "Super Duty Pontiacs," it sternly intoned, "are not intended for highway or general passenger car use and they are not supplied by the Pontiac Motor Division for such purposes."

Chevrolet, of course, had a head start with the 409, which dominated drag racing in the early sixties. At the time, it was the ultimate expression of the big-block Chevy,

***BELOW:* A 1969 Road Runner takes off. For a few years, Chrysler's Hemi was almost unbeatable over the quarter mile. Very few drivers actually bought one (it was never a cheap option), but the Hemi's glamour reached beyond its numbers, and trickled down to put a shine on quite mundane Mopar cars.**

which had been launched in 1958 as a 348, itself available in hot 315 hp form, with three two-barrel carburetors, solid lifts, and 11.0:1 compression. By 1961, make that 350 hp, but even that 348 had been overtaken by bigger-cube V8s from Ford and Chrysler, so Chevy bored and stroked it to create the classic 409. Slotted into the downsized Impala, this had immediate drag racing potential, maybe not the two-barrel 340 and 350 hp Turbo Thrust, but the Turbo Fire was a different story.

This offered 360 hp with a single four-barrel, 380 hp (triple two-barrels), or 409 hp (twin four-barrels). As well as scoring the magic 1 hp per cubic inch, the ultimate 409 proved super-fast on the strip. Even in standard form, owners could expect a mid-14 second quarter, and modified Impala 409s were running in the mid-13s in 1961. The following year, with more engine changes and more power, the top Impalas were down to the high-12s, and in 1961–62, a Chevy 409 was definitely the car to beat.

For 1963, Chevrolet offered a more radical strip-ready Impala direct from the production line. The Z11 shed weight via an aluminum front end and did without soundproofing, heater, and radio. Even the 409 was stroked out to a full 427 ci, and equipped with modified heads, a 12.5:1 compression, and twin four-barrel carbs. Only fifty-seven of these 430 hp Z11s were actually built. It was so specialized that the NHRA made it the first entrant in the new FX class.

If people saw the Impala 409 as the car to beat, Pontiac evidently thought so too,

BELOW: Thankfully, some owners of classic muscle cars are still keen to indulge in a little weekend racing, as this near-stock Belvedere testifies, though it's a fair bet that not many of these these cars are used as day-to-day transport any more. In the sixties, many muscle cars performed the double role.

and made a determined assault with its Super Duty parts, designed for the Catalina and Grand Prix coupe. A whole range of engine parts was available over the counter for Pontiac's 389 ci V8. Choose the right combination of cylinder heads, cams, high compression pistons, and headers, and a '61 389 could be coaxed up to 368 hp.

That was fine until the NHRA ruled that special parts had to be factory-fitted, but Pontiac complied to the letter, by fitting all the Super Duty parts on the production line. The result was not cheap, and certainly not suitable for grocery runs, but it was effective. Now beefed up to 421 ci, the V8 also came with big valves and heavy-duty springs, forged aluminum pistons, and solid lifters, among other things. It was also stronger and more durable than the street engine, thanks to a forged steel crankshaft, bigger main bearings, and a six-quart oil pan. Weight was pared off with aluminum wings, hood, and bumpers, with Plexiglas replacing real glass in the windows. The final Super Duty 421 Catalina of 1963 made an estimated 540–550 hp, with a 13.0:1 compression and another 100 lb. shed through the use of more aluminum and Plexiglas. Sub-14 second quarters were possible, but just because the Super Duty was factory-built, didn't mean that just anyone could order one: Pontiac assembled only eighty-eight of these cars in 1963, which underlines just how specialized they were.

Meanwhile, Chrysler wasn't standing idly by. It was still working on the second-generation Hemi, but in the meantime the big Max Wedge V8 kept the Mopar flag flying. The 413 Max Wedge came with a 11.0:1 or 13.5:1 compression, and 410 hp or 420 hp respectively. Depending on whether it was powering a Dodge or Plymouth, the motor was referred to as a Ramcharger or Super Stock. Chrysler's official line was that this race-tuned Max Wedge was for those who wanted maximum street performance. "The engine," said Dodge's chief engineer George Gibson, "is designed for maximum acceleration form a standing start and should be excellently suited for special police pursuit work." "Police work," of course, was a euphemism.

The Max Wedge was taken out to 426 ci, now offering 425 hp with the optional 13.5:1 compression, plus 480 lb ft. That was the top tune of three stages, including a single four-barrel carb version with 400 hp, intended for the oval circuits, where durability over a whole race was just as important as sheer power. Drag racers, of course, had to produce their prodigious power for seconds at a time. Powered by this 426R Max Wedge, Dodges and Plymouths began to score drag race wins, which in turn helped attract the top talent to drive them, men like Bill Golden and Roger Lindamood. For maximum effect, the V8 was fitted to the smallest, lightest Mopars that would take it, the Plymouth Savoy or Dodge 330 two-doors.

The second-generation Hemi was launched in 1964 and effectively took over from the Max Wedge as Chrysler's top drag motor. Details of the latest Hemi's development can be found elsewhere, but it's worth reiterating that the Hemi's secret was combining the deep-breathing hemispherical combustion chambers of the previous Hemi with the sheer cubic inches of the Max Wedge. Chrysler might claim 425 hp for the new engine—the same as for the top 426R—but the true figure was more like 500 hp, with more to come later. As a limited road option through the

Below: It wasn't just the compacts and intermediates that went racing. Full-size cars like this Fury would often race against a Galaxie or Impala as well. But ultimately, the smaller muscle cars proved more competitive, especially once the manufacturers went in for radical weight reduction.

sixties, the Hemi was exotic enough, but this original race engine was special indeed, with a magnesium inlet manifold, 328-degree cam, and 12.5:1 compression.

As such, it would power some truly radical factory drag racers. In an attempt to outlaw flimsy racing bodies in the Super Stock class, the NHRA had ruled that fiberglass panels could not replace steel ones. So when Mopar's A990 drag weapon was launched (either a Plymouth Belvedere or Dodge Coronet), it kept the steel panels, but of half the standard thickness. All the windows were acrylic, while minor items like door hinges were made of aluminum—Chrysler was going as far as possible within the rules to shave off the ounces. The A990 had no sound insulation or even seam filler. The small, basic seats (lighter than stock) came from the Dodge A-100 pickup, and the rear seat was taken out altogether. It goes without saying that a radio, heater, sun visors, and other convenience items were nowhere to be seen. There was some very thin carpet though, and to a casual observer the A990 looked almost stock. But it didn't accelerate like a standard Belvedere or Coronet. At the 1965

Winternationals, Bill Jenkins in an A990 was quickest of the day, at 11.39 seconds and 126.05 mph.

Not that the A990 was Chrysler's most radical drag racer. The new FX classes opened the doors to just about anything, and Mopar took advantage of that by building a small number of "AWB" Coronets and Belvederes. The AWB part stood for "Altered Wheelbase." On a drag racer, moving the rear axle forward shifts weight distribution to the rear, thus improving traction, and the AWB's axles were 15 inches ahead of the standard position. In the event, this was held to be too radical even for FX, though the American Hot Rod Association (AHRA) did accept the AWBs, one of which managed a time under 10 seconds at York, Pennsylvania, in April 1966. The top drag racers were becoming more and more specialized, and just a few months later, Jim Thornton of the Ramchargers team took an AWB through the lights in 8.91 seconds, with the considerable help of Hilborn fuel injection, nitromethane fuel, and high-intake risers.

ABOVE AND RIGHT: Those AWB Coronets and Belvederes, not to mention the overhead cam Mustangs and Super Duty Pontiacs, started something. In an attempt to keep "Super Stock" within shouting distance of stock, a new FX class catered for the radically modified dragsters—the funny cars came later.

What was Ford doing all this time? Surprisingly for a company with such a strong sporting reputation in the later sixties, Ford played little factory part in early drag racing, and when they finally did step in, they lagged behind in the early sixties. This was partly a hangover from the presidency of Bob McNamara, who was not a racing fan and ensured that Ford stuck with that 1957 AMA ban.

When McNamara left to join the Kennedy administration, the company began to look again at drag racing, though it had some catching up to do. The 352 ci V8 was opened out to 390 ci, then to a 406. With a triple two-barrel carburetor setup, this was claiming 405 hp, though it was still hampered by the weighty full-size Galaxie that Ford chose to take racing. Even special lightweight Galaxies, commissioned by Ford for the 1962 A/FX class, with fiberglass body panels, weren't truly competitive.

But the new 427 V8 of the following year was a different matter. Although it would be used as a street engine, this also slotted neatly under the NHRA's weight limit (and for that matter, NASCAR's). It had clearly been designed with high outputs in mind, with a tremendous amount of strength built in. Impact-extruded pistons, reinforced con-rods, and cross-bolted main bearing caps were clues that Ford didn't see this engine restricted to commuter duties. It also came with solid lifters, a high-lift cam, exhaust headers, and an aluminum intake. The result, with the optional twin four-barrel carbs, was 425 hp at 6,000 rpm, plus 480 lb ft at 3,700.

The 427 was a huge improvement, but didn't reach its full potential on the strip until Ford fitted it into the Fairlane in 1964. Smaller and lighter than the big Galaxie, the Fairlane Thunderbolt weighed only 3,225 lb. in drag racing guise, aided by fiberglass body parts. Whether fitted with a four-speed manual transmission or a modified Lincoln automatic, it proved capable of sub-12-second quarter miles. One hundred Thunderbolts were built until the Mustang came along and became Ford's drag weapon of choice. Good though the 427 was, Chrysler's Hemi still had the edge in drag racing. Ford thought it had the answer, in the form of an overhead cam version

for the 427, for which it claimed nearly 600 hp, and that with a single four-barrel carburetor. There was a single overhead cam per cylinder bank, and hemispherical combustion chambers (Mopar didn't have a monopoly on these), not to mention a long (6 feet) timing chain to drive both cams of this tall engine.

In fact, the "Cammer" 427 was far larger and taller than the original, so when Ford commissioned Holman-Moody to build a short run of Cammy Mustangs, it wasn't just a case of slotting in the new engine. At that time, the stock Mustang wouldn't even accept the standard big-block V8, so Holman-Moody had to take out the front shock towers altogether, using a leaf-spring front suspension instead. The rear axle was moved forward three inches, and the doors and entire front end were of fiberglass. In short, there wasn't much of the original Mustang left in a Cammer, though the resulting machine was able to turn in quarter miles between 10.0 and 10.7 seconds, so it was probably worth it.

Eleven of those Cammer Mustangs were built, and the engine stuck with drag racing only, as it was banned in NASCAR. But there were milder Mustangs too, notably fifty with the 428 Cobra Jet V8, lighter drum brakes, and no heater, radio, or soundproofing. The battery was moved to the trunk. It was all tried and tested stuff, and rewarded Ford with 13-second times in Super Stock. Not bad for a substantially stock production line car, and one of these Mustangs won at its debut event, the 1968 Winternationals. If one of those was too radical, showroom buyers of 429 Mustangs

BELOW: Quite unlike circuit racing, the sport of drag racing has always provided a few seconds of high excitement, noise, and adrenaline . . . over and over again. And of course, the cars are always in view, so it has always been a good spectator sport. Track aficionados might prefer the long-distance tactics of a circuit race, but for some, nothing can compete with the sheer power spectacle of drag racing.

LEFT: For the muscle car, drag racing has always provided that vital spur to development, as this Road Runner convertible demonstrates. The Road Runner was a single-minded acceleration machine, as were all the muscle cars—drag racing made them what they were.

and Torinos could order an optional Drag Pack, which brought an oil cooler and lower gearing.

Ford might have succumbed to the racing bug in the early sixties, but AMC was made of sterner stuff. Always seen as the "sensible" face of Detroit, the American Motor Corporation stayed well out of racing of all kinds right up to 1968. Then, with the Javelin and AMX on the strength, it discovered a need to impress younger, hipper buyers. Competing on the drag strip was the obvious way to do it.

It was actually Hurst Performance Research who approached AMC and suggested building a drag racer based on the AMX. With its short wheelbase and light weight, the two-seat AMX was a good starting point, especially with AMC's own 390 ci V8.

Hurst did the work (which suited AMC just fine), adding 12.3:1 compression heads, an Edelbrock intake manifold, and modified rear suspension. To cut weight, some items were ditched, and the drag racing AMX proved quite competitive. The best-known car was one campaigned by Shirley Shahan, better known as the "Drag-On Lady."

The Hurst AMXs were pretty special, but for weekend drag racers, AMC also offered the SC/Rambler. According to AMC's advertising this could not only cover the quarter in 14.3 seconds, but "make life miserable for any GTO, Road Runner, Cobra Jet, or Mach 1." Best of all, the SC/Rambler cost just $2,998 in basic form.

But really, AMC had appeared at the tail-end of factory involvement in drag racing. Within a couple of years, they had dwindled to nothing as Detroit wrestled with challenges of an altogether different sort—new emissions and safety legislation, and a public that was showing less interest in horsepower and elapsed times, and more in practicality and gas mileage. Drag racing, of course, would always survive, but the big-name factory involvement that helped fuel the muscle car boom was over.

1948 1950 1952 1954 1956 1958 1960 1961 1962 1963

1949—*Oldsmobile Rocket V8 launched; Cadillac offers an overhead-valve V8.*

1960—*The last year of big fins: the Plymouth Belvedere has them, as well as a 330 hp V8 with two four-barrel carburetors.*

1961—*Chevrolet Impala 409; the 409 could be ordered with any full-size Chevy until 1965.*

1962—*The unassuming Ford Galaxie 427 provides startling performance; the Studebaker Hawk GT challenges the Big Three.*

1951—*Chrysler Hemi V8 (first generation): the real beginning of muscle.*

1963—*Ford Galaxie 500XL wins NASCAR; the Chevrolet II Nova SS, Chevrolet Corvette Sting Ray, Studebaker Avanti R2, and Buick Riviera Gran Sport all provide more or less affordable performance.*

1955—*Chrysler C300 with legendary FirePower Hemi small-block V8 makes big horsepower available to the masses for the first time; Chevrolet Corvette gets the V8; Ford Thunderbird is introduced and has a far more successful debut than the Corvette.*

1964 1965 1966 1967 1968 1969 1970

1964—*A vintage year: the inspired package that is the Pontiac GTO, based on the midsize Le Mans coupes and convertibles; arguably the most successful car launch of all time, the Ford Mustang; Oldsmobile's answer to the Pontiac GTO, the Cutlass 4-4-2, similarly based on a midsize car, the F-85; Plymouth Barracuda S.*

1965—*Buick Skylark GS has the division's 325 hp 401 V8 shoehorned under the hood for an extra $450; Shelby Mustang R is specifically designed for racing, right down to plastic windows.*

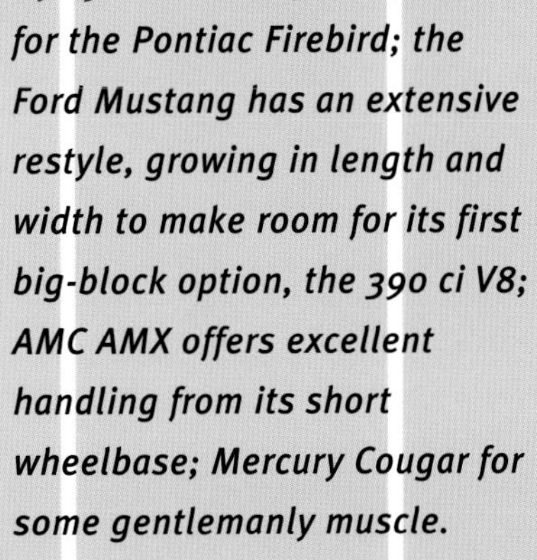

1967—*Seven engine options for the Pontiac Firebird; the Ford Mustang has an extensive restyle, growing in length and width to make room for its first big-block option, the 390 ci V8; AMC AMX offers excellent handling from its short wheelbase; Mercury Cougar for some gentlemanly muscle.*

1969—*Two serious performance cars, Pontiac Trans Am, based on the Firebird, and the aerodynamic Dodge Charger Daytona, designed to win back the NASCAR crown from Ford.*

1968—*AMC Javelin; Dodge Dart GTS; three body styles and two versions of the 428 ci Cobra Jet engine available on the Ford Torino 427; Dodge Charger is updated, as is the Chevrolet Corvette; the Plymouth Road Runner is a bargain-basement muscle car, as is the Dodge Super Bee.*

1966—*Chevrolet Camaro is available with various engine options, from V6 mild to 400 hp 302 ci V8 wild; Chrysler Hemi V8 (new generation); AMC Rambler Rogue V8; Chevrolet Chevelle SS396; Dodge Charger, the best-looking fastback; Dodge Coronet/Satellite, the Coronet R/T offering 480 lb ft; Plymouth Belvedere GTX even has an impressive top speed of 130 mph; Dodge R/T.*

1970—*Chevrolet Camaro completely restyled and gets the new LT-1 350 engine; Buick GSX is the GS special edition, only 678 sold; Plymouth Road Runner Superbird wins the Daytona 500; Dodge Challenger, the R/T package brings the 440 Magnum engine; Ford Mustang Boss 302, developed for SCCA, offers a rare muscle car combination of acceleration and handling—Boss 429 cleans up in NASCAR.*

1971 1972 1974 1976 1978 1980 1982 1984 1986

1978—*Henry Ford II fires company president Lee Iacocca, which is indirectly good news for Chevrolet—he takes over; implementation of Corporate Average Fuel Economy (CAFE) regulations, which specify 18 mpg average across each company's range.*

1984—*Chevrolet Corvette update: shorter, lower, wider, lighter, and much faster (140 mph).*

1974—*Ford Mustang II even offered a tragic 170 ci four.*

1979—*Third-generation Ford Mustang is a hit, boosting sales by more than 80 percent—it will become an eighties drag-strip star once the V8 returns; oil prices rise by 25 percent in two months; Congress bails out Chrysler with a $1.5 billion loan.*

1985—*Buick Grand National with a turbo V6 almost displays muscle car credentials: 0–60 under 9 seconds.*

1971—*Ford Mustang gets even bigger; compact performance in the 340 ci Dodge Dart Demon; Plymouth GTX/Road Runner updates, and the last year for the Plymouth street Hemi.*

1976—*The Corvette is only offered as a coupe because of the predicted banning of the convertible on safety grounds (which never materialized).*

1980—*Nothing happens; oh, apart from a fall from 8.4 million units produced across the US industry in 1979 to 6.4 million. And you thought 1979 was bad.*

1977—*Dodge Lil Red Express pickup brightens a sad year for muscle; the Chevrolet Camaro Z28 returns after a two-year absence.*

1982—*Chevrolet Camaro update and 6,380 replicas of the Camaro Indy 500 pace car are sold; Pontiac Firebird/Trans Am also restyled; Buick Regal Grand National and the Ford Mustang V8 return.*

1988 1990 1992 1994 1996 1998 2000 2002 2004

1993—*Pontiac Firebird/Trans Am update; Cadillac Allanté achieves 0–60 in 6.7 seconds with the all-aluminum Northstar 290 hp 4.6-liter V8.*

1997—*Dodge Dakota pickup R/T option adds 30 hp more than the 5.2-liter V8, to 250 hp for the 5.8-liter; aluminum Plymouth Prowlers are soon being sold for twice the original $40,000 price; Chevrolet Corvette stretches 8.25 inches and reaches 173 mph.*

1999—*Chrysler and Daimler-Benz merge.*

2001—*The Plymouth name is dropped.*

1994—*Ford Mustang update has 215 hp 5-liter V8, and the running horse grille badge returns; Chevrolet Impala SS is back.*

2003—*Ford SVT Lightning is officially the world's fastest production pickup at 147 mph.*

1990—*Chevrolet 454SS pickup—of course it's not a muscle car in the true sense of the word, because it's not originally a sedan or pony car—but it is big ci for big hp; the Chevrolet Corvette ZR-1 finally beats the Europeans at their own game—not with cubic inches, but rather, with modern technology and a Lotus engine.*

1996—*Dodge Viper GTS offers 415 hp for $66,000.*

2004—*The all-new Pontiac GTO gets 0–60 in 5.5 seconds from the 350 hp 5.7-liter V8, the same LS1 powerplant as the Corvette.*

1992—*Dodge Viper really is modern muscle with its 488 ci V10; another update for Chevrolet Camaro; Ford SVT Lightning pickup fulfills the Special Vehicle Team criteria of "performance, substance, exclusivity, and value."*

Index

Figures in *italic* refer to captions.

O

P

R

S

T

V

W

X

Y

Z